JFK Assassination

From the Oval Office to Dealey Plaza

JFK Assassination, From the Oval Office to Dealey Plaza,

by Brent Holland

JFK Lancer Productions & Publications, Inc.
401 North Carroll Avenue, #204
Southlake, Texas, 76092
www.jfklancer.com

Printed in the United States of America

ISBN: 978-0-9883050-2-1

1. History, Twentieth Century, 1960s.
2. United States History
3. Crime

First Edition, 2014

Brent Holland

JFK Assassination

From the Oval Office to Dealey Plaza

JFK Lancer Productions & Publications, Inc.

CONTENTS

PREFACE

"A man may die, nations may rise and fall, but an idea lives on."

President John F Kennedy

November 22, 1963 saw the murder of a young father and husband: President John Fitzgerald Kennedy. The president left behind a young mother and two children. JFK was just 46 years old that day he was assassinated. His wife Jacqueline Bouvier Kennedy was 34 and mother of their two children: Caroline six years old, and John Jr. only three. JFK's funeral and death were everywhere, saturating the airwaves for weeks on end, especially those drums and riderless horse from the funeral procession. It made quite an impression on me, a young six-year-old who was also destined to lose his father.

A month later, a thousand miles away in Montréal, another young father, at the age of 34, was gone, just four days after Christmas. He also left behind a young wife of 33, with three children: a seven year old, a six year old and a nine month old baby. They, like Caroline and John Jr., would all grow up without a dad.

On the day of my own father's funeral, I asked my mom, "is Dad's funeral going to be on TV too?" The quest for knowing my own father began that day, forever entwined with the JFK assassination.

History is marked by defining moments. In the 20th century alone, man bore witness to both the best mankind has to offer, and, at the other end of the spectrum, the worst in all of our history. I speak of course of the

Shoa, The Holocaust. Never before had mankind had the industrial tools and organizational apparatus to achieve the complete annihilation of a single people. There were even those companies who bid on the ovens for the camps.

At the pinacle of our positive achievements is manned space flight, culminating, of course, with the walk on the moon. This bold endeavor united mankind in a single, common goal and a moment unlike any other. When Neil Armstrong walked down that ladder to put foot on an entirely new world, we were suddenly thrust out of our own little worlds and mundane problems. We stopped, for one brief moment, being a member of the White race, Black race, Yellow, Red, Purple, Green, Muslim, Protestant, Jewish, Hindu, or Atheist, and instead we all claimed legitimate membership to the only race that has ever mattered: The HUMAN race. This wasn't some miracle. We just thought it up and did it.

But there was a single person behind all of this; a visionary like the world had never seen before, or perhaps since: John F. Kennedy. It was his vision to go to the moon, and for all mankind to unite around the endeavor in peace. That is what John Kennedy's legacy must be, can only be: peace.

We choose to go to the moon. We choose to go to the moon in this decade and do the other things, not because they are easy, but because they are hard, because that goal will serve to organize and measure the best of our energies and skills, because that challenge is one that we are willing to accept, one we are unwilling to postpone, and one which we intend to win, and the others, too.. But if I were to say, my fellow citizens, that we shall go to the moon, 240,000 miles away, then we must be bold.

Many years ago the great British explorer George Mallory, who was to die on Mount Everest, was asked why did he want to climb it. He said, "Because it is there." Well, space is there, and we're going to climb it, and the moon and the planets are there, and new hopes for knowledge and peace are there. And, therefore, as we set sail we ask God's blessing on the most hazardous and dangerous and greatest adventure on which man has ever embarked."

John Kennedy's "Moon Speech" September 12, 1962

Everyone remembers where they were for that glorious moment when Neil Armstrong stepped onto the surface of the moon. It was an unforgettable moment, like VE day at the end of both World Wars, the fall of the Berlin wall, the end of apartheid, and most recently, 9/11.

Like you, I remember 9/11 all too clearly. It began with the phone ringing, incessantly. After the third attempt I finally rolled over and answered it.

Screaming in my ear hysterically was my friend, "It's the end of the world! World War III has begun, and the United States has just been attacked!" Of course my first reaction was to think that the Russians had nuked the US somewhere, probably Washington or New York. Alarmed, I said, "What's happened!?" My friend responded, still screaming, "They've hit the twin towers."

"How did they get through?" I was desperate to know the details. How could the world's most formidable defensive system be circumvented and bombarded, allowing the Russians to invade New York? Then she said, "No, no, no, they flew into the towers." I said, "What a Cessna?" "No two airliners. Turn on CNN."

CNN popped up on my screen for a few seconds where they were showing people leaping from the windows to their death. I couldn't take the inhumanity of the scenes and flipped to CBC. Due to the large amount of expected casualties (upwards of 30,000), they would be sending as many as 5,000 of those to Montréal, where I was born and living then, due to our close proximity to New York. Above all they would need blood. Out of bed I jumped and headed to get dressed and to the blood donor clinic. As the TV blared in the background, the world stopped. The unthinkable happened: the towers fell.

I still went down to give blood, as it would be sent to New York as needed. All aircraft were grounded, and flights to the States were disallowed. Canadians took hundreds of passengers into their personal homes, fed them, clothed and made beds for them, and most importantly, comforted them, not as strangers or neighbors, but as our family. Americans are our family. They are our brothers, our sisters. Although I would never want to live with my brother or sister (even my real siblings, and I love you both), nobody comes to them but through me. I know that most Canadians feel this way as well.

9/11 inspired me to suck the marrow out of life, to do more than I had ever imagined I could hope to do, to go for it no matter what. If you're in a job, watching the clock wind down every day, quit. This is your life winding down; get going.

I also researched the Middle East and the reason everybody hates Jews. It was an epiphany for me. Bottom line, antisemitism is alive and breeding on a global scale like never seen before. I kid you not, demonizing Israel and Jews is a lie that is sexy and in vogue with those who have not done the research or worse.

America is an idea, like what JFK coined "Camelot." It is an ideal that all countries, including my own, aspire to. It is an idea that can never die as long as there is a single person who seeks freedom. It is a dream realized by the blood of the brave who fight every day in Afghanistan, some who wear the maple leaf and some who wear the stars and stripes. Brothers for all times. As JFK thundered in Ottawa:

> *Geography has made us neighbors. History has made us friends. Economics has made us partners, and necessity has made us allies. Those whom God has so joined together, let no man put asunder.*

These were the words President Kennedy thundered for all to hear when he addressed the Canadian Parliament in 1962. With them, he virtually brought down the house...The Canadian House of Commons, of course.

The mention of Camelot and JFK brings me to the most earth-shattering moment of my life: the death of my father. In some attempt to find closure from that horrible day that my dad left the house and never returned, just days after Christmas, my developing brain somehow associated the death of President John Fitzgerald Kennedy, age 44, with the death of my own dad, Gerald Emerson Holland, age 34.

If there ever was an ad for the Canadian Medicare System, this would be it. Like most of our neighbors in a 1960s working class section of Montréal, known as Verdun, every month brought new challenges to make ends meet and pay bills. I suspect for many, things remain the same. I do remember, in the fall of 1963, just prior to my dad's death, we were looking for a home. To this day, the smell of fresh cement brings me right back to the unfinished basements in the homes we were looking at. I'm not exactly sure when my dad had started to complain about a pain between his shoulder blades and an unbearable ache in his left arm that spread to his right.

In Canada, in 1963, we hadn't implemented our free Medicare system yet. (I should qualify "free." Our hard-earned taxes pay for it; nothing is free in a democracy.) Consequently, unless you were really sick or had ample money, you simply stayed away from doctors. Money was always tight. If you felt ill, the common prescription for any ailment was to "wait a few days and see how you feel." In an unwritten rule, you would wait and see if you felt better. If not, and you were noticeably worse, you wouldn't go directly to an emergency ward like you would today, but you would make a doctor's appointment and see him in his office. So my dad made an appointment. The doctor wanted to see him before Christmas, but my father wanted to wait until after Christmas to see if he might feel better. No doubt he took into consideration sacrificing the funds it would take to buy Christmas presents for his young family.

On December 29, 1963, a little over a month since JFK had died, my father kept his snowy Montréal afternoon doctor's appointment. My mom and dad were already planning supper as he left the house, and I was too busy playing with my brand new "Fort Apache" Indian and Soldiers set that Santa had brought me (which I still have to this day, my last gift from my dad saved all these years) to look up.

Upon entering the doctor's office, he had a massive heart attack, a clot broke free and went straight to his heart and he died right there in the office. I still remember the two detectives coming to the door to break the news to my mom. My seven-year-old brother, Glenn, in a sheer act of honor and bravery, went and got the step ladder from the basement, went out onto the gallery, and proceeded to take down the Christmas lights, as we were now in mourning. At seven! I suspect there are many moments that would earn the description of "life's insanity." This would certainly be one of them.

Because of a shared age and experience of losing a father, I somehow felt empathy with Caroline and John Jr. I used to get mad at the public and press every time they would hound them and their mom, Jackie. "Just leave them alone," I would bellow. But, like my own mom, brother and sister, they were a cut above and always, always were the most honorable and courageous in the face of adversity. Talk about role models. In December 2010, I had a chance to meet Caroline while attending Ted Sorensen's memorial in NYC.

This book shares behind-the-scenes stories of "Camelot" as told to me by Ted Sorensen and Abraham Bolden. Most importantly, it will uncover the Kennedy administration's peaceful resolve of the Cuban Missile Crisis as told by a first-person witness responsible for saving the world. You see, Ted Sorensen was the only person JFK trusted to draft the actual letter to Khrushchev to remove the missiles. You will be shocked by his explosive disclosures on the assassination in Chapter 3 "Ted Sorensen, The Man Who Saved The World, Really."

"Night Fright" A Brief History of the Show; No Other Show Covers the Assassinations Like Night Fright — Not One

In October 2007, I moved from my home in Montréal to Sudbury, Ontario, Canada. The people living there are top-notch. In July 2007, 10 months after arriving, and going somewhat stir crazy during the previous winter months, a communiqué from CKLU Laurentian University radio went out for volunteer radio hosts. On a lark, I decided, in order to "stay busy," I would volunteer as a host for a radio show and have some fun.

Having been an avid fan for 12 years of legendary paranormal & conspiracy radio show "Coast To Coast" with host Art Bell, but now finding that the show could only be heard in major urban areas in Canada (Montreal, Toronto, Vancouver) and not in Sudbury or the rest of the country for that matter, I decided to start a show in similar format called "Night Fright," but, with a significant difference. I sought out primarily Canadian filmmakers, documentary makers, authors, and artists of this genre to give them desperately needed exposure at home in Canada. Until "Night Fright," this had been alarmingly unavailable to them from any of our national broadcasters. I also wanted the show to be "smart," having been a fan of Charlie Rose for years. The show reflects the personal stories of my guests, regardless of the subject matter. I speak with them respectfully and authentically. I spent close to three and a half years broadcasting weekly from Sudbury, having seen the show become syndicated through the National Community Broadcast Association, around 80 stations.

Next came a move to a small city, by Canadian standards, of 117,000 people called Kingston. (Canada has only 35 million people living in the second largest country in the world, spread out from coast to coast to coast). Kingston is wonderful and is an overachiever as a city. It oozes culture from every crevasse. It is home to one of Canada's most prestigious universities, Queens. It is also our version of "West Point" where our military trains and educates its officers. It has seven, count 'em, seven prisons in the area, including the notorious Kingston Maximum Security Penitentiary. Built in 1830, it now houses five of Canada's worst psychotic serial killers. Despite that, Kingston remains the second most common destination for retirees in Canada (Victoria BC being the first), and also boasts being the safest city in Canada. It's an honor no doubt attributed to all the prison guards and military living in the neighborhoods.

Once settled, I made the leap to television. I approached the local community access television station and they agreed to broadcast the show. I had never hosted a TV show before, but then again, when I started "Night Fright," I had no previous broadcast experience whatsoever. The show was, and still remains, totally unscripted. It allows room to breathe something new into the show every week and for the guest to say what they need to. As I often say, we fly by the seat of our pants. "Night Fright" is now broadcast through local community cable stations throughout the country.

Another radio show I host is called "The Brent Holland Show." It was started October 2009. The show was started purely to inspire university and college-age students, who listen weekly from coast to coast to coast, into service in the global village. The track record of guests who have given of their time speaks for itself. Guests don't come on "The Brent Holland Show," like they do mainstream shows on national broadcasters, because they are guaranteed to sell books; they come on the show because they care. They care to inspire this generation of thinkers into service. There is something about the spark in a person's eyes that transcends all else. I have been blessed to have interviewed Canadian Prime Ministers, Speakers of the House, attorney general, Nobel Peace Laureates, and Ted Sorensen. Not bad for a volunteer show of one person and no funding. Two of our national broadcasters here in Canada had interviewed Ted Sorensen themselves and had embarrassed themselves. They had no idea who Ted really was or what he had accomplished. I was embarrassed for Ted as they launched into their cliché questions and phony laughs. I was elated when, several months later, Ted agreed to meet with me in his Manhattan apartment where we spent the afternoon together.

"It is the message that is important, NOT the messenger"

Brent Holland

Today, "Night Fright" is the number one show of its genre in Canada and is growing by leaps and bounds through America and beyond. There is something about being authentic, and not pulling the wool over the audience's eyes, that keeps the best and smartest fans in the world tuned in.

JFK Assassination Researchers

The Kennedy assassination was simple in its execution, but absolutely convoluted in its characters and their connections to each other. I stand on the shoulders of many who have come before: JFK assassination researchers and authors who have given their lives to investigate every aspect of the conspiracy.

Since the Internet has come into global use, the amount of data and speed that information can be accessed, has increased exponentially. In the early days, until around 1995, researchers would have to snail mail documents to each other and then wait for the responses to be snailed back. I am not speaking hyperbole when I say that what now can be accomplished in seconds using search engines would take six weeks or more back then.

> In the 80's, at Montréal's McGill and Concordia Universities, I would have to trudge over to the library (always through a blinding snow storm and uphill...both ways), go through the stacks to find a book, check the chapter titles, check the index, and flip to the page to find the info I was looking for. That was just for a single source. Four hours later I might have the beginnings of a single paragraph for a paper. And no laptops then, baby! When we wrote a paper in university, we would "write" a paper using pen and paper and copious amounts of white out. Especially me. No spell check back then either. With the advent of the Internet and "data mining," we now know more about the assassination than ever before.

For researchers, there's no private jets, no limousines picking people up, no penthouse hotel suites and luxurious meals. These are not rock stars. Many folks release their research and their books and don't even break even. It's a fact. What's more, they are called "conspiracy nuts" or worse.

They do the research because they're patriots. They want the truth. So many folks have put their lives on the line so that I can write this book and do my show, drinking a cup of coffee. In democracy, you have to be proactive. You have to get out there and challenge the government, because they work for us. "Why doesn't the government do _____?" In democracy, the government is us. We are the government, and the government is for the people. Imagine that. You all have your own small business and the Prime Minister and the president work for you. It's a fact. Don't let anybody ever tell you any different. We have the right, bought and paid for by those brave men and women of the Armed Forces, and the freedom to challenge what our government does and says.

Why The Truth Still Matters

I was pondering what to include in this segment; some high, lofty ideals about keeping history from repeating itself, bringing justice to those responsible for the murder of a president, patriotism and honor. But, then, I received an email from Abraham Bolden.

Abraham Bolden was the first ever African American Secret Service agent to be selected for White House detail. He was handpicked by JFK himself to protect the president and his family. Mr. Bolden was not on duty in Dallas on November 22, 1963. If he were, this book would not be written and none of this would matter; President Kennedy would not have died in Dallas that day if Mr. Bolden was guarding him. I can unequivocally guarantee it. Unfortunately, chances are, in protecting JFK from the fatal head shot, Mr. Bolden would have succumbed to the fatal bullet himself. Mr. Bolden would have gladly traded places with JFK that day; that is why he is a true American hero. (Please see Chapter 10 "Secret Service Abraham Bolden A Real American Hero" for the complete story of this great man, Abraham Bolden.)

The email I received from Mr. Bolden defines what it means to be a free person and why we have to find the truth. The email is in response to a Facebook post by David Patrick Kennedy (David is also my friend). The post stated how all of the talk of the conspiracy and murder of his uncle, John Kennedy, and his own father, Ted, upsets the entire Kennedy family; he wishes it would all stop and go away. Mr. Bolden's response is as follows:

Mr. Kennedy:

I read, with great compassion, your Facebook statements regarding the John F. Kennedy assassination from your perspective as a family member of the Kennedy Clan. I am in deep sympathy with both you and all of your sisters, brothers, and other relatives who are constrained to suffer the lurid details of the assassination of your esteemed uncle who was unfortunately murdered while serving as the president of These United States of America. It must be highly disturbing to you and other family members to constantly hear and rehear about the details of the misfortune in Dallas, Texas.

Although I agree wholeheartedly that the motivations of a few of the researchers and investigators are questionable, I humbly request that you and all of the Kennedy family understand that when John F. Kennedy placed his hands on the Holy Bible and became the president of The United States of America, the actions of those who took his life in Dallas, Texas mortally wounded the constitutionally elected leader of this nation and the free world, and the crime committed was against the People of These United States and the citizens of this country, and not against the Kennedy family as the main focus of their acts of treason.

What these researchers and investigations are focused upon is who assassinated a democratically elected president of These United States, in bright sunlight, at 12:00 noon, in view of the general public, while our president was fulfilling his duties of the office to which the American People had chosen as the Chief Executive of the United States…who happened to be your uncle. As a result of this magnanimous criminal deed against the people of the United States, measurements are being taken, reels are rolling, people are being interviewed, reenactments are occurring, books are being written, people have suffered their entire lives…..not because some person or persons murdered your uncle, but because we, the people democratically elected a great man and placed our hopes for a better America, a more peaceful union, an equitable and just society...our nation placed our hopes and dreams on his shoulders; I saw in his eyes when I spoke with both the president and your uncle, The Honorable Robert Kennedy, that President John F. Kennedy was not going to let the American People down.

If this matter is not pursued to its just end, the next sound of muffled drums that you hear could be those lamenting the death of our constitutional democracy. God Bless America.

DEDICATION

This book is dedicated to single moms everywhere, like Jackie and my mom. They stand strong and firm, hold the family together in crisis and raise children every day under duress and extreme circumstances. They are to be applauded.

CKNOWLEDGMENTS

My deepest regards to Afsaneh Hosseini, Norma Holland, Glenn Holland & Laurie Roch, Lorri Holland, Tyler& Ryan Reid, Jon Holland, Pat Best, Mary Holland, Garry & Lois Gosse, Mathew & Emily Gosse, Bev Nickle, Shari, Darren, Warren Nickle, Debra Conway, Sherry Fiester, Mark Lane, Arman Razavi, Mehdi & Azin Razavi, Perry, Lucy, James, Thomas Gingerysty, Rick & Carol Bell, Doug Bearisto, Anthony Mann, Ted, Michelle, Alexis, Chloe Dubien, Wayne & Rose Franks, Michel Deschamps, Deborah Frankel, Scott Meyers, David Gentile, David Yateman, Ronald Handfield, David McSherry, David Teasdale, Lee, Andrew, Eleanor Dixon, Kelly Logue, Sarah Costa, Joel Zazulak, Julianne Carson Rhodes, Alan Dale and Afsaneh Hosseini, without whom none of this would have been possible. Words will never do justice, and Baruch HaShem.

Thanks to all who I am honored to have in this book and who have been my guests on "Night Fright." I invite you to read their books and join the discussion.

Ted Sorensen, "Kennedy," "Counsellor," Dr. Robert McClelland, Dallas Parkland Hospital surgeon, Mark Lane, "Plausible Denial," Beverly Oliver, "Nightmare In Dallas," James Tague, Dealey Plaza first-person witness/third-person shot, Abraham Bolden, "The Echo From Dealey Plaza," Robert Groden, "The Killing of a president: The Complete Photographic Record of the JFK Assassination, the Conspiracy, and the Cover-up," Jim Marrs "Crossfire: The Plot That Killed Kennedy," Jim DiEugenio, "Destiny Betrayed" Lamar Waldron, "Legacy Of Secrecy" Jim Douglass, "JFK & The Unspeakable" Dick Russell, "The Man Who Knew Too Much," G. Paul Chambers," Head Shot," Sherry Fiester, "Enemy of the Truth, Myths, Forensics, and the Kennedy Assassination," Mark Sobel, Director of "The Commission" film starring Martin Sheen, Sam Waterston, Ed Asner, Martin Landau, Joe Don Baker, Larry Hancock, author "Someone Would Have Talked" regarding John Martino, who knew about the pending assassination, Rick Nelson, Oswald Expert, Lisa Pease, "The Assassinations," Debra Conway, president of JFK Lancer Productions & Publications, Inc., JFK historical research and publishing company, Casey Quinlin, "Beyond the Fence Line: The Eyewitness Account of Ed Hoffman and the Murder of President Kennedy," Brian Edwards, "Beyond the Fence Line: The Eyewitness Account of Ed Hoffman and the Murder of President Kennedy," Tom Lipscomb, Publisher of "House Select Committee on Assassinations," William Law, "In the Eye of History, Medical Evidence in the Assassination of President Kennedy," Peter Dale Scott, "Deep Politics and the JFK Assassination," known as the "Dean" of JFK research, Mathew Randazzo V, "New Orleans Mafia & Marcello, JFK Stewart Wexler, "Seeking Armageddon: The Effort to Kill Martin Luther King, Jr.," Len Osanic, "The Complete Works of Col. L. Fletcher Prouty," John Kelin, "In Praise of a Future Generation," Donald Scott, "AIDS: Common Cause Medical Research," Colin McSween, "Through the Door of History: The Aubrey Rike Story," Phil Nelson, "LBJ: The Mastermind of JFK's Assassination," Deidre Marie Capone, "Uncle Al," David Von Pein, "JFK" Youtube Channel, Jesse Ventura, "63 Documents the Government Doesn't Want You to Read."

INTRODUCTION

In the days immediately following the Kennedy assassination, I felt it was imperative to investigate the murder of my president. For a year, there was not a single television or radio network show in the United States that would broadcast any information that ran counter to the government position, that Lee Harvey Oswald killed the president and that he acted alone. There was one way that I could get to more than one city at a time. I appeared on Canadian radio, out of Windsor, Canada, across the border from Detroit. That was the only way I could communicate to a large number of my own countrymen, by leaving my country and going to Canada.

Brent Holland carries on the courageous work of his Canadian predecessors. It is not often easy for such a genial man to carry out a pointed mission, but Brent is persistent and, because he does his research, thorough. I have enjoyed listening to his interviews and I very much enjoy talking to him for those reasons. His passion and his scholarship are evident in his work, and for that I think we should all be grateful.

Mark Lane

This book is intended solely to inspire a new generation to "question everything" and, as a consequence, achieve more than they ever thought possible of themselves. The disclosures in this book are unsettling and bring the assassination from the outer fringes of wild conspiracies into the heart of the mainstream. These events really took place. This isn't just rhetoric. I can now confirm that the assassination of President John Fitzgerald Kennedy WAS a conspiracy. It was not, however, a coup d'état. So "who" was behind it and most importantly "why"?

The Torch Has Been Passed To A New Generation

"Let the word go forth from this time and place, to friend and foe alike, that the torch has been passed to a new generation of Americans—born in this century, tempered by war, disciplined by a hard and bitter peace, proud of our ancient heritage—and unwilling to witness or permit the slow undoing of those human rights to which this nation has always been committed, and to which we are committed today at home and around the world."

President John F. Kennedy from his inaugural speech January 20, 1961

This book is written to a new generation. A generation that has no emotional link to President Kennedy, Jacqueline or their children, for they were not yet born. It's a generation that knows little of the assassination other than some scattered rumors about a "grassy knoll" somewhere. It's a generation that is chastised by their teachers for entertaining original thought and is forced into complacency in order to advance. It's a generation seeking answers, truth. This is a book that bridges yesterday's history with today's generation. All the players and plots are brought together in a clear, concise chronology.

Why This Book ?

I will show confirmation of a conspiracy in the JFK assassination at last. This is the biggest and most important admission about the Kennedy assassination from the lips of JFK's closest and most trusted confident and aide, Ted Sorensen.

This book brings first-person, in-depth interviews and the work of over 32 researchers (many with their own books and expertise on each aspect of the assassination) under one umbrella. It is written in four parts.

Part One: The Grassy Knoll

Part Two: The Magic Bullet

Part Three: The Conspiracy

Part Four: Why

"The problems of the world cannot possibly be solved by skeptics or cynics whose horizons are limited by the obvious realities. We need men who can dream of things that never were."

President John F. Kennedy: Address to the Irish Parliament, June 1963

In any research, it is essential to get as close to the original source as possible. As events fade into the past and time marches forward, historical figures that bore witness can be lost or misinterpreted by third-person authors and researchers. For authenticity and historical accuracy, I have chosen to print the original source's interviews with me from my TV/radio show "Night Fright."

This book contains actual first-person interviews with the following historical figures. The words are their own. They are there for you to quote, analyze and draw upon for your own ideas.

- Ted Sorensen, JFK closest aid and speech writer. Sorensen passed away on October 31, 2010, after taking a stroke two weeks previously and just after getting off the phone with the White House. 04-21-2010 & 09-15-2010

- James Tague is the third person wounded in Dealey Plaza that day, inadvertently responsible for "The Magic Bullet Theory." Many people today are completely unaware of his story. 11-18-2009

- Dr. Robert McClelland, one of the Dallas surgeons who attended JFK and Lee Harvey Oswald. (Imagine having the opportunity to speak with the doctor who worked on Abraham Lincoln.) 03-16-2011

- Beverly Oliver (Massagee) is a 1st person witness to the assassination. Oliver can be clearly seen in film footage of the assassination, not 10 feet from JFK. She also filmed the assassination that day but had her camera confiscated by the FBI, because, it is believed, she had accidently filmed the actual shooter on the grassy knoll. 11-28-2011

- Abraham Bolden, 1st African American on JFK Secret Service Detail, handpicked by JFK himself. Though not on duty that day, he reveals there were other plots afoot before Dallas that were illegally covered up so the Secret Service could save their own hides. 05-05-2012

- Attorney Mark Lane was JFK's New York City campaign manager. Later, hired by Oswald's mother to represent alleged assassin Lee Harvey Oswald's interests before the Warren Commission. He produced the 1st JFK assassination documentary "Rush To Judgment" and co-wrote the film "Executive Action." Lane won libel law suit against CIA operative E. Howard Hunt over an article naming Hunt as being involved in the Kennedy assassination. 09-21-2012

- Jim Marrs, whose book "Crossfire: The Plot To Kill Kennedy" was made into the Hollywood feature film "JFK" by Oliver Stone. 10-17-2011

- Robert Groden, senior consultant to Oliver Stone on Stone's "JFK." 04-24-11

- James DiEugenio, consultant to Oliver Stone's "JFK" DVD. 06-10-2009

- Lamar Waldron, whose book "Legacy Of Secrecy" is being made in the Hollywood film of the same title starring Leonardo DiCaprio and Robert Deniro. 2013

- Sherry Fiester, a senior Crime Scene Investigator (CSI) who has used modern 21st century forensic techniques on the JFK crime scene and has found a frontal shot. 2013

- G. Paul Chambers, NASA physicist who has examined the Zapruder film using the laws of physics and also has determined a frontal shot. 2013

This book will definitively state:

What forces were behind the assassination.

Why the assassination.

Why the cover up then and until now.

1st person witnesses and researchers, including for the first time ever in a book on the assassination: the explosive statements from my personal interviews with JFK's closest aid and speech writer Ted Sorensen.

7 smoking guns.

CHAPTER 1

THE MOST BIZARRE THING HAPPENED IN DALLAS

"But, in today's world, freedom can be lost without a shot being fired, by ballots as well as bullets." November 22, 1963 [undelivered] remarks prepared for President John F. Kennedy, Trade Mart in Dallas

The most bizarre thing happened in Dallas, Texas on November 22, 1963, the day President John F. Kennedy was assassinated: *it stopped raining*. You would think, given the horror and evil that were about to unfold, that huge black storm clouds, gale force winds, thunder and lightning would be whipped into a cinematic frenzy. Instead, the clouds parted as if on cue and the sun came out basking the whole city in glorious sunlight and warmth. And so it began.

"The devil can cite Scripture for his purpose" – William Shakespeare

The hours and days that followed would seem controlled by the "gods of fate" themselves. In truth, a better analogy would be the Devil himself dutifully following a script ripped right out of the *Book of Revelations*.

"Something Wicked This Way Comes" – *William Shakespeare*

It had poured all morning in Dallas, where the 35th President of the United States, John Fitzgerald Kennedy, onboard Air Force One, was about to touch down. If the raging storm had indeed continued, AirForce One would have been, at the very least, diverted, waiting for the storm to subside. It would have resulted in delaying or maybe even cancelling the scheduled motorcade carrying the president of the United States that was destined to inch through the streets of downtown Dallas. The motorcade was scheduled to make an unorthodox turn into Dealey Plaza and past the Texas School Book Depository, then arrive at the Dallas Trade Mart, where JFK was expected give a rousing, inspiring speech on his favorite subject: world peace.

"Hell is empty and all the devils are here" – *William Shakespeare*

Unfortunately, AirForce One was not delayed. The president of the United States, husband and father, had minutes left to live. The president's limo had its convertible roof down and the plexiglas bubble top attachment off, leaving the car wide open and the president vulnerable and exposed from the torso up. It was perfect weather for anyone contemplating an assassination. If the rain had continued its onslaught, then things would have been different. Indeed, the country and world as a whole would have been different.

"So wise so young, they say, do never live long" – *William Shakespeare*

Accompanying the president was his beautiful wife, Jacqueline Bouvier Kennedy. The couple was married on September 12, 1953 and had two kids at home in the White House. Caroline was about to turn six on November 27, and John Jr. was going to celebrate his third birthday in three short days, on the 25th. Instead, history records John Jr. in a solemn black and white photo, saluting his dead father's casket on his third birthday. Their first child, Arabella, was stillborn on August 23, 1956 (I was born one year later, to the day). Seven years later, Patrick Bouvier Kennedy was born on August 7, 1963 with Hyaline Membrane Disease, now more commonly called Respiratory Distress Syndrome. After living only two days, Patrick would sadly succumb to this disease and pass away on August 9. How in the world could evil not have a hand in this, when such repulsion is allowed to prey on children?

"I have a bone to pick with Fate" – William Shakespeare

Along on the trip to Dallas were Vice President Lyndon Johnson and his wife Lady Bird, Texas Governor John Connally and his wife Nellie, and Senator Ralph Yarborough. The trip was political. Some infighting in the Democratic Party had to be mediated, but I suspect it was also to shore up JFK's popularity within Texas for the coming 1964 election, in which he was vying for a second term. There is never just one reason in politics. Every step and movement is assessed, calculated, spun around and reassessed again. When the plane landed, the president, with the First Lady directly behind him, descended the stairs down to the tarmac. There the couple did a "walk about," greeting and shaking hands with enthusiastic well wishers who were only held at bay by a steel fence. After a few minutes, it was time to leave, lest they be late for the speech at the Dallas Trade Mart and their rendezvous with destiny. The entourage climbed into their awaiting cars.

"Why then tonight let us assay our plot" – William Shakespeare

The president's limo was a 1961 dark blue Lincoln Continental four-door convertible with two single jump seats that would fold down just in front of the back seat. The back seat was able to raise 10.5 inches in order to give the president a higher profile.

In the president's limo, in the driver's seat, was Secret Service agent Bill Greer. Beside Bill Greer was Secret Service agent Roy Kellerman. If Kellerman had been on alert, as he should have been, he would have jumped over the front seat to cover the president the instant he heard or even suspected shots. Instead, he didn't even motion in that direction and remained seated. This was another stellar performance by the men tasked with protecting the life of the president that day.

Behind Secret Service agent Roy Kellerman was Governor John Connally sitting in the passenger's-side jump seat. Governor Connally was sitting in front of President Kennedy, slightly lower, as the president was elevated 10.5 inches on the back seat. Connally sat just to the left of the president because the jump seat, when folded down for use, did not fit snuggly against the passenger's-side rear door. I mention this tedious seating alignment of Governor Connally only because some use it to justify the possibility of the "magic bullet" entering Kennedy and then Connally. It does not. Try as they will, the angles are still wrong.

Nellie Connally was situated in the driver-side jump seat, directly beside her husband John Connally, to his left. Governor Connally was badly wounded by none other than the legendary, magic bullet, which we'll get to later as it needs quite a bit of room for all the smoke and mirrors. Mrs. Connally was responsible for saving her husband's life that day. When he slumped sideways, to his left, into the lap of his wife, she bent over him to hold him closely, and unintentionally stopped the flow of blood and loss of air that would have caused his death.

Directly behind Mrs. Connally, in the driver's-side back seat, sat Jacqueline Kennedy. Beside the first lady, on the passenger's-side of the back seat, was her husband and father of their two children, President John F. Kennedy.

"The crack of doom" – William Shakespeare

Despite the hectic pace the two had kept during their Texas tour; both President Kennedy and Jacqueline seemed relaxed and jubilant at the sea of well wishers along the motorcade route. Thousands waved, snapped photos, filmed with home movie cameras and generally dispelled any negative rumors about how Texans despised JFK. Instead it was Texan hospitality at its best.

Coming straight along Main Street (headed west) they would make a right hand turn (north) for a single city block along Houston Street, turn left onto Elm Street (west, again) then travel a few hundred yards until they reached the "triple underpass" below the train tracks as it is called. Once they passed the triple underpass, they were free and clear. The motorcade was to accelerate onto the on-ramp for Stemmons Freeway, then on to the Dallas Trade Mart.

"Like a fountain with a hundred spouts, Did run pure blood" – William Shakespeare

However, the 120-degree turn onto Elm forced the motorcade to slow almost to a standstill. The president had unknowingly just entered the kill zone. He had seconds to live. Every time I see footage of the motorcade, I want to reach back into the past, stop the motorcade, and change the outcome of those six seconds. Such is never to be the case.

The first shot rang out...

CHAPTER 2

Seven Smoking Guns: Proof Positive of Conspiracy

The term "smoking gun" is dirived from the image of a murderer caught standing over the body of his victim, the pistol in his hand still hot from firing, smoke pouring out of the barrel. No matter *why* the murderer is standing over the body, the bottom line is that he has the murder weapon in his hand (complete with the chemical residue on his skin from firing the gun) and is guilty beyond a shadow of a doubt.

The term comes from the 1893 Sir Arthur Conan Doyle's Sherlock Holmes classic "The Gloria Scott."

> *"We rushed into the captain's cabin and there he lay with his brains smeared over the chart of the Atlantic while the Chaplain stood with a smoking pistol in his hand."*

Although there are many smoking guns in the Kennedy assassination case, I have laid out seven that provide the absolute best proof of a conspiracy behind the JFK assassination.

Public opinion polls have consistantly shown that the vast majority of Americans believe there was a conspiracy to kill President Kennedy. However, on the question of government knowledge and complicity in the assassination and cover-up, there seems to be no firm conclusion in the polls. It is my belief that there was no government involvement or a coup d'état. I will explain this clearly in Chapter 14 "My Own Perspective" and offer my conclusions.

- A 2003 Gallup poll reported that 75% of Americans do not believe that Lee Harvey Oswald acted alone.
- A 2003 ABC News poll reported that 70% of Americans thought that the assassination was a conspiracy.
- A 2004 Fox News poll reported that 66% of Americans believed that there had been a conspiracy.

But what of the 30-44% who believe that there was no conspiracy and the assassination was committed by the lone-nut assassin, Lee Harvey Oswald?

These polls are based on people's assumptions, as most of those polled know little about the facts of the case. What's more, if they have relied on the news agencies mentioned above, they certainly have not been presented with any alternative view, other than the standard "Oswald did it alone." I would argue that mainstream media, in general, has done itself a disservice by presenting only its own biased stance.

Perhaps the best opinion on polls comes from Conservative Canadian Prime Minister John Diefenbaker. On November 1, 1971, he was asked about his party's standing in the polls. He summed it up best when he stated "only dogs know best what to do with polls."

I believe that those who, since 1963, have dismissed the idea of a conspiracy behind the Kennedy assassination, will struggle to counter these facts.

Below is a wonderful quote by JFK regarding our basic right to think for ourselves, free from persecution. His thoughts are an apt way to lead into the "Seven Smoking Guns."

> *"In 1946, the United Nations General Assembly passed a resolution reading in part, "freedom of information is a fundamental human right, and the touchstone of all the freedoms to which the United Nations is consecrated." We welcome the views of others. We seek a free flow of information across national boundaries and oceans, across iron curtains and stone walls. We are not afraid to entrust the American people with*

unpleasant facts, foreign ideas, alien philosophies, and competitive values. For a nation that is afraid to let its people judge the truth and falsehood in an open market is a nation that is afraid of its people."

John F. Kennedy February 26, 1962 "Remarks on 20th Anniversary of Voice of America"

1. TED SORENSEN - JFK'S CLOSEST AID AND SPEECH WRITER – CONSPIRACY CONFIRMATION

Very few know of the following confidential information from a videotaped interview with Sorensen in March 2010:

> *"I think this country, as I said in the big forum, this country was changed by...in all kinds of harmful ways, both domestically and internationally, by the loss of John F. Kennedy. And without inviting a lot more questions, because I won't answer them, we're all going to learn more, this year, about why he was killed."*

That, my friends, is explosive. What Ted Sorensen said that day in March 2010, implicates conspiracy in the assassination of JFK. I would argue that it remains, to date, the most important statement about the assassination coming from JFK's closest aid.

"We are all going to learn more, this year, about why he was killed." This indicates that Ted knew the real reasons behind the assassination, though perhaps he was waiting for the go-ahead for disclosure from the White House, at least that was my impression. At that period in time, March 2010, it was thought the passing of Fidel Castro was imminent. I suspect full disclosure will be revealed with the death of Castro.

It has been my thesis, since I became interested with the research of the assassination, that nuclear missiles are still in Cuba, never removed as they were supposed to have been after the Cuban Missile Crisis in October 1962. The cover-up of the assassination remains in place for national security. Why open that can of worms again and invite the possibility of nuclear war? Nuclear holocaust is a pretty good reason for national security and a cover-up.

It was only recently that my thesis was confirmed by ABC investigative reporter Chuck Goudie's ominous report on April 5, 2012. The headline reads:

> *"It was widely thought that all the missiles were removed and taken back to the Soviet Union, and the silos all dismantled. That does not appear to have been the case."*

Ted Sorensen passed away on October 31, 2010, after having suffered his second and final stroke only two weeks previous. Oddly enough, he suffered the stroke just after taking a call from the White House.

One thing seems certain from his "real reasons" quote, Ted had finally learned the truth behind the assassination and *why* his best friend Jack Kennedy was murdered. It is the *why* that is imperative to know, so we can prevent it from ever happening again.

2. Kenny O'Donnell & Dave Powers – JFK's personal friends and aides

Two impeccable witnesses saw the shots come from the grassy knoll in front of JFK. This is important because the official Warren Commission government report concludes that Lee Harvey Oswald acted alone, and all shots originated from behind JFK, specifically from the sixth floor of the Texas School Book Depository. Both of these witnesses were seated in the Secret Service car directly behind JFK's limousine, not more than a few feet from the president. These witnesses were none other than two of JFK's top aides and closest friends: Dave Powers and Kenny O'Donnell.

Dave Powers first met John Kennedy in 1946, when JFK was looking for help in running his first political campaign for Congress. Powers was immediately taken with Kennedy's sincerity in helping constituents. Kenny O'Donnell was introduced to JFK by his friend Bobby Kennedy in 1946, also to help with JFK's run for Congress.

Both Powers and O'Donnell became personal advisors to Kennedy when JFK was elected president. They remained a close-knit unit, often called "The Irish Mafia" in the administration circles due to their similar Irish heritage.

Both men were close friends and advisors to JFK for 17 years of political battles to get JFK into office. Their loyalty and belief in JFK were unwavering. They would often accompany Kennedy when he traveled and were both on that trip to Dallas. Both men were seated in the Secret Service follow-up car, little more than 10 feet from JFK when he was assassinated. Accordingly, what they witnessed and testified about the assassination should be taken as gospel.

Both men have stated that they clearly saw the shots coming from the front of President Kennedy, on the right side (the grassy knoll). According to "Legacy of Secrecy" author, Lamar Waldron, they were both told to change their story "for the good of the country." ("Legacy of Secrecy: The Long Shadow of the JFK Assassination" by Waldron, Lamar and Thom Hartmann, 2009)

Why the silence and cover-up? The FBI asked both of them not to mention it for fear of starting WWIII. This was November 1963, and it is essential to remember that the Cuban Missile Crisis had taken place only a year prior, in October 1962, when we came "that close" to nuclear holocaust.

The following is an interview I did with author and researcher Lamar Waldron, one of many from "Night Fright."

> Holland: Kenny O'Donnell and Dave Powers, two of President Kennedy's closest aides, right in the car directly behind the president, saw the shots coming from the grassy knoll. Why was this never brought out to the public? This is explosive.
>
> Waldron: It is amazing that the mainstream media in America certainly does not cover that, even though we got the information directly from Dave Powers when he was the head of the JFK Presidential Library in Boston.
>
> We arranged for Thom (Thom Hartman) to have a private sit-down with him. Thom went into the office and Powers pointed to a rocking chair and so Thom sat down in that nice rocking chair with the presidential emblem. Dave Powers said, "That's one of JFK's rocking chairs from the White House." Thom was actually there to interview Powers about Cuba and something else...
>
> Thom was asking questions about Cuba and so [he] was just stunned when Powers started telling him about seeing the shots from the what is called the "grassy knoll." Thom was also stunned when Powers said he and O'Donnell were told they had to change their stories for the good of the country. Powers said he did not know what that meant at the time but it was made clear to him this was national security. It was for the good of the country.

Dave Powers further verified this story to Waldron.

> Powers: The same bullet that hit JFK did not hit John Connally. ("Legacy Of Secrecy" Pg. 214)
>
> The Warren Commission was handed this theory on a platter and anything that didn't conform with it, they didn't take. ("Legacy Of Secrecy" Pg. 307)
>
> Waldron: If you go back and look at Powers and O'Donnell's testimony… in a weird affidavit from Powers and the Warren Commission volumes – it's not the report but the many volumes of

supporting material – they kind of "hem and haw" and sort of say what they were supposed to: "a shot from the back." But they each try to get in something about the shots from the front. And it was really not until Thom sat down to talk with Dave Powers all those years later – I believe it was 1990 – that Powers finally realized why it was for the good of the country, to prevent World War III. Just one year after the Cuban missile crisis, he had to lie about what he saw.

Now again, if people should wonder, "Why should we believe Lamar Waldron and Thom Hartmann on Powers and O'Donnell?" Actually, we've got a pretty good backup in Tip O'Neil.

The head of our lower House of Congress in the 1980s, Tip O'Neil from Boston, was the most powerful congressman in America at the time. He was close to JFK as were Powers and O'Donnell. Powers and O'Donnell told their story to O'Neil, and he put it in his autobiography years ago.

O'Neill wrote that at a dinner with Powers and O'Donnell, the assassination of President Kennedy was approached.

I was never one of the people who had doubts or suspicions about the Warren Commission's report on the president's death. But five years after Jack died, I was having dinner with Kenny O'Donnell and a few other people at Jimmy's Harborside Restaurant in Boston, and we got to talking about the assassination. I was surprised to hear O'Donnell say that he was sure he had heard two shots that came from behind the fence (the grassy knoll).

"That's not what you told the Warren Commission," I said.

"You're right," he replied. "I told the FBI what I had heard, but they said it couldn't have happened that way and that I must have been imagining things. So I testified the way they wanted me to. I just didn't want to stir up any more pain and trouble for the family."

"I can't believe it," I said. "I wouldn't have done that in a million years. I would have told the truth." "Tip, you have to understand. The family – everybody wanted this thing behind them."

Dave Powers was with us at dinner that night, and his recollection of the shots was the same as O'Donnell's. Kenny O'Donnell is no longer alive, but during the writing of this book I checked with Dave Powers. As they say in the news business, he stands by his story. And so there will always be some skepticism in my mind about the cause of Jack's death. I used to think that the only people who doubted the conclusions of the Warren Commission were crackpots. Now, however, I'm not so sure. "Man of the House" by Tip O'Neill, 1987, page 178

An exceptional portrayal of Kenny O'Donnell and his close friendship and loyalty to JFK can be seen performed by Kevin Costner in the film about the Cuban Missile Crisis "13 Days," a 2000 feature film directed by Roger Donaldson.

3. Ed Hoffman – An Exceptional Witness

Ed Hoffman is probably the most important eyewitness to the assassination. He remains the only person who actually saw the shooter behind the picket fence on the grassy knoll, rifle in hand, pointed over the picket fence and taking a shot at President Kennedy.

Ed was deaf and mute and so he communicated through American Sign Language and by jotting down cryptic messages on paper. It is important to remember that American Sign Language is a language unto its own, in the same manner that French is a language unto its own. It is not merely signed English sentences. As a result, when someone is asked to "translate" American Sign Language into English, it is the same as asking someone to translate French into English. Every translator has their own unique interpretation as to what is being said.

Here's a great example. French-speaking Canadians will often say "ca marche bien." Its English Canadian translation essentially means "things are going well." If, however, the translator is from France and is asked to translate "ca marche bien" to English in Britain, they would likely interpret it to mean "It's walking well." You see the verb "marche" comes from "marcher" which means "to walk." Consequently one can already see the problems of extracting an accurate translation from any language.

This is precisely what has plagued Ed's eyewitness account over the years, with people declaring that Ed is not reliable, as he keeps changing his story. Ed has never changed his story; however, various translators have interpreted it inaccurately. Consequently, his story has been bastardized over the years, until now.

Casey Quinlan and Brian Edwards, two impeccable researchers and friends of Ed's, came on my show, "Night Fright." They had both interviewed Ed on several occasions and have penned a book telling the true account of the events that Ed witnessed that day. ("Beyond The Fence Line" by Casey J. Quinlan and Brian K. Edwards, 2008)

Casey Quinlan has contributed, as a historian, to A&E Network, The History Channel and Oliver Stone's Hollywood feature film, "JFK". He has both a BSE and a Master's in American History.

Brian Edwards has a Master's in Criminal Justice and served on the Lawrence, Kansas Police Department as a sniper on their Tactical Unit (See Chapter 7 "Frontal Shot, JFK & CSI").

Both men give back to the community by teaching a course on the JFK assassination to High School students. In short, they know this subject matter inside out.

Ed's story was told succinctly in my interview with Brian Edwards. What follows is the interview transcript from our show together on "Night Fright."

> Edwards: Ed worked at Texas Instruments. And on his morning break, was drinking a Coke and chewing ice, as was his habit. And he broke a tooth, just serendipitously, you know. This, just from a broken tooth, all this stuff I'm about to describe, happened. He asked for permission to go to his dentist in Grand Prairie, which was on the other side of downtown Dallas. And he was given permission. On his way towards his dentist, he noticed that there were some cars parked along Stemmons Freeway.
>
> He told us that he remembered at that point that President Kennedy was in town and there was going to be a parade. So he pulled off into Dealey Plaza looking for a place to park. And of course, the police had blocked most of the main streets and there was no place for him to park and get out and watch. So he drove through Dealey Plaza, out onto Stemmons Freeway, the same route that President Kennedy's motorcade would take within the next hour or so. He parked his car along the shoulder of the road, just underneath the railroad trestle that went across Stemmons Freeway.
>
> While he was walking back – and you mentioned that he was deaf – he was, you know, he wasn't bothered by traffic zooming by at 70 miles an hour – and his first vantage point was underneath the underpass, and realized that he would get a better vantage point, a better view from above, so he went up on top of the overpass so he could look down on the entrance ramp onto Stemmons Freeway.
>
> While he stood there, he said he got there about 12 o'clock – and he said that as he was watching the activity behind the fence, he noticed one man wearing a suit, heavyset, with a hat, like a fedora hat, walking along the fence line. Ed paid no particular attention to

him because he wasn't doing anything unusual. But what he did see subsequently after 12 o'clock, 12:05, a car pulled into that parking lot and drove around as they were looking for a parking space. Ed said that it eventually didn't find a place to park and drove out the same way it had come.

Within five minutes Ed then saw another car pull through the lot. This was a different car, completely different. Ed described it as a green two tone Rambler Station Wagon. The Rambler Station Wagon will come into play later in the story, but Ed described it specifically as a Rambler. We asked him, "How do you know it was a Rambler?" He said, "Well, my good friend has one exactly like that, and I recognize the model and make."

Five minutes or so later, after that car drove around, Ed said he lost sight of that car, the Rambler. He said another car pulled through, didn't pay much attention to it. But then he noticed the man that he had seen earlier, with the hat and the sport coat, walking along the fence. He had walked in Ed's direction, and stopped and talked to a man who was standing by one of the railroad switch boxes. Ed said that it appeared that these two men were conversing. Of course, Ed being deaf, wouldn't be able to hear them. But he did notice the two men appeared to be together. A few minutes later, the two men separated and the man went back by the fence.

It was right at 12:30, Ed said he noticed the man stand up and had a rifle. He saw this man with the hat point this rifle over the fence. Of course, Ed wouldn't be able to hear the shot, but he said he saw smoke. Ed's immediate reaction was that maybe this guy was smoking a cigar or a cigarette. But he said that it was too much smoke to be from a cigarette or cigar. He said as soon as this man turned in Ed's direction, he was holding the rifle up across his chest. He could now tell it was a rifle.

Then, when Ed turned his attention back, away from the motorcade, he noticed that this man, who had held the rifle up, and had fired it over the fence, was running towards the man who was standing by the railroad overpass. Ed said the man suddenly stopped, just dead in his tracks and tossed underhand that rifle to the man in the railroad outfit who was standing by the railroad tower or the railroad switchbox. That man caught it, took it apart, and put it in a soft canvas-type bag and walked north out of the parking lot.

Ed realized that the connection was this man fired a rifle. The irony is that Ed was the first civilian to see the president's wound. President

Kennedy had a giant hole in his head. Maybe the two were connected. So Ed ran towards where his car was parked because he remembered seeing an officer, at least one officer in uniform, standing on top of the railroad trestle. As Ed ran down the road, he was waving his hands. Well, by now the follow-up car had come up and Ed told us – and he's always maintained the same story – that one of the men in the car had a machine gun and had pointed it at Ed as he was running toward his car.

Ed got back to his car – his motive was to get behind the fence to see if he could find either one of those two men that he had seen earlier: the man with the rifle, or the man who took the rifle out of Dealey Plaza. And of course, Ed couldn't get back there. He told us that it took him almost an hour to go two blocks because of traffic congestion, and also the police were trying to seal off the area. So Ed continued on to his dentist.

And a funny part of that story is that when he got to his dentist's office, the radio was playing. Of course, Ed couldn't hear it, but he told the receptionist that he had seen President Kennedy assassinated. In his inability to communicate effectively, he had to write it on a piece of paper. And, of course, the receptionist and her assistant had no idea what he was talking about.

He finally got into the dentist's chair, and he told his dentist that he had seen President Kennedy killed. Well, the dentist didn't believe him, so he went out and listened to the radio and, of course, now the radio broadcasts were – that's all they talked about. He came in and told Ed. He said, "President Kennedy's been shot." And Ed said, "I know. I saw that. I was there." And so Ed got four of those things I described in this story. A sub-compact version is that:

There's only one way that he would have known those things, is if he was there. He couldn't have known about the back of the head being gone. He couldn't have known about the Rambler Station Wagon which was seen by six other witnesses. He couldn't have known about the man in the suit. That man in the suit was later confronted by Officer Joe M. Smith of the Dallas Police Department, and he showed Secret Service Credentials. Ed saw that event.

So I guess to answer your question, I think he's honest. He's very sincere. He knows what he saw. But the first time he contacts law enforcement in 1967, the case is closed, and law enforcement doesn't care.

4. False Secret Service Agents in Dealey Plaza

Seconds after JFK's motorcade bolted from Dealey Plaza toward Parkland Hospital, Dallas Police Officer Joe M. Smith raced behind the picket fence on the grassy knoll. There he encountered a "suspicious man" lurking just behind the fence where many witnesses believed the fatal shots originated. Patrolman Smith pulled his side arm from his holster and demanded to know what the suspicious man was doing. The man then took out a Secret Service badge and told Smith to keep looking.

Several other witnesses reported running into Secret Service agents. The reason to focus on Smith is because he is a trained law enforcement officer. The same scenario played out moments later at the rear of the Texas School Book Depository. Dallas Police Department Sergeant D.V. Harkness also ran into several, as he describes them, "well dressed men." Police were sealing off the entire area at that point, including the rear of the suspected shooting location: the Texas School Book Depository. It didn't seem suspicious when these "well dressed men" simply told him they were Secret Service agents.

> **Here's the problem, there were no Secret Service agents anywhere in Dealey Plaza. Let me repeat for all the nay sayers: There were no Secret Service agents anywhere in Dealey Plaza. They were all accounted for at Parkland Hospital with President Kennedy and Vice President Johnson.**

NASA physicist G. Paul Chambers said, "I had the chance to talk with G. Robert Blakey, heading the 78 House Select Committee on Assassinations. He said he checked every federal agency. There was no federal agents of any kind on that grassy knoll. So someone was there with official credentials who no one wants to take responsibility for, someone who shouldn't have been there!"

Who was impersonating the Secret Service in Dealey Plaza where the president had just been assassinated? More importantly, why at that specific location on the grassy knoll and the Texas School Book Depository? Both are locations believed to be where the shots originated. What was the plan for these false Secret Service agents? (See also "Secret Agents on the Knoll" on jfklancer.com)

As an addendum, a fellow by the name of Malcolm Summers also raced up the grassy knoll. Upon reaching the fence, he encountered a man in a suit with his coat over his arm who sternly warned Summers, "don't come up here. You might just happen to get shot and killed." This coincides with Secret Service agent Abraham Bolden's theory that a stolen badge from his Chicago Secret Service office just may have been the badge in use by the false Secret Service agents in Dealey Plaza that day.

5. JIM BRADEN, CON MAN

Jim Braden, aka Jim Brading, Eugene Hale Bradley, was arrested by the Dallas Police Department just outside of the Dal-Tex building located in Dealey Plaza behind the motorcade. That building, in particular, is also believed to be one of the locations where shots originated. The Dal-Tex building aligns perfectly with the bullet trajectory that hit the curb, splintering off and wounding bystander James Tague, the third person injured by a bullet that day in Dealey Plaza. Tague was standing near the triple underpass. (See "Chapter 5: James Tague, the man responsible for the Magic Bullet" for more information) What's more, in 1977, a spent shell (meaning it had been fired from a rifle) was found on the roof of the Dal-Tex building.

Minutes after the assassination, Braden was found lurking inside this same Dal-Tex building by an elevator operator. He summoned the Dallas Police Department about a suspicious man who was out of place in the building. Braden was interrogated and bizarrely stated that he just "happened" to be in Dealey Plaza and wondered what all the commotion was about. Someone had told him the president had been shot, so he decided that he should call (are you ready for this?) *his mom*.

> **Being a dutiful son, I guess he wanted to let her know about the assassination. So into the building he scurried to look for a phone. At least that's the tale he gave the Dallas Police. Unknown to the DPD at the time, Braden had just changed his name. Consequently no records turned up for his new name, and he was released.**

So who was Jim Braden? Braden, was a long-time criminal with ties to southwest oil business and organized crime. Braden had an arrest record as long as your arm, having been arrested no fewer than 35 times. He had been convicted of bookmaking, burglary and embezzlement.

It is documented that Braden and a fellow by the name of Morgan Brown checked into the Dallas Cabana Motel on Thursday, November 21st, 1963 and stayed in Suite 301. He arrived in Dallas only one day before the assassination would take place.

Braden would maintain he was in Dallas on oil business and kept an appointment with Texas oil billionaire H.L. Hunt at Hunt's office on the afternoon of the 21st. It is widely believed that none other than Jack Ruby (who would murder and silence Oswald on November 24, 1963) was also in attendance at this same meeting. Hunt was well known to hold Kennedy with utter disdain and had even gone to great lengths to place a "Wanted For Treason" poster with JFK's face on it in Dallas newspapers on November 22, 1963.

After the meeting on the 21st ended, Braden went back to Suite 301 at the Cabana Motel. At midnight, there was a knock on the door. Braden opened it and there stood Jack Ruby who had come for a midnight "visit." JFK now had less than 13 hours to live. (See also, spartacus.schoolnet.co.uk/JFKbrading.htm)

If you still think this is just a bunch of disconnected coincidences, fast forward five years to June 5, 1968, Los Angeles, the Ambassador Hotel. Bobby Kennedy lay in a pool of his own blood, dying from an assassin's bullet to the head. Guess who was found in close proximity to the scene, picked up and interrogated once again. Our very own Jim Braden. (See also "Testimony of Jim Braden, May 16 and June 27, 1978 to the House Select Committee. Courtesy of the Mary Ferrell Foundation and Bill Kelly)

6. Dealey Plaza Target Practice

Have any of you hunters out there ever gone to a major urban center's downtown city park to scope your rifles and emulate firing on a parked car on the street? No? This is exactly what happened in Dealey Plaza on November 20, 1963, only two days before the assassination. This information comes from both an FBI report dated November 26, 1963, and a military intelligence report stating that two Dallas Police Department Officers chased two men with rifles who were targeting their rifle scopes and emulating firing into Dealey Plaza on a parked car with two silhouettes in it. The DPD did not capture the two would-be "hunters" who had sped away in an awaiting car.

Can you guess from which location in Dealey Plaza these two shooters were targeting the parked car and scoping their rifles? It was from behind the picket fence on the grassy knoll.

7. Rose Cheramie - Forewarned that assassins were on their way to Dallas to kill Kennedy one day before JFK was assassinated.

Rose Cheramie was a prostitute who had worked for Jack Ruby. (Louisiana State Police report of 4/4/67) As we have shown, Ruby gained infamy when he gunned down purported JFK assassin Lee Harvey Oswald while Oswald was being transferred in the Dallas Police Department basement on Sunday, November 24, 1963. The shooting took place on live television and in front of 70 Dallas Police Officers who were supposedly there for security, and only two days after the JFK assassination.

It was revealed that Ruby had a criminal background with friends in the Dallas Police Department, many who frequented his night club in search of "nocturnal pleasures." You see, Ruby's club was also a strip club. When Ruby took out

Oswald, it was heavily presumed he killed Oswald on behalf of the Mafia, in order to silence him. When you silence the assassin, he takes all his dirty little secrets to the grave. And that's exactly what happened. Oswald would die in Parkland Hospital at approximately 1:07pm.

Rose Cheramie was caught up in this insanity. In fact, on Wednesday, November 20, 1963, while our two hunters mentioned above were in Dealey Plaza scoping their rifles, Cheramie was enroute from New Orleans to Dallas with two Cuban exiles and potential snipers in the assassination. She was also involved with the underworld and the heroin trade. She later remarked that Oswald and Ruby not only knew each other, but were bed partners.

On this day she was a "heroin mule" with money in tow for a connection in Dallas. Along the way she got into a fight with the two Cuban exiles who subsequently threw her out of the car and ran her down. Hurt, but able to walk, she managed to get to a hospital. Accompanied by State Trooper Francis Fruge, she was transferred from the private facility where she was, to a public facility, due to lack of funds. Along the way she told him her plight. She nonchalantly added that the two Cuban exiles were on their way to Dallas for a different reason than drugs. They were on their way to kill JFK. Remember, this was *before* the assassination took place.

But perhaps the best way to tell Rose Cheramie's story is with Jim DiEugenio. When it comes to the JFK assassination, Jim may be the most knowledgeable person on the face of the earth. Oliver Stone turned to Jim to contribute his research to the DVD version of his Hollywood blockbuster "JFK." I had the great pleasure of interviewing him for "Night Fright" on several occasions. This is what he told us about Rose Cheramie:

> Holland: You just mentioned Rose Cheramie. Would you like to tell that story?
>
> DiEugenio: All right, Rose Cheramie is the woman who's depicted at the beginning of Oliver Stone's movie "JFK." She is depicted on this freeway from New Orleans to Dallas being thrown out of a car by these two guys who talked about killing Kennedy. Now this story – it's really kind of funny because a lot of people who watched the film a) didn't know what to make of it and b) didn't think it was true. Well, it is true.
>
> Rose Cheramie had been associated with these two guys who were doing at a drug deal, going from New Orleans to Dallas. And an Officer named Francis Fruge had actually interviewed her a few days before the assassination. She was a drug addict who was going through withdrawal symptoms when she started talking about this stuff.

Holland: And Francis Fruge was a Louisiana State Trooper.

DiEugenio: So, he came down to this hospital, and they were going to escort her to another hospital, and so he drove her there. On the way, she started talking about the Kennedy assassination. Now, this is a few days before the assassination, remember. Fruge dismissed it all as being - she's just making this stuff up, etc. So, he took it all with this giant grain of salt.

Then, of course, November 22, 1963… he just about jumped out of his seat. He says, "Wait a minute. What's going on here?" This woman was basically predicting that stuff. And so he goes back to see her and she starts filling him in on the whole story about how she had driven with these two guys to this place called the "Silver Spur," how she'd been thrown out, how they had talked about killing Kennedy, about this drug deal that they were going to do.

The incredible part of the story is that she actually said that Oswald knew Ruby. He gets in contact with his two superiors. After they talk to her, they call up the Dallas Police and they say, "Look, we've got this witness who knew about the Kennedy assassination *before* it happened and says that Oswald knew Ruby. Do you want to talk to her?" And guess what the answer was.

This is important because Jack Ruby murdered Lee Harvey Oswald, the purported assassin of JFK. The Warren Commission, which was set up by the government after the assassination to investigate if there was a conspiracy, said that Oswald acted alone. The Warren Commission specifically stated that Jack Ruby and Lee Harvey Oswald had no connection together and did not know each other. Now, we know this is simply not true. (A good example and parallel to this commission is just after the 9/11 attacks the government set up a commission to investigate. It was called The 9/11 Commission)

Holland: It was a "no."

DiEugenio: "No. We've solved the case."

Holland: Yeah, unbelievable. *No, we don't need a witness.*

DiEugenio: *Nah, we don't. It's Oswald.* So Fruge turns to her and says, "Okay, do you want to pursue this? Do you want to go to the FBI or anything?" And she says "No." So when New Orleans District Attorney Jim Garrison goes back to his investigation this is one of the things that he uncovers, because there were more people who had worked in the hospital where Chermie was treated who heard about this story, who also heard about her predicting the assassination. So, they heard Garrison was re-investigating the case.

Jim Garrison's true story is depicted in Oliver Stone's film "JFK." Kevin Costner plays Jim Garrison. Garrison, a New Orleans District Attorney, brought charges of conspiracy to assassinate President John F. Kennedy against a person by the name of Clay Shaw. There was an investigation by Garrison and he gathered enough evidence to bring the case to trial. We will cover the Garrison case and the movie JFK in Chapter 11 "JFK, The Movie."

DiEugenio: So, these hospital workers wrote Garrison a letter. He, of course, finds this utterly fascinating. He tracks down Fruge and hires him. He says, "Look, I want you to find this woman, okay? I don't care what it costs. I don't care how long it takes. I want you to find her for me. I want her in my office. I want to talk to her myself." So Fruge tries to find her, finds out that she had died in a kind of "funny car accident in 1965."

Many researchers feel she was murdered. Evidently, a car had hit her as she walked on the side of a highway, then stopped and backed up over her.

The circumstances are kind of weird. I don't want to say it's a mysterious death, but I'm not going to dismiss it either. So she had died, and [the report] comes back. Garrison actually wanted to go ahead and excavate the body. That's how suspicious he was about the way she died.

Garrison then says, "Okay, let's try and find out who were the two guys in the car." Fruge goes to the place she had mentioned, this "Silver Spur" or whatever it was – this bar. And he finds the guy, a guy named Mac Manuel who was actually there that night.

Holland: He was the bartender, I think.

DiEugenio: Yes, he was actually the bartender. And Fruge starts laying out all these pictures from Garrison's investigation. What's really funny about this is when Fruge was interviewed by the House Select Committee On Assassinations (1976 – because of public outcry the government set up yet another investigation into the assassination, its result was that Kennedy was killed by a conspiracy), he said, "I didn't even know who these guys were because Garrison had just given me these pictures. So I just started laying out these pictures in front of this guy, and he picked out two of them."

They were Sergio Acarcha Smith and Emilio Santana. Those two guys, of course, were two very high up Cuban exiles in the whole CIA apparatus. Sergio Acarcha Smith was the head of the CRC, the Cuban Revolutionary Council in New Orleans.

Holland: Which also had an office at 544 Camp Street.

After Fidel Castro's revolution took over Cuba in 1959, many Cubans fled to the US. They are called "anti-Castro Cuban exiles." They wanted to go back to Cuba to overthrow Castro and reclaim Cuba. The CIA agreed and ominously, so did the Mafia. The Mafia had been operating most of the night clubs in Cuba and making a fortune before Castro took over. Now suddenly that source of revenue was cut off. They wanted it back and were willing to do anything to achieve that goal including working along their nemesis the CIA. So the anti-Castro Cuban exiles, the CIA and the Mafia all ended up working together on a common goal: to topple the Castro regime and take back power and control. CIA agents who were involved with this were David Phillips and E. Howard Hunt. This was called "Operation Mongoose."

544 Camp Street, New Orleans, 1963, Oswald had an office there, the anti-Castro Cuban exiles had an office there and a fellow by the name of Guy Banister had an office there. Guy Banister was an ex-FBI agent who was organizing the anti-Castro Cuban exiles for US intelligence. Banister was also responsible for overseeing shipments of weapons into Cuba in order to arm the covert anti-Castro Revolutionaries there who were committing acts of sabotage against the Castro regime. Why Oswald had an office there is significant as both the anti-Castro Cuban exiles and Guy Banister were anti-Communist and anti-Castro zealots. Oswald, we are told by the Warren Commission, was pro-Castro and pro-Communist. It simply doesn't make sense that either Banister or the anti-Castro Cuban exiles would have put up with a pro-Castro and pro-Communist with an office across the hall from them. A more likely scenario is that Oswald was not really pro-Communist or pro-Castro, but, was actually working for the US intelligence community and Banister. More than likely he was creating a "cover" for himself so he would be accepted into Cuba on a mission for US intelligence without any problems. (See "Chapter 8 CIA: Guilty As Charged / Mark Lane" for more information.)

DiEugenio: Sergio Acarcha Smith knew both David Phillips (CIA) and Howard Hunt (CIA). During Fruge's interview with the House Select Committee, he stopped the interview and he goes to Jonathan Blackmore, the guy who was interviewing him, and "Oh, John, did you hear about the maps of the sewer system that Sergio Acarcha Smith had of Dealey Plaza in his apartment?"

It has been thought that the assassins in Dealey Plaza may have used the storm drains underneath the plaza as a way to escape after shooting President Kennedy. It most certainly is more than coincidence that these blueprints were found in the hands of the head of one of the most radical and violent anti-Castro Cuban exile groups. These groups certainly had motive to assassinate JFK. After the 1962 Cuban Missile Crisis, President Kennedy told the CIA to stop supporting the anti-Castro Cuban exile's efforts to regain control of Cuba. It is said that the Cuban exiles were filled with rage at JFK over this and wanted revenge.

DiEugenio: I'll never know how you can get more suspicious than that, actually having maps of the sewer system of Dealey Plaza in your apartment. Emilio Santana is one of the guys who Garrison actually polygraphed. It turned out either Santana, or a friend of his, actually had a rifle that looked like Oswald's, the Mannlicher Carcano rifle (believed to be the rifle Oswald used against JFK).

Note for the top photo on next page:

SSA Lem Johns had exited the follow-up car behind VP Johnson and was temporarily stranded in Dealey Plaza immediately following the assassination. In addition, the SS had ATF agents and others (including at least two Customs agents who worked at the Post Office) engaged as security reinforcements in and around Dealey Plaza. If questioned by uniformed DPD, any of these reinforcements may have stated their assigned affiliation with SS.

Please add the following IF space allows: SSA Lem Johns had leaped from the follow up car behind VP Johnson when he heard the first two shots and ran towards Johnson's car. The third shot rang out and the motorcade sped away. A quick thinking Johns aboard a press car and made his way to Parkland.

The north grassy knoll with the wooden fence showing at the rear. This is the area where many witnesses reported hearing shots fired. There were also sightings of Secret Service agents, however there were no agents assigned to Dealey Plaza and all were accounted for at Parkland Hospital with President Kennedy and Vice President Lyndon Johnson.

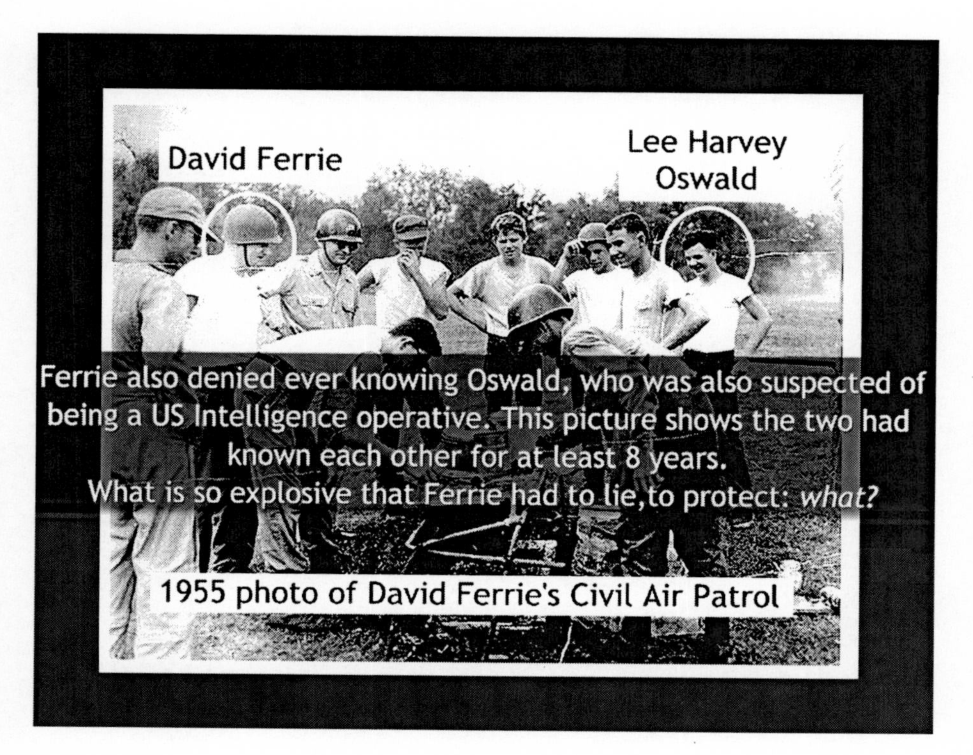

1 by the name of the Silver Slipper.
2 MR. BLACKMER: Do you know who manages that lounge?
3 MR. FRUGE: The manager at the time was a
4 fellow by the name of Manual, Mac Manual.
5 MR. BLACKMER: Now, after you were traveling --
6 while you were traveling to Jackson from Eunice, and I
7 understand that's a drive of approximately one to two
8 hours?
9 MR. FRUGE: Yes, at least.
10 MR. BLACKMER: Could you relate to us then
11 anything further Rose Cheramie told you?
12 MR. FRUGE: Yes. I asked her what she was
13 going to do in Dallas. She said she was going to, number
14 one, pick up some money, pick up her baby, and to kill
15 Kennedy.
16 MR. BLACKMER: And after you heard this, did you
17 question her further about those statements?
18 MR. FRUGE: No, because the answers she'd come
19 out with were -- in other words, to start with when she
20 came out with the Kennedy business, I just said, wait a
21 minute, wait a minute, something wrong here somewhere.
22 Now, bear in mind that she talked; she'd talk
23 for a while, looks like the shots would have effect on her
24 again and she'd go in, you know, she'd just get numb, and
25 after a while she'd start talking again. I was more or less

-9-

This is Officer Fruge's interview to the House Select Committee on April 18, 1978 where he relates when Rose Cheramie told him about the trip to Dallas. (Donated to JFK Lancer by Robert Dorff)

1 MR. FRUGE: I came on back home.

2 MR. BLACKMER: This, [redacted], was a day or so

3 before the Kennedy assassination?

4 MR. FRUGE: Yes.

5 MR. BLACKMER: On Friday, November 22,

6 President Kennedy was assassinated. When did you learn

7 of the assassination?

8 MR. FRUGE: I was watching it on TV. I was

9 home.

10 MR. BLACKMER: And as a result of hearing of the

11 president's assassination, did you do anything with respect

12 to Rose Cheramie?

13 MR. FRUGE: Immediately got on the phone and

14 called that hospital up in Jackson and told them by no way

15 in the world to turn her loose until I could get my

16 hands on her. And I talked to Dr. Armistead, and he

17 said that she was still kicking pretty hard, and he said

18 as soon as she gets the monkey off her back, he said, I'll

19 call you.

20 MR. BLACKMER: And did you later receive a call

21 from anyone at the East Louisiana Hospital?

22 MR. FRUGE: Yes, the following Monday morning.

23 MR. BLACKMER: And who called you?

24 MR. FRUGE: I believe it was Dr. Armistead.

25 I'm not positive.

-12-

Officer Fruge states he immediately called the Jackson, Louisiana hospital as soon as he heard of the assassination of President Kennedy.

1 MR. BLACKMER: And as a result of your conversation
2 with Dr. Armistead, did you then go back to the
3 East Louisiana State Hospital?
4 MR. FRUGE: Right.
5 MR. BLACKMER: And at that time, did you interview
6 Rose Cheramie?
7 MR. FRUGE: Right.
8 MR. BLACKMER: How did you find her condition
9 the next time you went back to the hospital?
10 MR. FRUGE: Very normal.
11 MR. BLACKMER: And this would have been on what
12 day, sir?
13 MR. FRUGE: It would have been on the Monday
14 after the assassination, the first Monday after the assassi-
15 nation.
16 MR. BLACKMER: That would have been November 25th.
17 What did you learn from this next conversation
18 you had with Rose Cheramie?
19 MR. FRUGE: She gave me -- she went more in
20 details. They had to go to Dallas. The president was
21 going to be killed; they were going to kill him.
22 MR. BLACKMER: Excuse me, sir; they, you mean --
23 was she indicating the men that she was traveling with
24 from Miami?
25 MR. FRUGE: That's correct.

-13-

Officer Fruge questions Cheramie again regarding her earlier statement about going to Dallas to kill President Kennedy.

1 said, "Come on out."
2 I waited for Mr. Guterres. He arrived. We go into my
3 office and we sit down. He started right off telling me he
4 is a homocide detective and was I in Los Angeles at the time
5 that Bobby Kennedy was shot. I said "Yes, I was." He
6 said, "Where were you?" "At the Century Plaza Hotel."
7 "With whome?" I said, "I was in bed with my wife at the
8 time. We were watching television and saw Bobby Kennedy
9 shot."
10 He dropped that line of questioning immediately and went
11 into Jack Kennedy. He said, "You were in Dallas at the time
12 John Kennedy was shot." I said, "That is correct." He said,
13 "Where were you?" I told him I was in the United States
14 Probation Office checking out with -- I forget what I told
15 him, whether I was checking out with anybody or not, but I
16 was reporting I was leaving.
17 He said, "Can you name whom you saw in there?" I thought
18 this was a little unusual that he got off the track of
19 Robert Kennedy and on to John Kennedy. I said, "As I recall,
20 the man's name was Mr. Flowers", to him. Then he got off
21 into other questions of insignificance ---
22 Mr. Purdy. Mr. Braden, did you see a Mr. Flowers in the
23 Probation Office?
24 Mr. Braden. No. As I recall, there wasn't any Mr.
25 Flowers. As a matter of fact, I had even forgotten Mr. Roger

ALDERSON REPORTING COMPANY, INC.

Jim Braden Testimony to the House Select Committee May 16, 1978, page 41. (Mary Ferrell Foundation)

CHAPTER 3

Ted Sorensen: The Man Who Saved The World...Really

"I think this country was changed, in all kinds of harmful ways, both domestically and internationally, by the loss of John F. Kennedy. And without inviting a lot more questions, because I won't answer them, we're all going to learn more, this year, about why he was killed."

Ted Sorensen, March 2010

JFK's Closest Advisor & Speech Writer

My show "Night Fright" primarily targets university, college and high school age students; although I would argue we are all students in life. I have been privileged to speak with Prime Ministers, speakers of the house, Governor Generals, attorney generals, Pulitzer winners, historical icons, civil rights legends, Nobel Peace Laureates. Each one has achieved greatness for all mankind. But Ted, he was light-years beyond that. He was the personification of idealism and what it is to be a true visionary for humanity itself.

I am honored to have had three interviews with Ted, which includes a filmed interview which took place September 18, 2010 in his Manhattan living room. He was so freely giving of his time because he cared; he just cared so deeply about the world and today's youth. His sole reason was to pass along his knowledge and what he had learned from his time spent directly beside his friend Jack Kenndy in the frying pan of whether the world would survive or not during the Cuban Missile Crisis, in the hopes that those listening would gain from that experience and integrate it in their own lives. I can't speak for my audience, but my time spent with Ted Sorensen changed me forever. If I had to describe what I came away with, it would come down to "dialogue before bullets".

Ted passed away on October 31, 2010, only two weeks after taking a fatal stroke just after receiving and hanging up from a phone call with The White House. It is essential in all research to get as close to the original source as humanly possible. There was no one closer or more knowledgeable about President John F. Kennedy and his administration than Ted Sorensen. More importantly for all of us right now and future generations, Ted Sorensen was: *The man who saved the world...really!*

In addition to Bobby and Ted Kennedy, many say Ted Sorensen was the fourth Kennedy brother, kind of like genius music producer George Martin was for the Beatles. It is said that the Beatles wouldn't have been the Beatles without George Martin. I believe the same can be said about President Kennedy and Ted Sorensen. JFK said that Ted was his "intellectual blood bank." As was evident, he also relied on Ted for moral fortitude. He remained a dreamer for the betterment of mankind and simultaneously stayed grounded on the world political stage.

Ted was devastated the day his friend Jack died. It was the worst day of his life. In 2000 Ted suffered a debilitating stroke that left him almost blind and slow in speech, but Ted never lost his quick mind. Not even close. There was a discussion with Noam Chomsky in which Ted, in his early 80s and after his stroke, chastises him for belittling a student and spreading untruths about JFK.

I had done two interviews with Ted for my radio show, and edited them into a four-part series. He was kind enough to spend two hours on the phone with me. When I was in NYC in September 2010 to interview Nobel Peace Laureates Jody Williams, Mairead Maguire and Shrin Ebadi, I called Laurie Morris (to whom I am eternally grateful) who handled Ted's appointments and asked if I could have a simple meet and greet with Ted. Laurie called back and said, "be at Ted's Manhattan apartment tomorrow at 4 PM."

> **I couldn't sleep that night, no kidding, due to sheer panic and nervousness. I was about to meet a long-time hero of mine, a living legend, who sat right beside JFK and wrote the letter to Khrushchev that saved the world. Talk about an OMG moment, for you younger folks. When I arrived at Ted's apartment, I was expecting a brief, "Hi, how are you? Thanks for coming, all the best." Instead, Ted invited me into his living room!**

On September, 18, 2010, I sat in Ted Sorensen's Manhattan living room. There was fire in his eyes, still and forever, when he spoke of Jack Kennedy. It was more than admiration. He spoke glowingly of a brother, forever bonded, like only brothers can be. He spoke with disdain concerning other administrations who had no vision for mankind or peace. To Ted, these weren't far-out, hippy, utopian dreams; they were possibilities, the possibilities of reaching the stars and beyond, as JFK had done for the world.

The most important aspect I want to get across about Ted is the idealism that both he and John Kennedy shared. I'm going to come back and repeat this "mantra" of idealism often. Ted's story is essential for today's generation as well as future generations. The Kennedy administration, like none before, would embark on a true *new frontier*.

Ted once wrote a speech, one of many, for President Kennedy:

> *"According to the ancient Chinese proverb, 'A journey of a thousand miles must begin with a single step'. My fellow Americans, let us take that first step. Let us, if we can, step back from the shadows of war and seek out the way of peace. And if that journey is a thousand miles, or even more, let history record that we, in this land, at this time, took the first step."*

President John F. Kennedy, Address to the Nation on the Nuclear Test Ban Treaty, 26 July 1963

The Cuban Revolution, Castro, The Mafia, Anti-Castro Cuban Exiles & US Intelligence

In 1959, Fidel Castro joined with his brother Raul Castro, and with Ché Guevara.The three of them led a successful revolution to overthrow a very corrupt Cuban government run by Presidente Fulgencio Batista. Batista's government was very pro-American corporations and pro-Mafia. The Mafia were running the hotels and gambling casinos in Cuba, earning enormous profits.

When Castro took over, Cuba became a dictatorship, a pro-Soviet and hostile anti-American regime. Castro shut down the main source of corruption: the Mafia casinos. The Mafia, which had been so well-protected by the corrupt Batista government, fled back to the United States. The Mafia was livid for being forced out of Cuba by Castro and wanted to return to their lucrative glory days, running the casinos in Cuba. They began searching for ways to do precisely that.

Many Cubans, as in every violent revolution, fled Cuba to get away from the new Castro dictatorship. Most went to the US, primarily to Florida, where their offspring reside today. Some of the Cubans that fled wanted to return to power in Cuba; they organized themselves in the United States in an effort to return and overthrow the Castro dictatorship. These folks are called anti-Castro Cuban exiles. They too were seeking a way back to their glory days in Cuba.

The American government was outraged by a pro-Soviet, Communist Cuba just 70 miles off of Florida and in such close proximity to the US. They feared that Castro, backed by the Soviets, would spread his revolution and turn the whole of Latin America pro-Soviet.

In 1959, the US president was Dwight Eisenhower. His vice president was Richard Nixon. That is the same Richard Nixon that would become president himself in 1968 and infamous for the Watergate Scandal in the 70s. The Eisenhower administration, with support from the CIA and military intelligence for logistics and supplies, trained 1,300 anti-Castro Cuban exiles in a secluded base in Guatemala for the sole purpose of invading Cuba and overthrowing Castro to remove the perceived Soviet threat.

The Eisenhower administration was at the end of their term in 1959, with the upcoming 1960 election looming. JFK represented the Democrats while Eisenhower's VP, Richard Nixon, represented the Republicans in the battle for the presidency in 1960. It was expected that Nixon would win and thus be able to carry on with the plan for Cuban exiles to overthrow Castro. Much to Nixon's disdain, Kennedy won the election and inherited the plan to invade Cuba.

The CIA told Kennedy that the invasion would be successful; Castro and Communism would be gone from the western hemisphere. What the director of the CIA, Allen Dulles, hid from JFK was that the assessment report of the invasion plan, done by the CIA alone, could not succeed. What the CIA had hoped to do was begin the invasion with the 1,300 anti-Castro Cuban exiles; when it inevitably started to flounder, they would trick Kennedy into sending in American armed forces to support the invasion.

> **When the invasion took place on April 17, 1961, and the anti-Castro Cuban exiles were floundering on the beach (at a place in Cuba called "The Bay of Pigs"), Kennedy refused to supply US military support, as he in no way wanted to escalate the failed invasion and potentially start a nuclear war with the Soviets. After it was over, most of the anti-Castro Cuban exiles who landed at the Bay Of Pigs were captured and put in prison in Cuba.**

Kennedy was livid with the CIA, who had lied to him; he fired its director Allen Dulles and its deputy director General Charles Cabel.

> **Bizarrely, Allen Dulles would end up being one of seven members of the Warren Commission in 1964, which was set up to investigate the Kennedy assassination, the murder of the very boss who fired him! Another weird circumstance was that Earle Cabell, brother to General Charles Cabell, was the mayor of Dallas on November 22, 1963, the day Kennedy was assassinated.**

The Bay of Pigs

Holland: Sir, I was wondering if we could talk about the Bay of Pigs; then I would like to jump to the Cuban Missile Crisis.

Sorensen: I am glad you keep them separate, because too many people don't.

Holland: Definitely they're separate, and I would also like to get to civil rights, Berlin, because these are all the problem-solving things for which you were right there in the Oval Office beside him, trying to find solutions, without causing a nuclear holocaust. Thank God there were people of your fortitude and vision in that Oval Office during this period, because we wouldn't be having this conversation right now without folks like you sir, and I say that with all sincerity.

Sorensen: Well that's good of you to say, and I give credit to Kennedy more than to me, but I certainly had a role in the peaceful resolution of the Cuban Missile Crisis. Historians still call it the most dangerous 13 days in the history of mankind, not just in the history of the United States, the history of all mankind.

Holland: That's right, we were sincerely "that close." But first maybe we can start with the Bay of Pigs. For those of the folks that are listening right now sir could you tell the story of the Bay of Pigs?

Sorensen: Pretty sad story, when Kennedy took office, January 20, 1961, he learned that the CIA and military chiefs that he had inherited from his predecessor, pretty good fellow, General Eisenhower – had been president before, he had inherited a plan to throw out Castro as the head of Cuba, by sending in to Cuba, an invasion of Cuban Exiles, men who had been recruited, trained, armed by the CIA, and then transported to Cuba to a landing site called the Bay of Pigs. Well, Kennedy kicked himself afterwards for believing all he had been told that it would be a success, that the people of Cuba, as soon as they heard about the landing would rise up and throw Castro out, forgetting or ignoring the fact that most of the anti-Castro people by that time were either in Miami or in jail, so word of this plot was widely leaked by the anti-Castro community in Florida, and Castro was ready for the invasion. He had his army, many, many times larger than this band of Exiles, waiting for them at the Bay of Pigs, and it was a one sided fiasco and everything the CIA had told Kennedy, that victory was sure, that no one would know that United States was involved, all that turned out to be completely false.

CIA hid the report from Kennedy stating that the Bay of Pigs was doomed to fail

Holland: There was something very alarming as well sir. The CIA, just prior to the launch of the Bay of Pigs, had done its own study of whether the plan would succeed or not and they came to the conclusion that it wouldn't succeed. But they never told JFK?

Sorensen: That's right. It was only long, long afterwards, that we heard about that study.

Holland: Were they trying to manipulate him somehow?

Sorensen: Who knows, the CIA has, first of all, let me say that the CIA gets some credit for the crisis we're going to talk about next, which is the Cuban Missile Crisis, because the CIA invented the aeroplane, the U2, that could take pictures at 50, 000 feet, and was able to detect the beginning of missile sites in Cuba. And it was the genius of the CIA photo interpreters, photo analysts that enabled Kennedy to call me in on October 16th 1962, and tell me that the Soviets had very secretly, swiftly put those missiles in Cuba. They had never put nuclear weapons outside their own boarders before in history, so, I give the CIA some credit for the fact that we had enough advance warning there to formulate our response.

But, the CIA was testing the new president I suppose, wanted to prove to him how tough they were. Cuba was not a threat to the United States, but it was an irritant and I suppose they wanted to show Kennedy they had an answer to this irritant: they weren't going to send in American troops, they were just going to let Cuban Exiles who wanted to reinvade and re-conquer their own country, let them go ahead. It may have sounded good to them on paper, but it was foolish from the beginning to think that this little band of Exiles could defeat Castro's army.

Holland: Many people speculate about the Bay of Pigs, that they were trying to draw the United States into an all-out war against Cuba, do you feel that…?

Sorensen: Oh, I think the Cuban Exiles were. Not so sure the CIA was...although the CIA was so confident of victory they might have been, but yes, the Cuban Exiles thought that they could go back and take over the government, take over the country, get back their land that Castro had taken from them, get back their business enterprises that Castro had taken from them. And they wanted Kennedy to be drawn into a war that the United States would win, forgetting that Cuba was backed by the other nuclear power, the Soviet Union and it would have been crazy for Kennedy to start a war with the Soviet Union's allies, Cuba.

Why JFK didn't commit US air support during The Bay Of Pigs

Holland: What made Kennedy step back from supplying that air support? Everyone says Kennedy didn't supply the air support and therefore the invasion was doomed because of that, what made him step back and say: "whoa... wait a second...?"

Sorensen: Number one, he realised, once it was underway and he found out that every single, every single premise on which that plan had been sold to him was false and he thought air support is just getting the US in deeper and the Exiles had already being vanquished at the Bay of Pigs and there was no way to reverse that through air support. But, it was a sure way of inducing the Soviet Union to come in with its nuclear weapons...

Holland: And that would have escalated...?

Sorensen: So Kennedy wasn't going to get in. He wasn't going to dig a hole deeper once he found himself in that hole.

Holland: You have to admire that, a young president like that, because all his peers, the people who have been there, are telling him to go one way and he says, no, I'm going to go the other way.

Sorensen: Well there's a clue, if I may say, in that same American University speech, commencement speech that I mentioned at the top of the show, when Kennedy said in that speech, "the world knows America will never start a war." I'm not sure they know that today, but

I'm talking about 1963, and his next sentence was, "this generation of Americans have seen enough of war." He was talking about himself. He had been in war and injured, and two of his best friends on his boat were killed, his older brother had been killed in the European theater earlier...

Holland: Joe Kennedy, Junior.

Ted Sorensen: Kennedy was not going to start a world war over Cuba or anything else.

Below are excerpts from what is, perhaps, the best speech that the world has ever heard: "The Peace Speech" of June 10, 1963 given at American University.

"What kind of peace do I mean? What kind of peace do we seek? Not a Pax Americana enforced on the world by American weapons of war. Not the peace of the grave or the security of the slave. I am talking about genuine peace, the kind of peace that makes life on earth worth living, the kind that enables men and nations to grow and to hope and to build a better life for their children--not merely peace for Americans but peace for all men and women--not merely peace in our time but peace for all time.

Some say that it is useless to speak of world peace or world law or world disarmament—and that it will be useless until the leaders of the Soviet Union adopt a more enlightened attitude. I hope they do. I believe we can help them do it. But I also believe that we must reexamine our own attitude--as individuals and as a Nation—for our attitude is as essential as theirs.

The United States, as the world knows, will never start a war. We do not want a war. We do not now expect a war. This generation of Americans has already had enough—more than enough—of war and hate and oppression.

For, in the final analysis, our most basic common link is that we all inhabit this small planet. We all breathe the same air. We all cherish our children's future. And we are all mortal."

President John F. Kennedy American University Address June 10, 1963

The following is an excerpt from JFK's inaugural speech given January 20, 1961. It demonstrates with crisp clarity JFK's desire for a new beginning and a fresh start on global co-operation and peace. It also touches on the consequences that the world would suffer if that challenge was not met.

"So let us begin anew—remembering on both sides that civility is not a sign of weakness, and sincerity is always subject to proof. Let us never negotiate out of fear, but let us never fear to negotiate.

Let both sides explore what problems unite us instead of belaboring those problems which divide us.

Let both sides, for the first time, formulate serious and precise proposals for the inspection and control of arms, and bring the absolute power to destroy other nations under the absolute control of all nations.

Let both sides seek to invoke the wonders of science instead of its terrors. Together let us explore the stars, conquer the deserts, eradicate disease, tap the ocean depths, and encourage the arts and commerce.

Let both sides unite to heed, in all corners of the earth, the command of Isaiah — to "undo the heavy burdens, and [to] let the oppressed go free."

And, if a beachhead of cooperation may push back the jungle of suspicion, let both sides join in creating a new endeavor -- not a new balance of power, but a new world of law — where the strong are just, and the weak secure, and the peace preserved.

All this will not be finished in the first one hundred days. Nor will it be finished in the first one thousand days; nor in the life of this Administration; nor even perhaps in our lifetime on this planet. But let us begin."

President John F. Kennedy, Inaugural Speech January 21, 1961

PT-109

It's important to understand what JFK had gone through, caused by World War II. His older brother, Joseph Kennedy Jr., had taken on the task of a secret "suicide" mission during World War II. He virtually flew a flying bomb (a bomber filled with explosives to the rafters) from England, on a mission to take out a V-2 Rocket site in Normandy, France. Needless to say, the mission was perilous, as explosives in those days were not as stable as they are today. Any extensive jostling could set them off. The idea was to put the plane into a steep dive on a direct collision course with the rocket site and then bail out. Tragically, the plane exploded before that took place. There were no survivors. President Kennedy's brother, Joe Kennedy Jr., was killed in action (K.I.A.) August 12, 1944.

> **The following story about how JFK became a war hero was yet another dramatic tale of the Kennedy family's seemingly unending waltz with the Grim Reaper himself, and can leave no question why Kennedy so despised war and all its horrors. I have to admire President Kennedy. With a bad back and his family's influence, he could have easily sat out the war. Instead, he hid his chronic back problem and turned his family's influence around.**

The Kennedy family twisted some arms and JFK was admitted to the Navy in October 1941. He transferred from his desk job to one where he would see combat. On April 23, 1943, Kennedy took command of PT-109 in the Pacific theatre to fight against the Japanese. PT stands for Patrol Torpedo boat. A PT boat was like an oversized fishing motor boat (not really, but close enough for our purposes). It was 80 feet long, with machine guns mounted on the front and back. It also had two torpedoes in tubes on either side of the deck and had an average crew size of 12. It had three 1,500 HP engines, each with its own, separate propeller. At 1,500 HP per engine, fueled by aviation gas (so it would burn hotter than standard diesel, thus giving more power), this boat was fast. It could reach speeds just shy of 50 MPH. PT boats were tasked with monitoring the Japanese shipping lanes and sinking any enemy ships that would venture into their path.

And so it was on the night of August 2, 1943, in the Blackett Strait near the Solomon Islands. PT 109 was on patrol, hoping to sink one of the supply vessels sent to reinforce the Japanese. The black of night smothered the small PT boat against the vastness of the sea. The crew had kept only one engine slowly rotating just to keep moving; the other two were off. It was a gamble. By operating on one engine, they could remain somewhat stealthy by not causing a lot of noise and churning up the sea. But that one engine was enough to mask all but the closest of sounds that night. Their worst fear was that they would come up against a Japanese destroyer. A destroyer out-gunned them in both fire power and size. If one were nearby, the only escape would be speed and maneuverability; but with only one engine engaged, barely above idling, it would take valuable time to get up to speed. With their low profile on the surface of the sea, their eyes strained to the edge of the darkness, ever on the lookout for a vessel.

The night sliced open and the Japanese destroyer Amagiri burst through. With the height advantage of the destroyer, its captain had spotted the PT boat some distance away, sideways, in front of them, and had ordered the destroyer to ram it. With no time to do anything, PT 109 was sliced in half. Crew members were trapped below deck unable to escape, and others were flung into the water. The aviation fuel, far more flammable than diesel fuel, spilled onto the surface of the water and ignited.

The air filled with an acrid smell of burning fuel and horrid screams as Kennedy's shipmates were burned. However, not all were screaming. Seamen Andrew Jackson Kirksey and Harold W. Marney lay dead. Kennedy organized his men. He knew that being in the middle of the Pacific Ocean, with a firey beacon burning and the Japanese hunkering down on them, was no place to await a rescue, if one was ever to come. Instead, they would swim to the closest island as quickly as possible; for there were other threats lurking just below the surface... sharks.

Off they swam. Kennedy ordered that a timber from the boat be placed in the water, and all the crew who could not swim would get on top. Those who could swim, leaned over it and kicked. Kennedy had been on the varsity swim team at Harvard University and was no stranger to the physical demands of long-distance swimming. He clenched a life jacket strap between his teeth and began to swim, pulling behind him the badly burned machinist, Patrick McMahon. The distance they all traveled; crew and timber; JFK with McMahon on his back; was 3.5 miles.

The Japanese were entrenched all over the islands in the area. No one knew for sure which islands were occupied. As it turned out, the one they swam to was clear. Exhausted, they crawled up onto the shore. It was a tiny island with no food or water, both of which they needed desperately, especially water for the injured. So, back into the sea Kennedy went. He swam an additional three miles to two other islands to check the feasibility of bringing his men there. He returned and led his men to one of the islands, which had coconuts and water.

They finally received help when two natives arrived on the island via dugout canoe. Kennedy made an engraving on a coconut (below) and gave it to the two natives to deliver to an Australian scout, Lt. Arthur Evans, who was in the area keeping an eye on and documenting Japanese shipping for the allies.

NAURO ISL

COMMANDER... NATIVE KNOWS POS'IT...

HE CAN PILOT... 11 ALIVE

NEED SMALL BOAT... KENNEDY

The message was delivered, and shortly thereafter, Kennedy and his men were rescued.

Kennedy kept the coconut, and it was kept on the corner of his desk in the White House during his presidency. Kennedy was once asked how he had become a war hero. His response was, "it was easy...they sunk my boat." That's why JFK hated all and anything to do with war. He was no coward.

Holland: Many people don't realize, also, President Kennedy was in charge of a PT Boat in the Pacific theater, and his boat was cut in half by a Japanese destroyer, he swam, geez I think it was five or six miles to shore with somebody on his back…

Sorensen: Not only did he swim to shore, or at least to an island, as soon as they found one, but he was swimming with one of his injured boat mates, towing him. Kennedy, fortunately, was a good strong swimmer, and despite his own injuries and exhaustion, he and his ship mates made it to that island, which was behind Japanese lines. Ultimately they were rescued, made it to safety. Ended up in the hospital. Kennedy also ended up with hatred for war.

The New Frontier

The "New Frontier" was a term that the press gave to the Kennedy administration. The term was derived from a speech JFK had given on accepting the Democratic Party's nomination as their candidate to run for president in 1960. The speech went as follows.

"We stand today on the edge of a New Frontier — the frontier of the 1960s, the frontier of unknown opportunities and perils, the frontier of unfilled hopes and unfilled threats. ... Beyond that frontier are uncharted areas of science and space, unsolved problems of peace and war, unconquered problems of ignorance and prejudice, unanswered questions of poverty and surplus." President John F. Kennedy, Democratic Party Nomination Acceptance Speech, Los Angeles Memorial Coliseum, July 15, 1960

President Lyndon Johnson's administration was labeled "The Great Society," also from a speech Johnson had made. Kennedy had some amazing people on his team and I thought it would be apropos to ask Ted about them.

Holland: I just want to mention the Kennedy team; he had put a "dream team" together, to coin a popular phrase. Certainly you had been with him for a while, then he brings in McNamara and Bobby, his brother. There was others as well, there was Kenny O'Donnell, Dave Powers, etcetera, etcetera. Can you talk a little bit about this dream team, and the dynamic, the "New Frontier" as he coined it?

Sorensen: Well, firstly, just look at the history afterwards, which is unlike most other American administrations; not one member of the Kennedy team was ever subsequently indicted for some kind of lobbying corruption; not one member of that Kennedy team ever wrote a book attacking or criticising Kennedy and his decisions. So it was a team of people who were dedicated to the best interests of a better country and a better world, they believed in Kennedy, he was loyal to them, and they were loyal to him. It was an unusual group of very able, committed people, I know that the song "Camelot," about mythical King Arthur is the song and a myth that was applied, but we weren't a mythical group. We were just ordinary flesh and blood human beings, but it was a very special time, and we had a very special leader.

Holland: And he brought everyone together. Was there an outrage from the public, or from his opposition when he brought Bobby in as attorney general?

Sorensen: Yes, and I suppose if I would look at it objectively today, and I said this in my book, "Counselor – Life At the Edge of History," I said it's probably not a good idea for any president, even John Kennedy to appoint his own brother, even Bobby Kennedy as attorney general. The attorney general is supposed to be, under the Constitution, a check on presidential power. He's supposed to be an independent source of law and order in a country that lives and is ruled by law. And I suppose if any other president appointed his brother as attorney general, there would be an outcry and I'd probably be leading the outcry.

We saw when George W. Bush appointed his pal and his personal lawyer to be his attorney general, it didn't work as a restraint on the president; it had just the opposite effect. The Justice Department, itself, under George W. Bush, was the leading law breaker. They were authorizing torture, which is against international law, and against the laws of the United States. They were encouraging the president that he could tap wires, that he could assume special powers as in chief, which is not provided for by the Constitution.

So, if I'm going to complain about other attorneys general, who were not at arm's-length independent, I suppose that I should say we were lucky that Bobby Kennedy turned out to be as good an attorney general as he was. He played a strong role in bringing about and supporting the revolution in civil rights that JFK finally led, after he had been in office for a couple of years.

The Cuban Missile Crisis

To be direct and un-dramatic, the Cuban Missile Crisis in the closest the world has ever come to non-existence.

The "Doomsday Clock" represents how close the world is to midnight; midnight represents extinction. The clock was started near the beginning of the nuclear age, 1947, by the board of directors of the Bulletin of the Atomic Scientists at the University of Chicago. It was set at seven minutes to midnight, at that point, and depending on the political climate of the world, it either moves closer to midnight or away. The closest recorded time to midnight (two minutes to midnight) occurred in 1953 when both the Soviet Union and United States had tested thermonuclear warheads within nine months of each other. I write "recorded time" because, during the Cuban Missile Crisis in October 1962, events between the US and Soviets were escalating so fast that it was impossible to keep up and adjust the clock. Estimates are that the clock reached 1 second to midnight! That is the stress and pressure JFK was assaulted by, around the clock. Tick, tock. Tick, tock.

It is imperative to understand the geo-political, as well as domestic, climate in which JFK found himself during October 1962. It is also imperative not to underestimate the impact that the Cuban Missile Crisis had on JFK. Understanding the Cuban Missile Crisis and the Cold War brings us to the precipice of understanding the abyss of nuclear holocaust. Conditions were analogous to the fearful panic that swept across both Canada and America just after 9/11.

> **We were raw nerves, pulsating in horror, waiting to be hit again from anywhere. The next attack could be a nuclear one, resulting in the death of millions of innocents, including our children. The panic was fueled by the knowledge that we had no control over the events that took place, or could take place. Vulnerability.**

In October of 1962, when nuclear missiles were found only 70 miles off the shore of the US in Cuba, JFK knew the missiles could reach and destroy most of the United States in minutes. There was no time to evacuate even the White House. There was no concrete nuclear-proof bunker under the White House in 1963.

Life was lived between deep sighs of relief that the missiles had not been launched between East and West ushering in a nuclear holocaust. New parents were home from World War II with rapidly growing families. It was a population growth spurt so unprecedented that their children were given the term "Baby Boomers." Although there was the constant threat that the world, quite literally, could end in an instant, there was still a hope and optimism for a world free of conflict and full of prosperity. They wanted a better life for their children than what they had.

That is America. There will be faltering along the way, but that eternal spark for new ideas, better ways and the pursuit of happiness are embedded in the psyche and spirit of all Americans. I love my country, Canada, and am a proud Canadian, but Canada could never produce a Lincoln, JFK, Martin or Bobby. Only America could produce a Ted Sorensen. G-d bless America.

Holland: Ted I was wondering if we could go into the Cuban Missile Crisis now, Tuesday October 16th, 1962. Can you take us through that momentous beginning of that crisis?

Sorensen: I certainly can, because it's still as vivid in my mind as if it had happened yesterday. The president called me in that morning, Tuesday, October 16. He told me that, to his astonishment and anger, because he had been– we'd all been lied to about it. Khrushchev had a back-channel means of corresponding with Kennedy. He lied about what he was doing in Cuba. The Soviet ambassador, not a bad fellow, Anatoly Dobrynin, called both Bobby and me in on separate occasions to lie to us about what was going on in Cuba.

The U2, not the band, was the name for the secret CIA's "spy" airplane. With a ceiling of 70,000 feet, its main purpose was taking high-altitude photos over the Soviet Union and Cuba, primarily to obtain troop and armourment deployments. It was flown by a single pilot and had extremely long wings for lift at high altitudes.

Some trivia: guess where the U2's first test flight took place. Area 51. Way back on August 1, 1955. Now, about U2 the band. It surprises me how many fans of their song "Pride," don't realize the lyrics are about Dr. Martin Luther King Jr. and his assassination. "Early morn, April 4, shot rings out in a Memphis Sky, Free at last, They took your life, They could not take your pride." Dr. King was assassinated on April 4, 1968 in Memphis.

Many suspect he was the victim of a conspiracy. Only three months later, Bobby would be murdered via a conspiracy plot on June 6, 1968. Stick around and read the rest of the book as the same names involved in the JFK assassination pop up over and over again in both Dr. King's and Bobby's assassinations.

Sorensen: These U2 airplanes took pictures 50, 000 feet above Cuba, then those pictures were developed by the geniuses who analyze and interpret photographs for the CIA. The photos showed, unmistakably, the beginnings of Soviet missile sites. These missiles carried nuclear payloads and had a range capable of devastating almost any part of the United States and most parts of the Western Hemisphere, including Canada.

Kennedy said he was calling a meeting for later that morning. He wasn't calling a meeting of the National Security Council, because that particular body is fixed by statute. A lot of people, because of their job, are invited to National Security Council meetings. Kennedy didn't want all those people, especially if they brought their deputies with them.

Sometimes people in Washington like show how important they are by bringing alone an entourage. Kennedy would have had a room full of people which makes it almost impossible to get the kind of crisp, precise decision that he liked to make, not to mention dealing with their inability to keep a secret.

He did not want everybody in Washington to know about this, because then, the Soviets, as he put it, would know that we know, and might take some pre-emptive action. They might use the missiles. They might send Khrushchev to the United Nations meeting in New York and have him try a little nuclear blackmail; or show pictures of the missiles and threaten to use them unless the West backed out of West Berlin (that was the testing place for freedom in those days).

The Berlin Crisis

Let's talk about West Berlin and the Berlin Wall. When Germany lost World War II in 1945, Germany was split into four regions. Each region was given to a victorious power to govern until a new German government, which was acceptable to all four powers, was created. The four governing powers were the United States, Britain, France and the Soviet Union. The city of Berlin was right in the middle of the Soviet section of occupied Germany. Berlin, too, was then split into four pieces, with each of the above powers taking a slice.

> **Great. So now you've got three Western democratic powers with ¾ of Berlin and the communist Soviets, never known to play nicely, with their own slice. And on top of that, they completely surrounded Berlin.**

In 1948, the Soviets decided they didn't want to be "friends" with the West anymore. You see, at the beginning of World War II, in 1939, Stalin's Soviet Union had signed a "non aggressor" pact with Hitler, meaning they would stay neutral in the war in return for parts of Poland, Romania, Latvia, Finland, Lithuania, Latvia, as well as Estonia. It stayed that way until 1941 when Hitler betrayed the agreement, which he had intended to do all along, and attacked the Soviet Union in an operation called "Barbarossa." The unprepared Soviets were caught completely off guard and almost lost their country. The Soviets immediately sought an alliance with Great Britain and all the Commonwealth countries (including Canada) who were already engaged in war, fighting against Hitler for three years. At this point the US was not in World War II. They were trying to stay out of what was called another European War. The US was ushered into WWII when the Japanese launched a surprise attack on Pearl Harbor. It was then that the US, Great Britain and the Soviets fought together against Hitler. They would defeat Hitler's Nazi Germany in May of 1945.

Back to the not-so-friendly Soviets in 1948. They decided, for a variety of reasons, that they wanted the whole of Berlin for themselves. Essentially, if they controlled Berlin, the Capitol, they controlled Germany. The Soviets cut off all ground transportation corridors (roads, rail and canals) leading into the now-besieged city of Berlin. Food and other daily living necessities were cut off. The one thing the Soviets couldn't control was the airspace.

Thus began the Berlin Air Lift. The allies had thousands of planes in operational order after the Second World War. They filled them to the rafters with baby food, medicine, clothes, and other needs. Over 200,000 flights were made in a single year with 4,700 tons flown into Berlin daily.

> **This certainly pissed off the Soviet Union. The Soviets' gamble completely backfired. This is important as they would take several more in the near future. By the end of the year there were more goods being flown into Berlin than there had been via rail before the blockade.**

Finally, the Soviets lifted the blockade in 1949.

The next crisis in Berlin would come a little over a decade later. It was called the "Berlin Crisis," and once more, the Soviets would flirt with nuclear war for the sake of power. The Berlin Crisis lasted from June 4, 1961 until November 9, 1961. JFK had become president in January of 1961. It was "Welcome to the majors," for the president, as this would be his first test in the international arena.

One of the main irritations for the Soviets was the constant emigration of East Berliners out of the communist-ruled section of East Berlin into the free West Berlin side. The Soviets seemed powerless to stop the flood.

Kennedy gave a televised speech on the night of July 25, 1961. He seemed to be preparing for the worst case scenario, a nuclear exchange with the Soviets, but offering an olive branch at the same time. He increased the military budget and increased the draft. He stopped the scheduled mothballing of older military ships and planes and brought them back into duty. He put together a plan to build fallout shelters for nuclear attack survival for the population. He was preparing for the distinct possibility of nuclear war.

"We do not want to fight – but we have fought before. And others in earlier times have made the same dangerous mistake of assuming that the West was too selfish and too soft and too divided to resist invasions of freedom in other lands. Those who threaten to unleash the forces of war on a dispute over West Berlin should recall the words of the ancient philosopher: "A man who causes fear cannot be free from fear." – We seek peace--but we shall not surrender"

President John F. Kennedy: Radio and Television address to the American people; The White House; July 25, 1961

The Soviets rolled the dice again and escalated the crisis; they built the Berlin Wall. In response, President Kennedy mobilized the Armed Forces. The world held its breath. There were several incidents with NATO upper echelon commanders being held up at border crossings between East Berlin and West Berlin. Under the agreement between the occupying powers, this was not permitted. Occupying personnel were to have free movement anywhere in Berlin, and, much to the Soviet's chagrin, that included East Berlin. In a show of bravado, American tanks were sent to the border and of course, Soviet tanks were sent to respond. Both Soviet and American tanks parked facing each other, guns loaded, only meters apart. Luckily Khrushchev and Kennedy talked to each other and the tanks backed off, thus averting further escalation. In the end, Kennedy said that a wall was certainly not worth a war.

> **There were some then, and some still now, that think that this was a weak response. Thank goodness they weren't in command, or I wouldn't be writing this, and you wouldn't be reading it.**

It's important to remember that one of the causes of the Second World War was appeasement of Hitler by the Western powers. They let him do as he pleased before the war, in the early and middle 1930s. So, most of commanders who had bravely fought in the Second World War did not want to make the same mistake with the Soviet Union, who was such an obvious aggressor. But, the stakes were incredibly higher now. Any war between two super-powers, like the US and the Soviets, would start with conventional weapons, but would not be contained. Within days, if not hours, it would inevitably escalate to nuclear holocaust; the doomsday scenario. JFK realized this. This was the first time he walked the razor's edge, but it would not be the last.

We continue with the Cuban Missile Crisis

> Sorensen: So we had to keep it secret. He didn't want a big group. So he was inviting me, and Bobby, and a couple of others who were not official statutory members of the National Security Council, to come to that first meeting later that morning.
>
> Unlike those presidents who go off and cut brush on their ranch (he's referring to George W Bush after 9/11) and leave everything else to their subordinates, he wanted everybody there face to face – to come up with a decision and later that morning we had a meeting.

And he told us that he wanted us to present to him every single option we had, military options, diplomatic options, combined military/ diplomatic – what were the pros, what were the cons, and that was the beginning of 13 long difficult dangerous days and it was not until the 22nd of October, six and a half days later that he was ready to go on national television and let the world know, let the Soviet Union, let all our Allies know, exactly what the group that he had assembled around that table, about a dozen of us, what we had decided on and what our decision was – was not the first automatic response, which was bomb those missile sites, get rid of them – no, that would have started a war.

No, our decision, his decision was to put the ball in Khrushchev's court, make him decide between annihilation for the world or possible humiliation for him, and that option, that's the second option that we chose was in effect a blockade of destroyers around Cuba to keep out any further Russian shipments. We didn't call it a blockade, because a blockade can be an act of war under international law also. We called it a "quarantine," a quarantine against offensive weapons.

He wasn't trying to keep medicine or food or gasoline, or energy out of Cuba – he wasn't trying to punish the people of Cuba, he just wanted to make sure Khrushchev understood that we were determined to react and resist.

Holland: You mentioned the quarantine sir, who was the person sitting around that table that brought that idea up? To me it was a stroke of genius?

Sorensen: Well thanks; I don't get any credit for it. I think there were two people who do, interestingly enough the head of the CIA at that time…

Holland: John McCone (Director of the CIA handpicked by Kennedy)

Sorensen: I can assure you that had changed since the Bay of Pigs that CIA chief was no longer around. (Ted is referring to Allen Dulles as the person who was head of the CIA but was no longer around.)

Sorensen: But the head of the CIA, at that time, had been a business man (McCone) and he'd been in the shipping business. And he said if you put up a blockade, it's an act of war, then under most insurance codes, any ship from Europe traveling across the Caribbean is going to have to pay three or four times as much insurance on that cargo as they usually do, and they won't be very happy about that. And then the legal advisor to the State Department remembered that during the...that before World War II, when Nazi Germany was threatening Western Europe, Franklin Roosevelt had proclaimed what he called a "quarantine of the aggressor." And basically it was an embargo as I recall, I don't recall, I was still a baby, but that the quarantine was a peaceful act. And later on, the State Department was able to get all of Latin America, the Organization of American States, to join with us in adopting and endorsing that quarantine and that made it a regional security arrangement, and regional security arrangements are permitted under the United Nations Charter and Kennedy wanted to abide by international law.

Holland: Also a very smart move. Were there those opposed to the quarantine, those that were adamant in going into Cuba?

Sorensen: Yes, Yes, during that first week of debate and discussion around the cabinet table, there were those who said the quarantine won't accomplish anything, how will that get rid of the missiles, those missiles are pointed at us, it's a threat, got to get rid of them. And I still remember the sentence of one of those "Hawks" as they were later called, he said "Mr. President, you got to go in there and take Cuba away from Castro." And there was a time before the 13 days ended, when it began to look as though maybe they were right.

The quarantine was proclaimed, the destroyers surrounded Cuba, but work on the missile sites continued. And then one of our U2 overfly planes was shot down, and by the time...on the 12th day, the Saturday the 27th of October, it surely looked as though war was likely to come and some of those "Hawks" were saying, "I told you so."

Even Lyndon Johnson, who was vice president at the time, I think this story is in my book, he slapped his hand down on the table, and he said "Well, I don't know," he said "all I know is that when I was a young man walking along a dusty road in Texas, if a rattle snake reared up his poisonous head, the only answer was to take a stick and chop its head off."

Holland: Boy, that would have been ominous, that's ominous.

Sorensen: So it was a little cool in the room after he said that.

Holland: Scary, scary, scary. Just a quick abide, did JFK have second thoughts about keeping Johnson on as vice president in the upcoming second term, '64?

Sorensen: No, because, Kennedy, by that time, had proclaimed his support of civil rights and had sent to the congress the most comprehensive civil rights legislative program since the days of slavery, and the South was against the program and against Kennedy. And Kennedy felt that he had to keep Johnson, his token Southerner so to speak, his hand of friendship, his link to the South. So I think it would have been the same team.

Holland: The same team okay. Ted today's generation, for better, for worse, tends to get their history, if you will, from movies. I think of the movie "JFK," I think of the movie "13 Days," I want to talk about the movie "13 Days." Do you feel that's in...?

Sorensen: First of all, the movie "JFK" was total fiction and I'm amazed how many young people today think its history.

"JFK" is a feature film made about the Kennedy assassination by director Oliver Stone. Kevin Costner starred as New Orleans District Attorney Jim Garrison. Garrison accuses Clay Shaw in the assassination of JFK. The movie concludes with JFK as the victim of a military coup d'état and the overthrow of the American Government, with Vice President Lyndon Johnson seizing power.

It is my feeling, for a variety of reasons, it was not a coup at all. I will explain that in a later chapter (See "Chapter 12 Assassination Noise" for more information). The movie is worth watching as Stone does a herculean task of bringing all the lore about the assassination into one narrative. It is also a masterpiece of filmmaking for film students.

"13 Days" is another feature film, also starring Kevin Costner, who this time plays a top JFK aide by the name of Kenny O'Donnell. The movie is about the 13 days of the Cuban Missile Crisis. I would say it is essential watching for a clear picture of the tension that everyone at the White House, and the world, was under. It shows just how close we came, and how the military continued to undermine Kennedy, trying to force him into war. It is worth noting again, as stated earlier in the book (Chapter 1, "7 Smoking Guns"), it was Kenny O'Donnell that was directly behind JFK's limousine in the motorcade in Dealey Plaza and saw the shots on the grassy knoll.

> Sorensen: On the other hand, the movie "13 Days" – it had a few imaginative changes from history, which we can talk about, but essentially it was accurate. It was based on the documents, it was based on a couple of long conversations that the producers and writers had with me, they conveyed pretty well the danger we were in, and the very cool, objective leadership that was provided by John F. Kennedy that steered our little group called the "ExCom" through those 13 days to a peaceful solution.
>
> Holland: In that movie Kenny O'Donnell plays a prominent role, many people say that really was you, do you agree with that?
>
> Sorensen: I don't know about many people, but I'm immodest enough to report to you that the Carnegie Endowment for International Peace had the courage to have a showing of that movie in Moscow. And they flew Bob McNamara (JFK's Secretary of Defense who played a decisive role as well in the peaceful resolution of the Cuban Missile Crisis) and me and one of the producers of the movie over for that showing. And at the press conference after the screening, and Bob McNamara opened the press conference by saying to the producer, "It's a fine movie but you have one fundamental flaw," and the producers swallowed, he said, "Well, I'm sure there are many, which one did you have in mind?" And Bob McNamara, bless his heart, said it wasn't Kenny O'Donnell who brought us all together, it was Ted Sorensen. By that I assume he means that the speech that I drafted for JFK before he made his decision whether to go with the quarantine or go with the bombing.

The group that wanted the quarantine asked me to give him a speech so he would see what the components were, what it would look like, and yes I did put in that speech eventually, all the arguments, all the components of their response, including the talk about negotiations and recognition of the importance of peace. Even the appeal to the people of Cuba to make clear that we were not trying to hurt them, and that did bring all the elements of everybody's thinking around the table together. But I want to stress that it was John F. Kennedy who brought us all together and led the way.

Holland: Let's talk about that speech, how did you manage to write that speech under such incredible pressure. I mean this was life or death, nobody knew the outcome, you were looking ahead hoping to make the correct decisions to keep the world out of a nuclear holocaust, virtually the death of the world, how did you come to write that speech?

The power of the pen is mightier than the sword

Ted is a man that fought for peace and humanity throughout his lifetime. When the world needed peace the most, we had President John F. Kennedy and Ted Sorensen. If it were not for the fortitude of Ted Sorensen and the power of his words, you and I would not be reading this right now. The world would still be reeling from the horrors of a nuclear holocaust. That holocaust was far too real, in October 1962, when it was discovered that the Soviets had placed offensive nuclear weapons in Cuba, missiles that would only take five minutes to reach Washington. In those days there was no nuke-proof bunker safely tucked away hundreds of feet below the White House. JFK handed Ted the future of the human race that night when he told him to draft a letter to Soviet premier Khrushchev in a last ditch attempt to resolve the crisis. Ted told me he was afraid but had no choice. The world depended on it.

Sorensen: Well, that was my job in those days, I was much more involved with Kennedy in terms of formulating his program, policy, messages, speeches, than I was involved in foreign policy, until he invited me to participate in the ExCom. So when the group favouring, as I did, the quarantine approach over the bombing approach, when they asked me to put a speech together I went to my office, which wasn't that far away from the cabinet room, and I sat there staring at the blank paper. And thinking to myself, what can I say, how's the quarantine going to get the...some of these were the same question the "Hawks" were asking, how was the quarantine going to get rid of the missiles, how was the quarantine going to diminish the danger, and so on and finally I went back to the "Dove" group and I told them I have these question and we sat around the table, and answered those questions. I went back to my office, by this time it was late in the evening, I had to cancel a dinner date with one of the grand dames of Washington whose home I was expected for dinner. When I told her, because nobody knew there was a crisis, I told her I couldn't explain what I was doing, but I just couldn't come for dinner that night. She was nice enough, an hour later to send her housekeeper over with a covered plate, with a delicious dinner that fortified me through the night. And thank goodness, because I worked through the night on that speech. I took a look at Woodrow Wilson's declaration of war, in World War I.

Holland: Could I just interrupt you for a second, because sometimes I'm faced with decisions like that, not of that magnitude, but I want to know what you ate that night, to give you that insight?

[both laugh]

Sorensen: I have no recollection, but I remember that it was hot and very tasty, but this series of questions your actually overlooking a much more difficult draft, under much greater pressure, and that was the draft letter to Khrushchev on Saturday October 27th, the ultimate day of the crisis. And that letter, I like to think, had a part in persuading Khrushchev that he had made a reckless gamble, as he called it later, and he pulled his missiles out.

In truth, I was being selfish in the interview. This was Ted Sorensen. I had fully intended to get to this most important letter, perhaps the most important letter the world has ever seen. It virtually saved the world. But as I said, I wanted to get every detail from Ted that I could, and that's why I waited to get to this subject. But I guess Ted figured that, like 99% of interviewers, I didn't know the subject matter.

I always read my guests' books before they come on my radio show, and I do extensive research myself, rather than rely on other researchers. Self-knowledge is important to me. I have a responsibility to inform the audience about the story and the environment surrounding it. Most of my audience is made up of a younger demographic, and things like the Cuban Missile Crisis, Bay of Pigs, etc. are unknown to them. That is also why, in this book based on the conspiracy, I am taking the time to inform readers of the reality of the times and explain the people behind the names and events. The threat of world annihilation played a key part in bringing about the assassination and the coverup. No single crisis best shows that than the Cuban Missile Crisis.

The letter Ted Sorensen wrote that saved mankind

Holland: Can we talk about that letter then?

Sorensen: Absolutely, go right ahead.

It was a little test from Ted to see if I had actually read his book. I was told that if I was to interview Ted, I had to have read his book, and I did, twice. I had also read several other books on the subject and had watched many a documentary.

Holland: Okay that was the letter... you had received conflicting letters from Khrushchev. The first letter you received was more or less him under great stress. The CIA said it was written by Khrushchev himself. The second one looked like it had been not written by him, but by the Politburo, and that was when...

Sorensen: ...or the military for him. You are absolutely right!

Whew! Looks like I passed the test! lol!

Sorensen: That first letter came in Friday evening, October 26th, and yes, it was a bit emotional; it meandered all around; it was full of threats, saying if we do this, if the US does anything, the Soviet Union will give us all that and more. In addition to threats, it was full of denials, "we don't have any nuclear missiles in Cuba," he said. "We have some specialists yes, but they're not offensive weapons, because we put them there for defensive reasons. And if we put them there for defensive reasons that makes them defensive weapons." But mixed in among the threats and denials was some indications that he wanted to end this dangerous crisis also. Some hints of a quid pro quo that might enable that to take place.

That letter came in Friday night, and we were sitting around the cabinet table Saturday discussing how to answer it. We had at least two competing drafts in front of us. One from the state department, one from a US mission of the United Nations.

And then a second letter, as you point out came in. This one much different in tone. And the message of that second letter was: "we're not taking anything out of Cuba, unless NATO, which Canada is a member, unless NATO takes its missiles out of Turkey." And we all knew that the NATO missiles in Turkey were an insult and a particular bone in the throat of Khrushchev and all the people of the Soviet Union. When they took vacations on the Black Sea, on the Ukrainian side, they could look up from their fun at the beach and see those missiles in Turkey pointed toward them.

Holland: Had Kennedy not ordered those missiles out of Turkey?

Sorensen: Yes, and he had been told the previous year that they were anachronistic, unreliable and what the United States really should do is move that portion of the regional deterrent into Polar, modern Polaris Nuclear Submarines under the Mediterranean. They were reliable, they were powerful, and best of all nobody could see them so they weren't provocative. But as things go in government bureaucracies, that order by Kennedy to remove them had never been fulfilled. So then we were faced with those two letters. How to answer them, what to do about the fact that the second letter was much tougher than the first...

Holland: I'm sorry Ted, was there a fear that perhaps a coup had taken place in Moscow?

Sorensen: There was a concern that the military Presidium had in affect overruled Khrushchev and put in this second letter, with much tougher demands, rather than anything in the first that hinted at a peaceful withdrawal. And finally the wisest man around the table, other than the president, Ambassador Llewellyn Thompson, who had been our ambassador in Moscow previously, knew Khrushchev, understood him, he said "let's ignore the second letter and answer the first letter."

And Bobby Kennedy supported that and I also did. In fact, I said there are some elements in that first letter that we can respond positively to. And the president said to me and Bobby, "Alright you guys go draft it." And we went down to my office, which as I say was just a few steps down the hall and sat there and that was the most difficult letter I have ever had to write in my life.

Sorensen: "I knew if I wrote the wrong letter, if I antagonized Khrushchev, if he was upset with my ignoring, our ignoring the second letter, who knows, he might just push a button and fire those missiles.

In those days the cabinet room in the White House was not a reinforced concrete bunker, today I'm told that it is, those days it wasn't. We knew that all of us sitting around that table could be sitting there in our last day on earth if we didn't solve this problem very, very quickly.

So the pressure was on me and it was made even more pressure by the president's brother (Bobby Kennedy) sitting there staring over my shoulder at what I was trying to write."

Holland: Can you take us into your thought process – you know words can sometimes have a double meaning and especially if they've got to be translated into Russian, the connotations of those words...

Sorensen: That's very true.

Holland: How did you begin?

Sorensen: Well I had been a – I wasn't a diplomatic letter writer, I had never written a diplomatic letter, except for the fact that this back channel correspondence with Khrushchev had begun a year earlier and Kennedy usually had me do first drafts for his letters to Khrushchev, in that correspondence. Basically I was a writer of speeches for Kennedy and earlier in my life as a member of the debate team in high school and in college I wrote speeches for myself.

Sorensen: And sitting there at that table, I remembered some advice from my high school debate teacher, Florence Jenkins, and she said "sometimes you do better in a debate by trying to adopt or adapt part of your opponent's case." And so I sat there and I took two or three of those positive elements from Khrushchev's letter of the night before, and I reworded them a little bit, "our way."

And I would precede that by the phrase: "as we understand your letter you propose"...and then later on, "as we interpret your letter you are proposing"... and Khrushchev may have wondered did I really propose that, because I changed...for example: his positive elements could be described as A, B, C, and I reversed the order, making it C, B, A, to make sure that they did the things we wanted them to do, before we did the things he wanted us to do, making it a little tricky, but it worked.

Holland: That's brilliant, sir! When you submitted the letter, did you have any second thoughts and said "well, maybe I should have worded it this way, that way"...what was that tension like, that apprehension, waiting for the response?

Sorensen: Well, first of all I gave it to JFK, who approved it. He had me read it over the telephone to our UN Ambassador, Adlai Stevenson, he approved it, it was circulated around the cabinet table to the other members of ExCom – they approved and then Bobby was sent off to present the letter to Soviet Ambassador Dobrynin – to convey to his masters in the Kremlin. But before he left, I don't know whether this is all in my book or not, but before he left...

Holland: Yes sir it is actually.

Sorensen: Before Bobby left, the president called a few of us, mostly it was the "Dove" group, into his office for a private meeting and left the others sitting out there, or getting themselves some food or whatever. And he and Secretary of State (Dean Rusk) gave Bobby instructions to accompany delivery of the letter with two oral messages:

Number one time is short. We're making the letter in a positive way, agreeing more or less with Khrushchev's letter so this should end it. And we better end it fast because you never know when the "Hawks" will rise. Presidents in charge of government, but we don't want the "Hawks" to take over and start bombing and invading by Tuesday – this was Saturday.

The other message was: we can't, in a matter of a few days, persuade NATO to - which acts by unanimous consent – we can't get that by Tuesday to pull out the missiles in Turkey. But because the president of the United States had previously decided to take those missiles out of Turkey - we're not going to do it at the point of a gun - or nobody will have any confidence in us after that. Well Mr. Khrushchev, if it makes him feel better, can be assured that it will be done in a matter of months, if we can just get this crisis finished.

Sorensen: So Bobby went to Dobrynin with the letter and with those two messages and I woke up the next morning and turned on my radio and Khrushchev was taking the missiles out.

Holland: Even though I know the outcome of the story, I have been on the edge of my seat, because "that's how close we came." And every time we deal with this subject and look back on it, really humanity was really on the brink – I mean it could have gone either way – we would not be having this conversation, I would not be looking out of my studio window right now at a beautiful blue sky. We all think of 9/11, but this was bigger I think in many respects…

Sorensen: Well it could have been. Could have been bigger, because we later found out that the additional Soviet troops that Khrushchev had put in Cuba, to guard the missiles and otherwise, had also been given authority to fire tactical nuclear weapons against any American attack, whether it came from air, sea, or land, and had not only that, the authority you know to launch those nukes at us on their own.

And had they launched the nukes at us, in those mad days, I say "MAD" advisedly, because of "Mutually Assured Destruction," M.A.D. was the doctrine of the day, and had they fired nukes at us, we would have returned by firing nukes, maybe tactical weapons came our way, we would have responded with tactical nukes, but once both countries are on that nuclear ladder of escalation they keep going up the ladder, and they would have responded with strategic weapons, we would have responded to that with strategic weapons and so on up the ladder until both sides have emptied their arsenals and devastated every inch of the other country.

And all those nuclear explosions in the atmosphere would have produced radioactive poisons that would have circled the planet by wind, by air, by water, by soil, until scientists tell us, the whole planet was uninhabitable for plant life, animal life, or human life."

Holland: Also, something that was really ominous sir, was the fact that you had revealed that Castro was pressing Khrushchev for a pre-emptive strike against the United States.

Sorensen: Oh yes. I shouldn't laugh when I say that but it turns out that…this is a two prod answer if you've got time?

Holland: Sure sir.

Sorensen: First is, believe it or not, due to some initiatives taken by Harvard and Brown academics, participants in the Cuban Missile Crisis from the United States, Russian, Cuba, had reunions to meet and talk about the lessons of such a crisis and how to prevent it from ever coming close again. We had one of those in this country, we had at least one in Moscow, we had at least one in Cuba, and then we had another one in Cuba on the 40th anniversary of the crisis, in 2002, and I attended. And Castro was there, as active as ever, not quite as healthy as the first time I met him, which was 1977, he invited the American delegation to lunch.

And that was quite a friendly affair, a certain amount of banter and some toasts. So I rose to give a toast, because it, by that time, had turned out that on that same Saturday October 27th, when we thought everything was dark and disastrous, Castro thought that it was too. He called in the Soviet Ambassador to Havana and dictated a letter to him that he wanted sent to Khrushchev saying he, Castro, thought the Americans were about to attack and he wanted Khrushchev to order those missiles fired, and eliminate this scourge from the face of the earth.

So at the lunch I arose to make a toast and I chastised Castro for referring to us as the "scourge of the earth" and ordering us to be wiped out. Now that man needed an interpreter to speak to us, but he understood English – he heard what I was saying – and half way through he interrupted me and said "that's because I thought you were about to attack." I resumed my toast to say that, yes, I understood his motivation for sending that letter, calling us such names, but in fact I was glad he had sent that letter, because that letter, even more important than the letter I had drafted, helped convince Khrushchev that he had made a mistake, that things were getting dangerously out of hand. Because that very morning, early October 27th 1962, his troops had shot down the American U2 plane, and pilot flying over Cuba, he had not authorized that, and the combination made him feel that everything was getting out of control, and so I said to Castro at that luncheon in 2002, "I'm glad you sent that letter."

Second, during the Cuban Missile Crisis, American U-2 planes kept up a steady stream of reconnaissance over-flights of Cuba, looking for more missile sites via the photos they were taking. It was a dangerous but essential intelligence gathering method, so that the Kennedy administration would know precisely what they were up against in Cuba and respond accordingly. On Saturday, October 27, 1962, a U-2 was shot down over Cuba by two SA-2 Guideline surface-to-air missiles, killing the pilot, Major Rudolf Anderson.

No one at the time was sure who had ordered the U-2 shot down from inside Cuba. Whether it was directly ordered by Castro, thus an open declaration of war or a local commander worrying about his own career if he took no action, or even a Soviet commander inside Cuba. When the American military found out they wanted to go in and attack Cuba. JFK, with nerves of steel and a vision for the future, said no that it could have just been an accident and said they would wait for confirmation of how the plane was downed and why.

Fear of a Military Coup in The United States

Holland: You had eluded to a fear that perhaps the "Hawks" could take over in this and this will be my final question for Cuban Missile Crisis, was there a real threat of that fear running through the administration, that perhaps, a coup could take place in the United States?

Sorensen: There had been, at that every same time period, a very good movie, called "11 Days in May," (actually "7 Days in May," directed by John Frankenheimer, starring Burt Lancaster and Kirk Douglas) which was total fiction about US Army takeover of the White House, based on a good book. It was a good movie and we used to joke about the movie, whether it could happen here.

It was no joke when the Joint Chiefs, before that first week was over demanded a session with Kennedy. Because unlike the more recent movie "13 Days," they did not attend our daily, nightly Ex-Com meetings, except for the Chairman of the Joint Chiefs, Maxwell Taylor, who was not a wild man like some of the chiefs were, he was on the contrary very scholarly, reasonable…

Holland: And handpicked by Kennedy wasn't he?

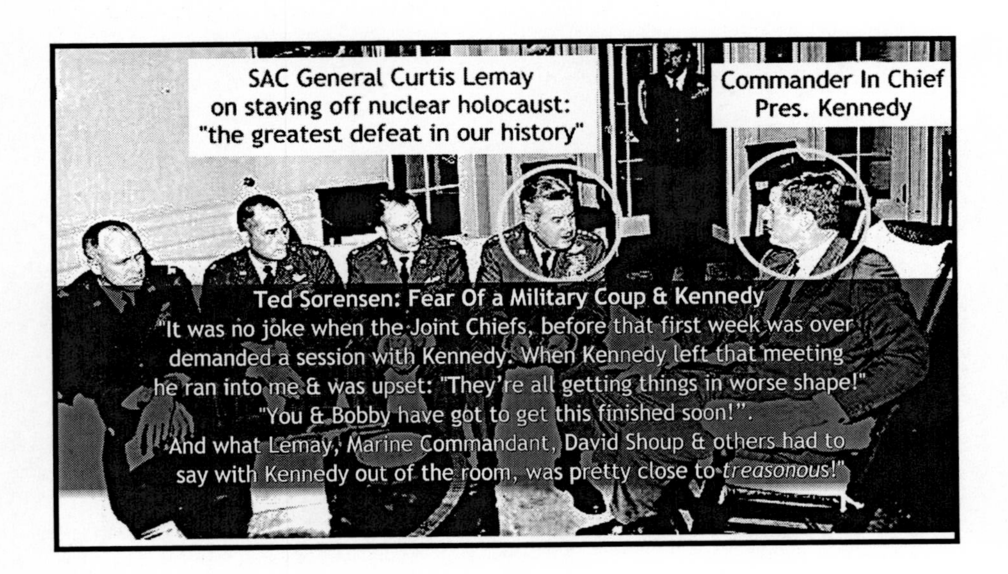

General Maxwell Taylor was an accomplished 4-star general with a solid background in diplomacy. He had commanded the famed 101st airborne in World War II, parachuted with his men into Normandy on D-Day, and was the first General on the ground. Taylor, like Kennedy, during the Eisenhower administration in the 50s, thought that Eisenhower's heavy reliance on nuclear weapons for the defense of the United States left far too few options to be used in case of war. Taylor, also like JFK, feared that any conflict, no matter how minor, would quickly escalate into nuclear holocaust. As a consequence of his thinking on nuclear weapons and the need for a wider range of conventional options, he was JFK's first choice for joint chief of staff when JFK fired General Lyman Louis Lemnitzer for his role in the Bay Of Pigs.

It is worth noting that it was JFK who created the Green Berets and the use of Special Forces to carry out stealthy essential military operations. The Special Forces would later branch out to the SEALS, Delta, etc. It is also worth noting that not only was Taylor handpicked by Kennedy, but he and Bobby Kennedy became such close friends that Bobby named one of his children after him. So, the threat of a coup was never from General Taylor, nor would he have stood still if one had taken place by Lyndon Johnson or anyone else. Nor would Ted Sorensen, CIA Director John McCone, JFK's brother Bobby, his brother Ted (a senator), or any of his aides. In a later chapter, I'll talk more about why a coup d'état was not the reason for the assassination nor the cover-up (See "Chapter 12 Assassination Noise" for more information).

> Sorensen: Handpicked by Kennedy, yes. Anyway, when the Joint Chiefs met with Kennedy, Curtis Lemay, a man who believed in nuclear war because he thought even if we suffered hundreds of thousands or millions of deaths, the Russians would suffer even more, so he…that was, Curtis Lemay, that's what he called his victory in war. And he lectured Kennedy on what he thought the quarantine, the combination of diplomacy and the blockade was too weak a response, and the American people wouldn't like it. Can you imagine a military chief lecturing the president of the United States on what the American people think!?
>
> When Kennedy finally left that meeting and went out into the hall, he ran into me, and he was upset and he said to me, bear in mind this is the Friday the 19th, he said to me, he pointed to that room and said

"they're all getting things in worse shape," he said to me, "you and Bobby have got to get this finished soon."

But it turned out that he left his tape recorder going when he left the room and we have recorded for history, a book called the "White House Tapes, the inside story of the Cuban Missile Crisis." (Actually titled: "The Kennedy Tapes: Inside the White House During the Cuban Missile Crisis")

And what Lemay and the Marine Commandant, David Shoup and some others had to say with Kennedy out of the room, was pretty close to treasonous, and blasting him. And I'm told that when Khrushchev finally pulled the missiles out of Cuba, without the United States firing a shot, not only was Castro upset that he hadn't been consulted, but the Joint Chiefs were upset that they didn't have their chance for a war.

But, John F. Kennedy was a strong and beloved president and I don't think there was ever a serious chance that the civilian control of the military – which is a fundamental principle of American government – I don't think there was a serious chance of that being overturned at that time.

The following is the actual transcript of the taped remarks that Ted mentioned above.

Friday morning, October. 19, 1963

General LeMay (condescending; superior tone): If we don't do anything to Cuba, then they're going to push on Berlin, and push real hard because they've got us on the run. This "blockade" and "political action," I see leading into war. This is almost as bad as "the appeasement at Munich."

Lemay mentioning the "appeasement at Munich" is an underhanded way of taking a shot at President Kennedy and calling him a "coward." Lemay knew full well that President Kennedy's father, Joe Kennedy, had been the United States Ambassador in England during the Second World War. Ambassador Joe Kennedy's attitude was that Hitler would win any war in Europe. The United States should stay out of another European conflict and should push Great

Britain to get any peace accord with the Nazis that Hitler would offer. Joe Kennedy supported British Prime Minster Nevil Chamberlain's initiative to give Hitler essentially whatever countries he sought, in order to appease Hitler and the Nazis and keep Great Britain out of another war with Germany.

This has gone down in history as a "cowardly act" by Chamberlain and is called "the appeasement at Munich." It is worth noting that a young John Kennedy thought any appeasement of the Nazis was the wrong thing.

General LeMay (continues): I just don't see any other solution except direct military action right now. A "blockade," and "political talk," would be considered by a lot of our friends and neutrals as being a pretty weak response to this. And I'm sure a lot of our own citizens would feel that way, too. You're in a pretty bad fix, Mr. President.

President Kennedy (no hesitation; challenging; angry; confrontational): What did you say!?

General LeMay (defensive and dismissive; superior; arrogant): You're in a pretty bad fix.

President Kennedy (sarcastically and in complete command): You're in it with me.

The meeting wraps up, and President Kennedy leaves, but, "forgets" that his tape recorder is still running. The following is caught on tape for all time unbeknownst to the generals. If this is any indication of what has been said behind the president's back and in the sanctity of the White House, one can only imagine what is contemplated behind closed doors by the generals outside of the White House.

General Shoup (kissing LeMay's butt; bold in absence of the president): You pulled the rug right out from under him. God damn.

General LeMay (playing along): Jesus Christ. What the hell do you mean?

General Shoup (boldly; posturing for LeMay): Somebody's got to keep them from doing the god damn thing piecemeal. That's our problem. Do the son of a bitch, and do it right.

The following is taken from actual taped recordings of Jacqueline Kennedy from the book "Jacqueline Kennedy: Historic Conversations on Life With John F. Kennedy." During an alarmed phone call from President Kennedy to Jacqueline Kennedy, Jacqueline described her husband's anxiety during the call, "There's something funny in his voice."

JFK: Please bring the children right now back to the White House.

Jackie was alarmed at the unprecedented request made by her husband to wake the children, "even though they were taking naps."

Jackie: Please, don't send me away to Camp David, you know, me and the children. Please don't send me anywhere. If anything happens, we're all going to stay right here with you. Even if there's not room in the bomb shelter in the White House...please... then I just want to be on the lawn when it happens, you know, but I just want to be with you and I want to die with you. And the children do, too, than live without you.

At the White House in those days, a "bomb" shelter was not a nuclear-proof shelter like it is now. There would have been no time to get on a helicopter, or anything else, to escape in the few minutes they would have if Castro launched. Both Jacqueline and President Kennedy believed the end was nigh, and they wanted to die together with their children by their side.

9/11 & JFK; Leadership in the face of adversity

I wasn't going to include this part of the interview because it was about 9/11, and JFK had long been passed away. However, I realized that it further illustrated JFK, his times and his vision, as opposed to leadership today. It emphasizes just what his assassination meant to the American people, and to the world. Just as 9/11 has impacted our world today, so did the assassination of JFK.

Holland: I would like to discuss the differences in leadership between George W. Bush and President Kennedy, and perhaps your speculation on how President Kennedy would have handled 9/11. But first where were you during that day sir?

Sorensen: Well, what you don't know about me Brent, is that I had a stroke that year, back in 2001, and it pretty well eliminated my eye sight which is why it took me a long time to write that book, couldn't handwrite it anymore, I dictated it. I was in bed here at home (only blocks from the World Trade Center in NYC) at that time and I heard about the first plane crashing into one of the Twin Towers, and I thought that's a terrible, terrible accident. It happened once before, many years ago, a plane crashed into the Empire State Building.

On a thick, foggy morning on July 28, 1945 a B-25 bomber piloted by Lt. Col. Bill Smith, on his way to Newark Airport crashed blindly into the Empire State Building.

Sorensen: But when I heard about the second one, I knew it was no accident, and it was an act of terrorism and that the United States was going to be a very different country if we started imitating what other countries under siege do, which is usually to crack down on civil liberties, crack down on free speech, crack down on immigration, and I regretted that.

And George W. Bush, who first of all, did nothing at all when he heard about it, he was reading a book to First Graders down in Florida and was too stunned to do anything for a while. But then he made a speech, which was, I suppose, what the speechwriters always call for, very nationalistic, chauvinistic, militaristic, vowing revenge, which a long time ago Thomas Jefferson said is the cheapest emotion there is.

Interestingly he didn't take any blame for ignoring the warning that he had had more than a month earlier, that Osama Bin Laden was going to strike at the United States in the United States. Perhaps if he had taken that one seriously, perhaps the administration would have alerted the Trade Towers, because they had once before been a target of terrorists, had they been alerted I'm sure the security people at the Trade Towers would have put in an evacuation plan, as a standby, there was no evacuation plan on 9/11 and as a result a great many people died unnecessarily, they didn't know where to go, they didn't know how to go, they didn't know whether to climb up higher or go down faster. They didn't know what to do about smoke or flame, and that I think is serious indeed.

The Twin Towers were attacked on February 26, 1993, by terrorist Ramsey Yousef. A van, filled with explosives, was driven into the basement parking lot of the North Tower and detonated. The hope was to destroy the tower's supports and bring it down at an angle, crashing into the South Tower, and taking them both down. The truck bomb did explode as planned in the basement, but the structure held fast. Neither tower fell that day. Tragically, the terrorists did murder six innocent people and 1,000 were injured, some seriously. All the conspirators including Yousef, were arrested and are still incarcerated.

> Sorensen: All the world was on our side after the attack on 9/11. Sympathy reports poured in, people at the United Nations and in the Western Alliance vowed that they would help in any way they could. But, in less than a month, all of that disappeared and in a matter of several months the world had turned against us. Because President Bush, unlike President Kennedy, defied the United Nations, he defied international law, he ignored the Alliance, he unilaterally invaded Iraq as his instrument of revenge when in fact Iraq had nothing whatsoever to do with 9/11.
>
> Saddam Hussein, the evil tyrant of Iraq, was a secular leader of a Muslim country. For that reason, Osama Bin Laden despised Saddam Hussein and had him on his hit list. We did Osama Bin Laden a favour when we got rid of Saddam Hussein. At the same time, the United States went into war against Afghanistan. There was at least a logical justification for that.
>
> The Taliban, who ran Afghanistan at the time, harbored and sheltered Bin Laden and his al-Qaeda organization. In fact, they were given positions in the security apparatus and police of the country, where they tyrannized the local Afghan population, who didn't like the Taliban and certainly didn't like al-Qaeda. But the United States bombed their homes and villages anyway, so the Afghan people turned against us too.
>
> No effort was made to find out whether there were moderate adherences to the Islamic faith, modernists in Islam, who had a different belief, who did not support suicide bombing and all of that. Kennedy reached out to leaders in Poland and elsewhere behind the Iron Curtain. And in his correspondence with Khrushchev, tried to

encourage peaceful solutions. But Bush wanted only to be a war time president to assure his re-election and sad to say that's what he did.

Holland: Do you feel JFK would have handled it differently, more diplomatically.

Sorensen: I think he would have. As I say I think he would have, it's not easy to negotiate with somebody whose headquarters are in a cave and there is no deterrent back in the works. Because he has deterrents depends upon the other side, like Khrushchev. Khrushchev had a whole civilization and urban and industrial empire to defend against a war. Osama Bin Laden, more of a religious fanatic in his cave, he has nothing to defend. He and his followers believe that dying in a suicide bombing, in which they blow up the infidel, then the United States, will guarantee them a place in paradise. No, I think that Kennedy would have... I mean after all Islam is a distinguished, classic religion, it has over a billion adherence in this planet, and I am certain Kennedy would have looked for a way to find someone with whom some understanding of a better world might be reached.

Holland: Sir, if you were in charge right now, how would you deal with the terrorism that's going on in the world and the knife at the United States' throat?

Sorensen: I would try to do all possible to regain the respect that the world had for the United States, at the time John F. Kennedy was president. Nobody was threatening or attacking us then, people loved the president and they loved this country and its values, and I think Obama is the man to regain that world respect. I think in Afghanistan we will achieve a solution there, not by increasing the number of combat troops we have in the country, but by increasing the number of schools and medical clinics and libraries they have in the country, so they can see the United States as it truly is.

Civil Rights

In 1957, nine little kids of high school age, lined up outside Central High School in Little Rock, Arkansas. As their white brothers and sisters walked before them and entered the high school, they were abruptly stopped by bayonets and armed soldiers. The only reason they were selected to be stopped that day was the color of their skin. Schools were White and Black. The historic US Supreme Court Brown vs Topeka Board of Education said, "schools are for children, not colors." Despite persecution and undue pressure, the nine attended and graduated from Central High. They are known as "The Little Rock Nine." (You can listen to my interview with one of the brave members of the Little Rock Nine, Mini Jean Brown, at www.brenthollandshow.com.)

Abraham Bolden is the first African American Secret Service agent on White House detail. He was handpicked by JFK. He was not on duty the day of the assassination and is haunted by that to this day, knowing full well that he would have kept the young president from the sniper's bullets. (See "Chapter 10 Secret Service Abraham Bolden, A Real American Hero" for more information.)

Holland: I had Minnie Jean Brown on this show, she was one of the original Little Rock Nine…I also had a fellow that used to work for your boss, on the show, his name is Abraham Bolden, do you remember him…?

Sorensen: Oh the Secret Service agent?

Holland: Yes sir, do you remember him?

Sorensen:I remember that there was such a person, but, to be honest with you, I didn't pal around with the Secret Service agents, so I did not remember him personally.

Holland: Folks today just don't understand the division that was in place in those days, and what Kennedy was up against, that your whole administration was up against in those days…was it very…?

Sorensen: Not just those days, because when Kennedy and Johnson put through a comprehensive civil rights program, they both agreed that that was the end of the Democratic Party in the South and maybe the end of the Democratic Party winning presidential elections. Since then, the only two Democrats who have won presidential elections up to before Obama, were two Southern Governors, Carter and Clinton, and every other presidential election was won by the Republicans with strong support from the Southern and border states and that anti-Democratic Party attitude continues to a considerable extent today despite the miracle, and it was a miracle, of Obama's victory.

Holland: Do you think a lot of those elements are still in place today?

Sorensen: Yes.

Holland: And you draw parallels between the anti-Catholic movement that was against Kennedy and the anti-African American movement that's against Obama?

Sorensen: Yes, if anything it was stronger against Kennedy. Because people thought that the Catholics exercise mind control and that a Catholic president would therefore be submissive to the Pope, that he would permit clergymen to tell their parishioners how to vote. They don't mind if Protestant ministers tell their congregations how to vote, but in those days the fear of a Catholic in the White House, which today seems incomprehensible, nobody things about it, it was very, very strong and that was one of the reasons why I thought Obama could win in '08, if a Catholic could win in 1960, and so they both faced formidable demographic obstacles, but, both were young, they both were articulate and eloquent, both had a good idea of how the United States looked from abroad, because both of them had spent time abroad, Obama when he was growing up, Kennedy when he was an ambassadors son. So I think Obama is more like John F. Kennedy than any president since.

Holland: I'm going to ask you a question now, just off the top of my head, did JFK ever piss you off sir, did you ever disagree with him?

Sorensen: No. He was a lot slower to lead on civil rights, which had been a subject very important to me when I was even younger, I was going to say when I was young, but I was pretty young when I was in the White House.

Holland: You sure were, 30.

Sorensen: But even younger, I had started out talking about and rooting for civil rights, and he came from a totally different background and was a little slower. But, my affection and admiration for him were such that I respected him always, admired him and can never say that whatever minor disagreements we might have had on other subjects from time to time, that anything ever became a major block between us.

In fact, just to take time for one other story, there was almost a lawsuit over the claim that I had been the author of his book, "Profiles In Courage." He was very upset and angry about that and when the lawyers for the other side, both he and his father were threatening the lawsuit, said "Well, maybe Sorensen himself talked about writing "Profiles In Courage"? JFK said, "No, he never would have said that." And the author said, "Maybe he said it when he was drunk"? "No, he doesn't drink." "Maybe he said it when he was angry at you?" And JFK said, "He's never been angry at me," – and that was the truth.

The Civil Rights Act of 1964

The Civil Rights Act of 1964 was enacted on July 2, 1964 after JFK's assassination. It established that discrimination against African American citizens was illegal and punishable. Some believe that JFK was assassinated because of his role in bringing about legislation for the Civil Rights Act. Some believe Johnson played a role in JFK's assassination. One of the reasons I believe Johnson was not involved in the assassination is because he fought to bring the Civil Rights Act into legislation, making it JFK's legacy. Indeed, Lyndon Johnson made a speech only five days after President Kennedy's assassination on November 27, 1963. "No memorial oration or eulogy could more eloquently honor President Kennedy's memory than the earliest possible passage of the civil rights bill for which he fought so long."

Johnson championed the act, twisted arms and gave the "Johnson Treatment" to those who opposed. He knew full well it could mean the end of the Democratic Party in the South, and no chance of him being elected as president in 1964. By pushing the legislation that supposedly got JFK killed, paradoxically LBJ would be signing his own death warrant, if, indeed, he was involved in the assassination. Those opposed to the Civil Rights Act would then be after the new president. It doesn't add up.

"This Nation was founded by men of many nations and backgrounds. It was founded on the principle that all men are created equal, and that

the rights of every man are diminished when the rights of one man are threatened.

It is better to settle these matters in the courts than on the streets, and new laws are needed at every level, but law alone cannot make men see right. We are confronted primarily with a moral issue. It is as old as the Scriptures and is as clear as the American Constitution.

The heart of the question is whether all Americans are to be afforded equal rights and equal opportunities, whether we are going to treat our fellow Americans as we want to be treated. If an American, because his skin is dark, cannot eat lunch in a restaurant open to the public, if he cannot send his children to the best public school available, if he cannot vote for the public officials who will represent him, if, in short, he cannot enjoy the full and free life which all of us want, then who among us would be content to have the color of his skin changed and stand in his place? Who among us would then be content with the counsels of patience and delay"?

President John F. Kennedy, Civil Rights Speech, June 11, 1963

Sorensen: But Bobby as Attorney General, was completely supportive of JFK's policies, particularly on civil rights, which was in Bobby's jurisdiction, and in the years after, Bobby continued as a United States Senator to forward JFK's policies on civil rights and on peace, instead of constant resort to war and military force. And that's why Bobby would have found a way out of Vietnam which JFK was on the verge of doing when he was killed.

The Assassination- ominous undertones revealed

Holland: Can I touch on his death sir?

Sorensen: Briefly, but it's the worst day of my life, so I don't like to talk about it too much.

Holland: Understood sir. You wrote something quite ominous in your book, you said that…I'll paraphrase, basically upon reflection you find it hard to believe now that perhaps some of Kennedy's enemies *were not* behind the assassination. Have I got that correct?

> Sorensen: Well, something like that, because I don't know, nobody really knows and I try to avoid reading most of these so called "conspiracy" books. The fact is that Kennedy had enemies in the Right Wing, particularly because of civil rights, and because his American University speech indicated that he was taking a more accommodating position toward the Soviet Union. He also had enemies among organised crime, as did his brother Bobby. He also supposedly had enemies among Communists in both the Soviet Union and Cuba – although I don't think either one of them would have thought that they would gain by Kennedy's removal.
>
> All I meant to say in the book was: Considering the number of enemies that he had, in the military and intelligence circles in the United States – Lord knows they had reasons to get rid of him – they had opportunities to have access to arms, to reach out to the kind of weird and confused individuals who can be recruited for that kind of work. I don't make any accusations, because I don't believe in making any accusations without proof.

Idealism. The idealism that both Ted and President Kennedy shared is contained in the American University Peace Speech from June 10, 1963. Indeed this may be the most important speech of all time. This clearly demonstrates that when people stand together with a common goal of peace, all is possible.

> *"For in the final analysis, our most basic common link is that we all inhabit this small planet. We all breathe the same air. We all cherish our children's futures. And we are all mortal."*
>
> ---
>
> President Kennedy, American University, June 10, 1963

The soaring adventure that both Ted and JFK traveled together can be best summed up by the true story of a flight they took when they first met.

> Sorensen: JFK and I, in 1956 – when he first became a national figure and we were traveling to every state – we had been in Idaho. And we were flying from Idaho to Nevada, in a little one engine plane and the local county chairman was the pilot. When the county chairman says he'll take you, you don't say "no" – when you're trying to get in good favor in Idaho.

And, he flew into, or started his descent into Reno, Nevada – the plane turned upside down. And JFK...I was sitting in the front with the pilot and turned around, looked at JFK, he looked at me, it was a kind of a "my God!" look...

The pilot straightened out. Righted the plane, the plane righted itself. He made it, went past the airport, made a turn, came back. And he apologized saying he'd been getting a little tired and he – I don't know anything about flying airplanes, much less aerodynamics – but he said that you're supposed to come in against the wind and he came in with the wind and that's what caused that momentary shock.

Holland: Boy, that's a bit of a metaphor for what was to come.

Sorensen: (laughing)...well, it might have...well, I think, we'd already been through quite a bit together and we knew more was to come, and it sure did!

Epilogue

Ted passed away on October 31, 2010, after a stroke, and only two weeks after a call from the White House. I was deeply moved and honored to have been invited to Mr. Sorensen's memorial in NYC in December 2010. Attendees rose to immortalize Ted on a personal level, and share what he meant to the country and how he saved the world. It seems Ted had indeed changed them, as I have also changed since our talks together. What he offered us is "dialogue before bullets."

Because the time is nigh, and night beckons.

Today the world struggles through similar life-or-death battles, decisions that race across the Internet instantaneously with little or no time for reflection. The world seems littered with those that entertain murder and death as the ultimate glory and servitude to God. I can only hope that the next person responsible for deciding whether or not to end the world will have the inclination to resolve ... and take a moment to reflect. Because the time is nigh, and night beckons.

"I can only hope that the next person responsible for deciding whether or not to end the world will have the inclination to resolve ... and take a moment to reflect. Because the time is nigh, and night beckons."

Brent Holland

Photos owned and copyright, Brent Holland, 2013

CHAPTER 4

Dr. Robert McClelland

"Kind of, a discrepancy. In general, the pictures we saw, 8x10 color pictures of the autopsy photos, showed a large wound in the back of the head. But in one of the photos, they were, I thought, pulling a flap of scalp up over this wound in order to [hide] a wound in the back of the head. We had not seen any other wound except this large gaping wound. I was later told by someone that this was not a flap of scalp being pulled up on the back of the head. This was just the way the back of the head looked. And I said, to whomever I was talking to, well that's not the way it looked, because there was a huge hole, where that, what I thought was a flap of scalp being pulled up over that hole. So, that was the only sort of inconsistent statement in that regard."

Dr. Robert McClelland

INTRODUCTION

Stop and ponder for a moment. If we had the chance to speak with the actual doctor who worked on President Abraham Lincoln after the fatal shooting, what an incredible resource for history and all time that would be.

This is the true story of Dr. Robert McClelland, surgeon, who was in Trauma Room One at Parkland Hospital on Friday, November 22, 1963, pulling out all the stops to resuscitate and save the life of young President John F. Kennedy.

Not only did Dr. McClelland work on the fatally wounded president on that day, but three days later on Sunday, November 24, 1963 he would have another rendez-vous with history when he worked on a mortally wounded Lee Harvey Oswald, the purported assassin of JFK.

When Dr. McClelland graciously agreed to be interviewed by me for "Night Fright," I asked him why he was still open to talk about his experiences. Like all I have interviewed on the JFK conspiracy, he replied that it was not for personal fame or monetary gain. He told me he felt a responsibility, a duty to the country and history as a whole to speak about his experience. That answer would repeat itself from person to person as I interviewed witnesses and research authors alike. A personal sense of integrity, honour and duty. We are indeed indebted to them all.

DR. BOB

Dr. Robert "Bob" McClelland is no lightweight, first-person witness. His credentials are impeccable, and his character remains beyond reproach. He was called upon to testify to the American government's Warren Commission in 1964, the US House Select Commission on Assassinations in 1978 (whose conclusion found a conspiracy in the murder of JFK), and on a 1990s PBS Front Line exposé on the assassination. Over the years, Dr. McClelland has come to believe that what the Warren Commission (the official government inquiry into the JFK assassination) presented was a lie, based on his own first-person witness.

> **To set up that day in Dallas, Texas, and to put us in context, I think it's important to portray the political climate and attitudes towards JFK in Dallas, leading up to the Kennedy trip. Dallas was somewhat of a "provincial" city in November of 1963 and according to Dr. McClelland, the political demeanour in the city was far "right wing." Many people in the power and money milieu felt that Kennedy's administration and policies were far "too leftist" in ideology.**

Dr. McClelland told me that there was a great deal of excitement due to the visit by JFK, but there was an ominous undercurrent of concern for his safety. In fact, a poster was openly circulating throughout Dallas declaring that JFK was wanted for treason. This same poster had also appeared as a full-page spread in the newspaper. This was the electrically charged whirlwind JFK was about to leap into.

November 22, 1963, the day of the assassination, began unassumingly for Dr. McClelland. He was at Parkland Hospital in Dallas, a university teaching hospital where he worked and taught, showing a film on hiatus hernias. Symbolically perhaps, there would come a knock at the door. That knock would alter his life forever as he became entwined in the events of the John Kennedy and Lee Harvey Oswald assassinations.

What follows is historic. This is the actual doctor who worked on John Kennedy and Lee Harvey Oswald. This is that true life testament, in his own words, by none other than Dr. Robert McClelland.

But I think the American people expect more from us than cries of indignation and attack. The times are too grave, the challenge too urgent, and the stakes too high--to permit the customary passions of political debate. We are not here to curse the darkness, but to light the candle that can guide us through that darkness to a safe and sane future. President John F. Kennedy, Presidential Nomination Acceptance Speech. 15 July 1960

PARKLAND HOSPITAL, DALLAS, NOVEMBER 22, 1963, 12:35 PM (APPROX.); IT BEGINS.

Dr. McClelland: I went to the door and looked out and standing there was Dr. Charles Crenshaw, who was one of our senior surgery residents. He said, "Dr. Mac, could you step outside here, I'd like to tell you something?" So I said I would. So I went in and shut off the movie projector and stepped out and he said, "They just called the emergency room and said that President Kennedy had been shot during the midst of his motorcade downtown and that they're bringing him, rushing him right now, to Parkland Hospital to our emergency room and they want all the faculty surgeons to come to the emergency room immediately." So that's what happened and that's where I first heard about it.

I was curious as to what I would be thinking if I was in Dr. McClelland's shoes at that moment...

> Holland: What was running through your mind; speculation on the wounds perhaps?"
>
> Dr. McClelland: No, not really, neither of us knew any of the particulars about it, and so we couldn't speculate about the nature of the wounds, but, as we rode down in the elevator, two floors down to the emergency room, immediately below the operating room, I said to Chuck, I said, well, you know, we often get these stories called into the emergency room that they're bringing in some horrific accident or problem like that and it turns out that it's not really as bad as its said to be on the phone.
>
> With that the elevator door came open and we walked around a little corridor, a corner in the corridor there, out into the big area that we call the "pit," which is the center of the emergency room, and it was filled with people in business suits all wearing hats. Everybody wore a hat back in those days. But there must have been fifty or sixty men like that in the center of this emergency room, something that I had never seen before. And as I took that in, that crowd spontaneously parted, made a little corridor from where I was, about fifty feet down to the area to where Trauma Rooms 1, 2, 3, and 4 were off the side of the emergency room.
>
> And there, sitting on a folding chair outside of Trauma Room One, was Mrs. Kennedy in her bloody clothing. So, I knew immediately, this is exactly what it was said to be. And it also occurred to me immediately, that "My God, here it is at noon and I'm the only faculty surgeon in the hospital."
>
> There were only four faculty surgeons at that time in Southwestern Medical School in Parkland, now they're more than fifty. But at that time there were four. My chief, Dr. Shares, I knew was in Galveston at a medical meeting. My two associates, Dr. Charles Baxter and Dr. Malcolm Perry, I didn't know where they were, but I thought it being noon time they were probably outside the hospital looking for better food than we had at the hospital. So I thought, I'm by myself and I'm the "senior," quote unquote, I was 34 years old, faculty surgeon. So I literally had to force myself to walk down there toward Trauma Room One to where Mrs. Kennedy was sitting.

It's interesting to look at the preparations that take place today for a presidential visit as compared to 1963. President Kennedy's Secret Service team had not contacted Parkland in advance to request that they stock up on JFK's blood type, or even to have staff prepared for any emergency that could jeopardize the president's life. Today, the president travels with all kinds of emergency equipment in the trunk of his car, including his own blood type. Not so in Dallas on November 22, 1963. Dr. McClelland had later asked the Secret Service why they had chosen Parkland Hospital to bring the president. He was told that generally the Secret Service would find out what the nearest hospital was along the motorcade route, particularly looking for a university hospital, and Parkland just happened to fit the bill.

TRAUMA ROOM ONE, TRYING TO SAVE PRESIDENT KENNEDY

In his own words, Dr. Robert McClelland takes us into Trauma Room One on November 22, 1963, where JFK has just been rushed after being shot.

> Dr. McClelland: I went to the door of Trauma Room One, and I was passed through by two Secret Service agents who were standing next to Doris Nelson, the nurse in charge of the emergency room at that time. She was telling them who to let go by or not – so, they signaled me through and I went into Trauma Room One.
>
> As I opened the door, the thing that struck me immediately was the terrible appearance of the president, who was lying underneath an operating room light on a gurney in the room with his face towards the door, the light in his face and his head completely covered in blood. And he was attached to respirators through an endotracheal tube that had been placed into his trachea immediately as he entered the emergency room and also to an electrocardiographic monitor.
>
> And, so, that's what I saw immediately. I was horrified, of course, by that. But, I was also simultaneously gratified in that I saw I was not by myself, that Dr. Perry and Dr. Baxter, my two associates on the faculty, had arrived immediately before I did and they had just placed a sterile surgical drape on the president's neck where there was a small wound in the lower right hand portion of his neck and they had just begun making a transverse or straight across an incision in his neck, as I walked into the door.
>
> As I walked by the gurney, on the left side of the gurney, Dr. Perry, who was starting to make the incision, dropped his scalpel and leaned over and picked up what's called an Army-Navy Retractor off a surgical tray and handed it to me as I walked by and he said, "Bob, would you go and stand at the head of the gurney and lean over the president's head and hold the retractor in this incision we're making so we can see?" as he and Dr. Baxter were doing that exploration of that wound.
>
> And so that put me in a position immediately above the president's head about, probably 16 to 18 inches above this horrendous wound

in the back of the head that I could look down into and into the inside of his skull from where I stood. So that gave me the best and the worst view of the wound of anybody in Trauma Room One.

And, so, I stood there while they completed that exploration of the wound that I'd pointed out here in the right side of the neck, for about... it took about 12 minutes to complete that. As they were completing that exploration, saw there was no damage to the internal jugular vein or the carotid artery, (which is what they were looking for) and had put in a tracheotomy tube to replace the endotracheal tube, Dr. (William Kemp) Clark, our neurosurgeon, who had entered the room and had been standing by the electrocardiographic monitor, looked at it just as they were completing the exploration and he said, "Mac, you can stop now," to Dr. Perry, "he's gone." Because he had just flat lined on the electrocardiographic monitor.

Holland: Was Mr. Kennedy clothed when you saw him, could you see the blood stains on his shirt, his jacket?

Dr. McClelland: No, when I entered the room, he had been cut out of his clothing by the nurses immediately. That's the standard practice for any injured patient so that you can see the entire body and be certain that you see where all the injuries are.

Holland: Can you walk us around the gurney and tell us who was standing where?

Dr. McClelland: When I entered the room, Dr. Baxter was on the left side standing just above the wound on his neck and Dr. Perry, who was the operating surgeon, was on the president's right side and had just placed a surgical drape on the president's neck. I was standing at the head of the gurney immediately above the presidents' head.

Holland: Mr. Kennedy was alive when he arrived at Parkland, was he breathing on his own?

Dr. McClelland: No, Dr. Jenkins, our anesthesiologist professor, was sitting right beside me at the head of the gurney and he was working an anesthesia machine and squeezing the bag to breath for the president. So that was moving his chest up and down. But, he had excellent cardiac activity on the electrocardiographic monitor. So he was, as you said, he was alive even though he had sustained an absolutely fatal brain injury.

Mrs. Kennedy, poise & grace as she watched her husband die

> **Given the profound opportunity I had to speak with a living historical figure, I wanted to get as much detail as possible about the scenario. It has been my experience that even the most mundane moments, which often get glossed over in interviews, can sometimes reap rewards in terms of the best information. I also wanted to humanize the events, to break down the barriers. Yes, this was a president and the first lady, but I wanted to get a picture of the concern and care that the doctors would have shown in any emergency situation and to any human life in the balance.**

I had often wondered about the well-being of Mrs. Kennedy during these insane moments, so I asked Dr. McClelland if she was in the room witnessing the actual death of her husband and father of their children.

Dr. McClelland: No, Mrs. Kennedy remained seated on the folding chair outside the room. However, she got up two or three times and came into the room and Dr. Clark, who had been standing there by the electrocardiographic monitor. Each time she did, he very gently ushered her back out again to try to protect her from this terrible thing that was occurring at that time and she didn't resist that and left each time and that was probably two or three times while we were conducting this exploration of the president's neck wound.

Holland: Did she ever ask about the condition of her husband?

Dr. McClelland: Not at that time but... after he was pronounced dead, by Dr. Clark, everybody in the room left. And, there had been a number of people other than Dr. Perry, Dr. Baxter and I, who had accumulated in Trauma Room One during this procedure and they all left immediately after the president was pronounced dead except Dr. Baxter and I.

Father Huber administers the Last Rites

Dr. McClelland: As the crowd was leaving the room, they moved the gurney with the president on it so that Dr. Baxter and I were pushed against the wall by the gurney and had to wait for everybody else to get out. And then after everyone left, and just as we were about to step around the head of the gurney and leave ourselves, the door of Trauma Room One came open and a Priest came in.

Then we later found out it was Father Huber, to administer "the Last Rites." And we would have had to almost push him out of the way in order to leave the room. So, we simply froze against the wall again and stood there. We felt inappropriate, but we couldn't get out without knocking the Priest down. So, we didn't try to do that and we had to stand there and listen to the Last Rites.

And all I could hear Father Huber say and he anointed the president's forehead, he uncovered his head which was covered with a sheet at that time and anointed his forehead and leaned over to him and the only words I could hear him say was, "if thou livest..." into the president's left ear, and then I couldn't hear anything else he said after that.

After he completed that, immediately after, Mrs. Kennedy again came into the room and stood by the side of the gurney, as Father Huber was putting all of his material that he had back into his little bag that he had used to perform the Last Rites. And I couldn't hear what Mrs. Kennedy said because she spoke in such a low voice, but from the context of Father Huber's answer to her, she apparently asked him if he had received the Last Rites and Father Huber said, "Yes, I have given him conditional absolution." And with that Mrs. Kennedy grimaced. She didn't say anything, but she, literally, was not pleased at having heard that sort of statement by Father Huber. But she didn't say anything.

With that she stood there for a moment silently and exchanged rings from her finger to his finger and back and forth between the two fingers. She stood there for a moment more, didn't say anything, then walked to the end of the gurney where the president's right foot was protruding out from underneath the sheet that had covered it. She stood by his foot for a moment then leaned over and kissed his foot and then walked out of Trauma Room One. And that was the last that Dr. Baxter and I saw of either President Kennedy or Mrs. Kennedy as we promptly left the room at that time too.

JFK & Addison's Disease

Something many people are unaware of is that President Kennedy suffered from Addison's disease. This is when the adrenal glands do not produce enough steroid hormones. The effects can be stomach pain and weakness. In severe cases, it can lead to low blood pleasure and coma. This was ever present on the mind of JFK's physician, Dr. George Burkley, who was in a separate car in the motorcade. He knew that due to the president's massive blood loss, his blood pressure would be critically low and coma would be imminent. I asked Dr. McClelland if Dr. Burkley came into Trauma Room One and offered any assistance.

Dr. McClelland: He came into the room and wanted to hand a vile of Adrenal Cortical Hormone to inject into the president. He was told by someone in the room that Dr. Charles "Jim" Carrico, who had incubated his trachea as soon as he had entered the emergency room, had been aware of the fact that the president had adrenal insufficiency and had already injected him with sadia-cortex, which is the name of the adrenal hormone he had used to give to the president.

JFK's Neck Wound

President Kennedy also suffered a wound to the center of his throat, near where the top button of his collar would be, a little above the Adam's apple, if you will. This wound has been a huge area of controversy in the assassination. It is widely believed that it is an entrance wound, and he was shot in the throat from a shooter in *front* of him.

Why do I emphasize the word "front"? Because, let's not forget that the official conclusion of the Warren Commission was that all shots originated from behind and above the president by one shooter acting alone. A shot causing a wound in the president's throat, coming from the front, would destroy their official conclusion. It would prove that there were at least two assassins shooting at the president, and therefore was, by definition, a conspiracy in the assassination of President Kennedy.

Dr. McClelland is a straightforward, no-nonsense and honest guy with no bias in any direction. He tells it like he saw it, and his integrity is beyond reproach. I asked Dr. McClelland about that wound.

Dr. McClelland: Actually, I didn't see that wound, because it was covered by a surgical drape. But, Dr. Perry and Dr. Baxter had and so they described it to me. It was a very small, about a ¼" in diameter, very clean wound, right where I'm pointing my finger, the right side of my neck, just above the collar bone and right next to the wind pipe, in this area.

Dr. Perry said that evening in the first interview he gave, that he thought, knowing nothing about the particulars at that time of Dealey Plaza, this was an entrance wound. We later were disaprised [*sic*]of that and knew that it was a wound that had been fired and it hit him in the back and it came out the neck, so this was an exit wound rather than an entrance wound.

This took me aback. I had always believed and still do, that this wound was caused by a frontal shot. Because Dr. McClelland was recounting what he had been told by Dr. Perry and Dr. Baxter and not personally witnessed, I asked him if he adhered to the thesis that the neck wound was an exit wound and not a frontal entrance wound. His response was honest, but still surprised me.

> Dr. McClelland: Yes, I do. And that's also based on my viewing of the Zapruder film some years later, as well as other things that I've learned since then.

The Zapruder film is the most viewed film of the assassination of the president. It was filmed by businessman Abraham Zapruder. It was used in the movie "JFK," where Kevin Costner played District Attorney Jim Garrison. Somberly, he repeated, "back and to the left, back and to the left."

> Holland: What are those things sir?
>
> Dr. McClelland: Well, I can probably go into those a little bit more later, because it was quite a train of other things down through the years that have led me to think that there was a shooter both on the sixth floor Book Depository – and that's clear – whether it was Oswald or someone else – I think fired a bullet from that point that hit him in the back and then came out his neck.
>
> And then on the Zapruder film, as you see, a good many seconds later – after he's already been hit – and you can see on the film – that when that first bullet hits him from behind and comes out his neck, that the president's arms and hands move up to his neck, like that (demonstrates his two hands at the middle of his throat). And it's obvious that something has happened at that time.
>
> Holland: I just want to ask you one more question about President Kennedy. Again, that is, with the throat wound – many people thought he was hit from the front, as well, but you think indeed, he was hit in the back and it went through and came out his throat?
>
> Dr. McClelland: Right.
>
> Holland: Now, one of the arguments against that of course, as I'm sure you're aware of, is the angle. That the angle where the bullet went into his back is below where it came out through his throat. Do you follow that thesis at all...I guess you dispute it.
>
> Dr. McClelland: That's a bit confusing and it is been, has been disputed. And, one of the things...We, first of all did not see the bullet wound in his back in Trauma Room One. The next day, I was in the office with Dr. Perry, we had an office together at the medical school. About 10 o'clock Saturday morning, Dr. Perry got a call from Dr. Boswell,

one of the pathologists at the (Besthesda) naval medical hospital, who had done the post-mortem on President Kennedy. And he wanted to ask Dr. Perry some questions about the exploration wound in the neck and then he also asked Dr. Perry – and I could see what was being said or hear what was being said – not by hearing Dr. Boswell, but by hearing Dr. Perry's response in answer to his questions.

So, Dr. Boswell apparently asked Dr. Perry did we know there was a wound in the president's back? And I heard Dr. Perry reply that, "no we didn't." Because we didn't think it was appropriate to do any further examination of the president after he had been pronounced dead. So, we didn't turn him over and look at his back.

Dr. Boswell said, "Well, there *was* a wound in his back." But he said it was high in the back, sort of in the middle, but over toward the right. But he didn't specify to us or to Dr. Perry, where that bullet was exactly as far as the height of the bullet.

Now some people have suggested that the president's coat, which had a bullet hole in it, had been sort of hiked up farther on his neck, you know, your coat gets pulled up higher sometimes when you're sitting down and that made the bullet hole appear lower in the coat than it actually was in his back. So, while I can't say from my own seeing anything, I do know where this bullet was in the front of his neck from what Dr. Perry told me. It was right here. (points to just center left above collar). And then I do also know that from the Zapruder film, that the president put his hands up to this hole and that was when the first bullet hit him, most likely from the back, from the Book Depository window or from one of the windows in one of the buildings around him.

Holland: From upwards and behind?

Dr. McClelland: Upwards, and what the exact angle was I don't really know.

President Kennedy's Back of Head Blasted Out

Dr. McClelland: And then several seconds later he disappears behind a sign along the edge of Elm street on the Zapruder film – and two or three seconds after being behind that sign, he comes out from behind it and a second or two later – Mrs. Kennedy at this point is leaning over to him – he still has his arms up to his neck – and she's concerned that something obviously has happened. And just as she is doing that, all of a sudden the president's head literally explodes and he's thrown violently backward and to the left.

So that was clearly an absolutely different shot from a different position, namely from the picket fence on the grassy knoll, is where that bullet came from that hit him – somewhere probably around the hair line.

Although we didn't see anything there because his head was covered in blood – and we didn't see anything. But, we saw this huge hole where I'm pointing (clutches his hand and fingers as if holding a softball and holds it places it at the lower back right hand quadrant of his head) in the back of his head that blew out probably a circular hole that was something like maybe 5 inches in diameter. And blew out most of the back part of his brain, that, so that I could look down into the empty part of his skull there.

Holland: When you were in Trauma Room One.

Dr. McClelland: Right. Trauma Room One.

EXPLANATION OF THE ZAPRUDER FILM

The Zapruder film is that most commonly seen film of the JFK assassination. There are other films of the assassination, but they are slightly out of focus, shaky, or too far away from the subject. The Zapruder film is by far the clearest and most complete, showing the entire assassination from start to finish, including the horrific head shot. The Zapruder film was shot by Abraham Zapruder, hence the name.

Destiny played its own role twice in Abraham Zapruder's story. The first time was when Zapruder left his office in the Dal-Tex Building and went back home to get his camera to film the motorcade which was due to arrive in Dealey Plaza around 12:30 PM.

For the second time, destiny came into play when Zapruder choose his spot to film the motorcade: on top of a concrete pedestal in the northside stucture of the Plaza (the grassy knoll). The pedestal was approximately 3.5 to four feet high at the structure level and just in front of the picket fence (where witnesses testified shots originated from and where the assassin was located). Because he suffered from vertigo, his secretary, Marilyn Sitzman, accompanied him on top of the concrete block, stood behind him and steadied him. This location, where Zapruder had innocently chosen to stand, was the perfect spot to take the most important film of the 20th Century.

Minutes after the assassination, Zapruder told a police officer he heard the shot come from behind him, indicating the picket fence on the grassy knoll, and from in front of the president's motorcade.

> **The Zapruder film was shot on an 8mm home movie camera manufactured by the leading company of such products in those days: Bell & Howell. It was shot on analog 8mm film. With no digital or instant playback in 1963, the film would have to be sent off to be developed before it could be viewed. Films were originally called "moving pictures" because a movie is really a series of individual photos being shown quickly, back to back, to give the illusion of movement, much like a flip book.**

For accurate examination, and to keep the correct sequence of frames, each individual frame, or photo, was given a number. The frames go from Z1 to Z446. (Z stands for Zapruder.) The film shows the entire sequence of the shooting of Governor John Connally and President Kennedy. The most talked-about and referenced is frame Z313, the head shot which killed Kennedy.

There are those that claim that the Zapruder film has been doctored, with frames painted and actors elaborately standing in place, and then inserted into the film, all as an attempt by the government to mislead us. If that were true, the Zapruder film would not line up with other films taken of the assassination that day, and *it does*. What's more, instead of allowing to exist a clear and accurate film of a frontal head shot, therefore proving two shooters and a conspiracy, they would have simply destroyed it.

Abraham Zapruder inadvertently captured on film for all time, from start to finish, the complete Kennedy assassination, giving us a priceless document for history and invaluable forensic evidence for investigators. The assassinations of Dr. Martin Luther King, Jr. and Bobby Kennedy had no such documentation of the complete scene of their murders and the moments of the shots being fired.

> **One day the technological expertise and indisputable scientific methods will exist to finally identify just how many bullets flew into the motorcade that day and from what directions. The day will arrive, I have no doubt, that highly detailed scanners and software will exist that can differentiate between the subtleties of shadows and light to unmask who is really standing behind that picket fence.**

THE BACK OF JFK'S HEAD BLASTED OUT CONFIRMED BY HIS BRAIN (CEREBELLUM)

Being ever the optimist and never wanting to surrender in any situation, even the inevitable and even though I knew the answer, I asked the question anyway...

Holland: Sir, when you looked down into the back of his brain, was there any brain left at all. In other words, was it inevitable that he was about to pass away?

Dr. McClelland: Yes, it was inevitable.

To this day, it still causes me grief. It's kind of like watching a movie about Jesus. I'll watch it right up to the part where he has just been sentenced to be crucified and then stop. I can't change the ending. It has already been cast. This is my struggle, to find a way to change history and save the president, not just the president, I suspect, but my own father as I have outlined before. Funny how the mind works. Perhaps all that has taken place in my own narrative has made me that ever optimist. Perhaps it was experiencing death at such a young age that has made me appreciate life and question why we don't aspire to more profound ventures. Does it really matter the reason you get together with your loved ones? It is the relationship and experience that count.

Dr. McClelland: Because there was nothing. I could look into the empty skull there. There was nothing there. And as I stood there, in fact, the right half of his cerebellum fell out through the wound onto the gurney in front of me there.

And there was some argument later between me and Dr. Jenkins and other people in the hall as to whether this was cerebellum or cerebrum. That's a significant point I think because if it is cerebellum, it means that the wound in the back of the head was farther [down] than some people have said. It would have indicated that maybe it was in the back of the head, but, *in sort* of a front part of the back of the head, whereby, it would be unlikely that cerebellum would come out (clutches his hand and fingers as if holding a softball and holds it over the upper most part, bordering on the top of the head, of the right upper quadrant of the back of the head); Well, the cerebrum was gone, that is the front part of the crane, but the cerebellum was the only thing that was left and that's what I saw clearly, to be cerebellum.

Although Dr. Jenkins changed his initial testimony in which he said it was cerebrum and later said, "Well, maybe I was mistaken, it probably was cerebrum, rather than cerebellum." He'd initially said cerebellum in his Warren Commission testimony.

DISCREPANCY WITH OFFICIAL JFK AUTOPSY PHOTOS

Holland: Sir, some years later, after that day, you were asked to go to the archives and look at the autopsy photos of President Kennedy.

Was there any discrepancies in the autopsy photos you saw and what you saw that day in Trauma Room One?

Dr. McClelland: Only one.

There shouldn't have been any discrepancies. The official autopsy photos should be identical to what Dr. McClelland witnessed in Trauma Room One. But what Dr. McClelland was about to reveal to me sent chills down my spine. You see, of all the possible photos that would show some sort discrepancy with what Dr. McClelland witnessed, it ended up being the exact photo that would indicate a cover-up.

Dr. McClelland: Kind of, a discrepancy. In general, the pictures that we saw, 8 x 10 color pictures of the autopsy photos, showed a large wound in the back of the head. But in one of the photos, the doctors were, what I thought, pulling a flap of scalp up over this wound in order to show a wound in the back of the head. We had not seen any other wound except this large gaping wound.

I was later told by someone that, well, this was not a flap of scalp being pulled up on the back of the head. This was just the way the back of the head looked. And I said, to whoever I was talking to, well that's not the way it looked because there was a huge hole, where that, what I thought was a flap of scalp being pulled up over that hole. So, that was the only sort of inconsistent statement in that regard.

This was the same wound Dr. McClelland has been describing in JFK's lower right quadrant at the back of his head, the same wound he saw cerebellum fall out of, the same wound he described as five inches in diameter, the same wound he looked down into in the president's skull. In other words, the wound was an exit wound indicating a frontal shot and therefore a second gunman and therefore a conspiracy.

In fact, as Dr. McClelland mentioned, that particular autopsy photo does indeed show what appears to be a bullet entrance hole in the back of President Kennedy's head. I have no problem with that. I believe JFK was hit by at least 4 bullets and never mind about Gov. Connolly getting pelted with his own set of bullets. The following are what I believe to be the minimum four shots in JFK alone:

1. Middle back, just to the left of the right shoulder blade, entrance wound, shot coming from behind, this bullet did not exit JFK's body

2. Throat, just above the Adam's apple, entrance wound shot coming from front

3. Rear head, just above neck line center right, entrance wound shot coming from behind

4. Head, front right forehead, entrance wound shot coming from front, exited JFK's rear lower right quadrant making a five inch diameter exit hole and cavity in JFK's skull

What is alarming is that the autopsy photos only show a bullet entrance wound originating from behind JFK. Therefore, the autopsy photo only succeeds into shoring up the cover-up of the Warren Commission's thesis, that all shots originated from behind the president, and none came from the front.

Let me play innocent here. Is it possible that, as Dr. McClelland first suggested, someone had simply pulled a flap of scalp up over the hole in the back of JFK's head so as to reveal the bullet entrance wound and get a clear, unobstructed photo for the autopsy photo folder? Absolutely. I think that this is the probable scenario. In fact, Dr. McClelland stated that all the other photos showed the head as he had remembered it. However, if the exit path of the fatal head shot bullet was in the back of JFK's head, then a 5-inch diameter hole leading into an empty skull cavity is pretty hard to miss. Therefore, why are there no photos of the rear exit wound in the "official" autopsy folder?

> **In truth, there were probably photos taken of the wound in the lower right quadrant of the back of JFK's head, but were omitted from the rest of the autopsy folder package, precisely because they did show an exit wound and therefore two shooters and a conspiracy. The cover-up was already underway.**

I don't believe the autopsy was coordinated, purposely planned to destroy evidence for a coup. A coup is far too complicated. Too many pieces would have to fall into place. When you design a covert op, you keep it as simple as possible, with the fewest moving parts, because one or more of those parts always breaks.

Think back to Seal Team 6 taking down Bin Laden. With two helicopters and thousands of hours of planning and training, one of the helicopters landed slightly off kilter and couldn't take off again. No operation goes according to plan. Even with modern technology, the highest quality operators, extremely smart guys, something inevitably finds its way to screw up. So, no, I don't believe in a government coup, or a military coup for that matter. I see no precalculated plan to destroy autopsy evidence. I will discuss the "why" of the cover-up and the "why not" of a coup d'état in a future chapter. (See "Chapter 12 Assassination Noise" for more information.)

Mrs. Kennedy Held JFK's Brains Cupped In Her Hands

> Holland: Sir, there was another story too; I wanted to get on tape as well. Mrs. Kennedy apparently came into Trauma Room One clutching something in her fist. Do you know that story Sir, can you tell us that one, please?"

> Dr. McClelland: Yes... Yes, Dr. Jenkins told me about that. I didn't see that. But, just before I came into the room and after Dr. Jenkins had seen it himself, there by the anesthesia machine, Mrs. Kennedy came in, she said – and Dr. Jenkins told me this right after we had finished what we were doing in Trauma Room One – he said she was holding a large portion of the president's brain and – again it was cerebrum – and handed it to Dr. Jenkins and just walked out after that, after she had handed that large portion of brain of the president to Dr. Jenkins.

In the Zapruder film, just after JFK was shot in the head, and his skull literally exploded (Z313), Mrs. Kennedy can be seen going onto the trunk of the limo. Many have thought that she panicked and was trying to get out of the car. You can see Secret Service Agent Clint Hill leap onto the trunk of the limo and collect Mrs. Kennedy back into the backseat of the car. Hill was assigned that day to guard "Lace," which was Mrs. Kennedy's code name. "Lancer" was President Kennedy's.

In truth, Mrs. Kennedy had not panicked. Indeed she showed the wherewithal to risk her own life amid the flurry of shots, and leap out into the open, onto the trunk to retrieve a piece of the president's brain. This was the same piece of brain that Mrs. Kennedy gave to Dr. Jenkins as related in the previous story.

> **It was just an insane moment of pure despair. She hoped against all hope that somehow they could put his brain back in his head. It was a nightmare that would not end. I have always been curious, if JFK had not been shot fatally in the head, were his other wounds survivable? If the Secret Service had been focused on doing their job professionally, would JFK, the father of two and husband to Jackie, been alive to celebrate his children's birthdays that week, instead of in a closed coffin?**

> Holland: If President Kennedy had not been shot in the head, and I point to the front as a frontal wound, as you had, could he have survived the initial shot in the back that came out his throat?

> Dr. McClelland: Oh yes! No problem at all with that!

DR. MCCLELLAND'S EYEWITNESS DISCREPANCIES

President Kennedy's rear head wound, that Dr. McClelland witnessed in Trauma Room One, was situated in the back of JFK's head in the lower right quadrant and was about the size of a grapefruit or five inches in diameter.

As I stated before, the significance of this wound is that it was an *exit* wound. This would mean the bullet that caused it had to come from in front of President Kennedy, entering the front of JFK's forehead and exiting in the back of his head. Therefore, this would indicate that there was a second shooter who shot the president from the front. Two shooters, one from the back and one from the front, would mean that people got together to make a plan to assassinate the president; a conspiracy. For you and me it's a no-brainer. What is the big deal?

The big deal is that the Warren Commission's official conclusion says that only one shooter killed the president. His name was Lee Harvey Oswald, who, they claim, acted spontaneously and alone. In addition, all the bullets that caused all the wounds that day, came from above and *behind* the president, exactly where The Warren Commission says Oswald was perched on the sixth floor of the Texas School Book Depository building. So, just how does a bullet shot into the back of JFK's head from *behind* him, not cause an exit wound in the *front* of the head where physics dictates it should? It can't be explained, plain and simple.

> **In this ridiculous scenario, this bullet defies physics (and I would argue logic) and enters JFK's head from behind, does an abrupt u-turn inside Kennedy's head and then exits from the same way it came in: out the back of JFK's head. (and believe it or not folks, this isn't even the "magic bullet" you've heard about. We will get to that amazing story coming up in a later chapter, (See Chapter 5 "James Tague, the man responsible for the Magic Bullet" for more information).**

Now there was a dilemma; the mounting evidence was showing a conspiracy. Even the Warren Commission knew they could never get away with something so absurd as a bullet that does a u-turn. So they simply took away all the evidence that would show an exit wound in the back of JFK's head, including any autopsy photos.

THE WARREN COMMISSION

The Warren Commission was set up by President Lyndon Johnson on November 29, 1963, only six days after JFK was assassinated. It is worth noting that the initiative for an investigation came from Kennedy's "New Frontier" team and did not originate with Johnson. Lyndon Johnson was the vice-president under President John Kennedy and became the president automatically after the assassination of JFK. Johnson was actually in the same JFK motorcade in Dallas at the moment of the assassination but was in a different car and was unharmed as no shots were directed anywhere but at the president's limo.

After the assassination, there was a strong urging by Kennedy's people for an investigation, like the Government did just after 9/11, to explore and reveal all there was to reveal about the catastrophe that has just befallen the American people. In truth, the Warren Commission was put together primarily to squelch the raging rumors that the assassination was indeed a conspiracy, that is, more than a single assassin.

Johnson also wanted to lay to rest the rumors that Lee Harvey Oswald was contracted to kill JFK by Cuba or even the Soviet Union. This was the height of the Cold War, let's not forget, and the Cuban Missile Crisis had taken place only a single year before (See Chapter 3 "Ted Sorensen, The Man Who Saved The World. Really" for more information). Americans were still immersed in the fear that a nuclear holocaust could take place at any moment.

Hell of a way to live; in fear 24/7.

To lead the Warren Commission, Johnson chose US Chief Justice Earl Warren. It seems clear to all JFK researchers, and those who have read all 26 volumes of the Warren Commission investigation, that the Warren Commission's official conclusion was already made long before the investigation even started. They were resolved that one lone-nut communist sympathizer and malcontent, Lee Harvey Oswald, assassinated the president.

The members of the Commission were:

- Earl Warren, Chief Justice of the United States – who repeatedly refused to take part in the Commission. But, Johnson was a powerful salesman and manipulator whose "Johnson Treatment," as it was known to all who worked for him, was legendary. Finally Warren got tired of Johnson's nagging and agreed to head the Commission.

- US Representative, House Minority Leader Gerald Ford – before he became the 38th president of the United States, after Watergate in the 70s. Ford would later reveal that the CIA had knowingly destroyed and/or concealed essential information from the Warren Commission because, he states, "certain classified and potentially damaging operations were in danger of being exposed. It was to hide or destroy some information, which can easily be misinterpreted as collusion in JFK's assassination." He also was illegally passing information along to the FBI on just how things were going with the investigation. He shockingly admitted to altering evidence by stating that a shot hit the president in the back of the neck and exited the front of his throat.

This was a pure lie. In truth the shot that entered the president's back was actually located six inches down from the hair line just to the left of JFK's right shoulder blade. Ford stated that he wanted to avoid any confusion with the Commission's report. He changed the location of the back wound up to the neck so that it would more closely match the Magic Bullet Theory. I jest not (See "Breach of Trust" by Gerald D. McKnight, 2005).

- Allen Dulles – the former director of the Central Intelligence Agency. This was a bizarre appointment for this Commission. Kennedy fired Dulles as head of the CIA for lying to him over the Bay Of Pigs fiasco which took place in Cuba in April 1961 (See "Chapter 3 "Ted Sorensen, The Man Who Saved The World. Really" for more information).

After this, Kennedy didn't trust Dulles or for that matter the CIA, and for Johnson to appoint him to the Commission is a red flag at the very least.

- Senator Richard Russell, Jr – who outright refused to sign the Warren Commission report as he did not believe the single bullet theory, or as it has become known, the Magic Bullet Theory.

- John J. McCloy – who was the former president of the World Bank.

- Senator John Cooper and House Majority Leader Hale Boggs – who were also in agreement with Senator Russell. They believed that Governor John Connolly of Texas, who was sitting in the limousine's jump seat directly in front of President Kennedy, was struck by a bullet unto its own (and maybe two). They believed that the "magic" bullet could not have entered Kennedy's back in the center of the shoulder blades, exited his throat, and then wounded Govenor Connally.

This bullet was conveniently found on a Parkland hospital gurney, by the way. To solve the problem, eventually some wording in the final section of the report was changed to a very absurd and self contradicting: "Although it is not necessary to any essential findings of the Commission to determine just which shot hit Governor Connally..." What!? Of course, it was essential to find out which shot(s) hit Connally! It was their mandate to account for all bullets, shots and their trajectory origins.

It would be like the 9/11 Commission stating it didn't matter how many planes crashed into the Twin Towers because the towers would have fallen anyways. Absurd. Of course it matters, otherwise there would be no way of knowing who flew the planes, what direction they came from and how, where and when they crashed that caused structural

failure with the inevitability of the collapse. How would we then know how to protect ourselves and prevent the same scenario from happening again?

By omitting which shot(s) hit Connally, the Warren Commission would not have to commit to the true number of shots fired at the president and the governor that day, and where they originated from (above, front, side, back and /or otherwise). Therefore, they were able to control the whole crime scene and fabricate the assassination shooting scenario to anything they wanted in order to shore up the lone shooter theory, with only three shots.

The above doesn't reflect a lot of confidence in the Commission members or their conclusion. I am perplexed. The Warren Commission was comprised of some the country's smartest and cleverest people. I would argue that they were patriots, who presumably would have the best interests of the country at heart. So, why would they knowingly, and illegally, omit evidence, and do a shabby job investigating the most heinous assassination of the 20th century? Let's not forget that John's brother, Bobby, was still attorney general of the US at that time. So why the obvious cover-up?

It is my belief that it was for one reason only: national security. Whatever was at stake in revealing the truth behind the assassination, was worth the consequences of the cover-up. What national security issue could prevent full disclosure to this day? I'll talk more about that in chapter 14 "My Own Perspective."

One last thing about the Warren Commission's conclusion: during a phone call from Senator Russell to President Johnson, when Russell would not sign the Commission's report because of the Magic Bullet Theory, Johnson told Russell that he didn't believe the Magic Bullet Theory either!

Dr. McClelland and Lee Harvey Oswald

President Kennedy was shot and killed on Friday, November 22, 1963 at approximately 12:30 PM Dallas time (CST). That same day, only an hour and a half later, the Dallas Police arrested Lee Harvey Oswald. On Saturday, November 23, they formally charged Lee Harvey Oswald with the assassination of President Kennedy.

On Sunday morning, November 24, at approximately 11:00 AM, Lee Harvey Oswald was mortally shot by a known underworld figure, Jack Ruby, while being transferred to a more secure facility. Oswald, like President Kennedy, was rushed to Parkland Hospital. In an unprecedented rendezvous with history, Dr. Robert McClelland found himself eerily in the same scenario as he had been only three days before. He now attempted to save a fatally shot victim of assassination, the very man charged with the assassination of President Kennedy.

Holland: Sir, I want to talk now about Lee Harvey Oswald, because you were instrumental in working on him as well. Folks, if you are unaware of Lee Harvey Oswald, he was the purported assassin of President Kennedy. He was arrested a little more than an hour after the assassination. Sunday morning the 24th, Oswald was shot by a fellow by the name of Jack Ruby when he was being transferred from the Sheriff's office to the county jail. In the basement of the Sheriff's office, as he was being brought out, this fellow by the name of Jack Ruby lunged forward with a pistol and shot him once in the stomach. Lee Harvey Oswald, was rushed to Parkland Hospital, sir can you pick it up from there for us.

Dr. McClelland: Yes. That Sunday, I was at home. I had been at Church with my wife and two small children and my mother visiting. And while they were upstairs getting ready to go out for diner, or for lunch, I sat down by our television set in our living room downstairs. And I thought well, I'll turn the television on and see what news is going on now.

And as I turned the TV on, the sort of picture began to form, I could hear voices. And the voices were saying "he's been shot, he's been shot!" And I thought to myself, now what? And the picture formed and I saw what everybody has seen many times, probably in various venues, the famous tableau of Ruby has just shot Oswald and he was slumping to the ground.

And so, having just seen that, I walked to the foot of the stairway in my house and called up to my wife, I said: "I'm going to have to skip lunch, because I've got to go to Parkland, they've just shot Oswald." And my wife called down and she said "Who is Oswald?" And I said, "He's the man they say shot President Kennedy." "Oh," my wife said. And she said, "Well, we'll see you later."

And, so I went and got in my car and drove as rapidly as I could towards Parkland. And on my way there, I saw Dr. Shire's car coming towards me in the opposite direction from Parkland and we stopped along the side of the road and looked out our windows at each other and said, "Did you see what or hear what we just heard"? And we [realized] that we both found out the same piece of information about Oswald and we...he turned his car around and we both then sped out to Parkland.

Inside Trauma Room Two, Trying to Save Lee Harvey Oswald

Dr. McClelland: We got there, probably about – oh – thirty minutes after Oswald had been shot. We stopped, parked our cars behind the emergency room. Ran into the emergency room, to Trauma Room Two. Right across the hall from where the president had been treated and looked inside and that was a beehive of activity with all the residences and nurses in the emergency room working on Oswald, getting him transfused and ready for surgery.

And so when we saw that was being taken care of, Dr. Shires and I ran upstairs, changed into scrubs and by the time we got that done, they had Oswald up in the operating room ready for exploration. So, that's where we started.

Holland: And sir, when you rushed into that emergency room, was there as big a crowd surrounding Oswald as there was Mr. Kennedy?"

Dr. McClelland: Almost. There was a large crowd of all kinds of people in there. The residents, the interns, the nurses and other ancillary personnel, were working around him getting him ready for exploration. So, it was very busy.

Holland: Were you aware, in the same sense as when you were looking at Mr. Kennedy, that Mr. Oswald was not going to make it as well?

Dr. McClelland: No, not to the same extent. He had – I would say in fact – a fatal wound, but never the less, it was potentially – and I underline potentially – salvageable.

Unfortunately, when Oswald was walking toward Ruby, he saw Ruby approaching with the pistol. There's also some evidence that he knew Mr. Ruby, and that he recognized him. In any event, when he saw him approaching with a gun, he turned to try to avoid it, as anyone would. In essence, that turn cost him his life.

Because, when he turned, instead of the bullet going straight through from the front of his abdomen to the back – where it would have caused non fatal bowel injuries – it instead coursed across – having come in somewhere towards the upper left of his abdomen. It went across the back part of his abdomen, the so called electro-parapodium and injured his venicava and aorta. The two main blood vessels in the body that carry blood to the upper and lower portions of the body. To and from the vein, vinicava and the artery, aorta. And that is really a fatal wound in the great majority of instances. People bleed out on the side on the injury.

But, as luck would have it, the way the hematoma, that is the blood clot formed around these injuries, he did not bleed out as they usually do. So, we were able to open his abdomen. And Dr. Shires, who was doing that exploration, with Dr. Perry and I being the first and second assistants, was able to get clamps on those vessels, after a period of, probably, 20 to 30 minutes from the time he got into his abdomen and he worked down through the top and got the clamps on the vessels, so that we could have controlled it.

But, at that time, he had had so much blood loss and so much injury to his heart muscle, that he had a cardiac arrest at that moment. And Dr. Perry and I dropped out of the operation.

Dr Perry opened his chest and we took turns massaging Oswald's heart, for probably about 30 minutes or so. Initially, it looked like maybe it was going to come back again and begin beating again, but, it stopped again and then it got flabbier and flabbier until finally we gave up and he was pronounced dead.

Holland: Another young man with children left fatherless. Just a horrible, horrible weekend. And sir, I'm sure on that Friday morning when you awoke, November 22, you had no idea the next three days that you would be virtually making and touching history.

There is first person eyewitness testimony the Oswald knew Ruby (See Chapter 6 "Beverly Oliver the Babushka Lady" for more information). Why is this important? For two quick reasons:

One of the first rules of assassination is "silence the assassin" so that the assassin can't talk to the authorities and tell what he really knows. When Jack Ruby killed Oswald, in a police station, of all places, with over 70 police officers present and hoards of press, cameras and live TV, it was an act of a pure desperation. Ruby knew he could never have escaped and would be arrested or even killed immediately. What could Oswald have revealed, while on trial, that was so explosive? Who was pulling the strings on Ruby behind the scenes? This act raised red flags everywhere and solidified, in most people's minds, that there was a conspiracy in the JFK assassination and the assassin had just been silenced by organized crime. It also raised many other unanswered questions, such as, were there others involved? Was it a coup d'état? How deep does the conspiracy go?

The second reason is important because the official US government position was, and is to this day, Oswald acted alone, and there was no known association of any kind between Oswald and Ruby. This was false then, and it is false now. The two knew each other very well indeed.

Oswald Refuses "Death Bed" Confession

Holland: Sir, back to Lee Harvey Oswald, how did the Secret Service react? I understand that they were surrounding them as well?"

Dr. McClelland: They did. Although, the most memorable thing that I have about that relates to the deputy sheriff who was handcuffed to Oswald as he was being led out of the jail and was standing beside him as he feel to the ground and he told us as we came out after Oswald was pronounced dead, the deputy sheriff I think I recall, his name was Leavelle. He was sitting out, waiting to hear to what was going on in the operating room. And so, we came out and told him what happened and then he told us, "You know, when [Oswald] was shot and slumped to the ground, I got down on all fours over his body, straddled him and put my face down in his, and said, 'Son you're hurt real bad, would you like to say anything to me now?" And he said Oswald opened his eyes very wildly with that and looked up at him for a long...several moments, like he was thinking about whether or not he was or was not going to say anything. After those few moments, Oswald shook his head, like that, real wide from side to side, like no, he definitely did not want to say anything.

And with that, he closed his eyes for the last time. So the deputy sheriff, Leavelle, said "I will believe to my dying day that he was about to say something, pertinent, about everything, to me at that time but then he thought better of it and shook his head."

Holland: It really does appear that when Lee Harvey Oswald was shot, Jack Ruby was acting like he was silencing somebody.

History Belongs to Everybody

Holland: Sir, all these years looking back, I'm sure when November 22 comes around, these memories must spring up and certainly I appreciate you coming on our show tonight, I can't tell you how much I do. But certainly folks like me always asking you the same stuff...how do you deal with that?"

> Dr. McClelland: Well, I fell like...and it's interesting Dr. Perry would never talk about it, under any circumstances, to me or anybody else. I never really understood why that was. My own thoughts about it are that this is a...a pertinent point of history that is...should belong to the public. So that when somebody asks me about it, it's sort of my duty if you will to say what I know rather than to say, well, this is my private information, because it's certainly far from being that, it belongs to everybody.

Dr. Robert McClelland doesn't have to tell anyone what happened that day in 1963. But as he says, in true patriotism, duty and integrity, that day "belongs to everybody."

Indeed.

Note: Dr. McClelland is a 1954 graduate of The University of Texas Medical Branch in Galveston. Following his internship at the University of Kansas Medical Center and two years of military service in the Air Force in Germany, he completed his residency in general surgery at Parkland Memorial Hospital. He then completed a one-year fellowship in splanchnic hemodynamics with Dr. Fouad Bashour, in the Department of Internal Medicine, at UT Southwestern. He was appointed to the faculty of UT Southwestern Medical Center in 1962 and is the first faculty member to hold the Alvin Baldwin Jr. Chair in Surgery, an endowment designated for support of surgical education. His primary interests lie in gastrointestinal surgery and in postgraduate medical education. As originator and editor of Audio-Journal Review ¿,General Surgery, his influence as a medical educator extends beyond the department into surgical training programs throughout the country.

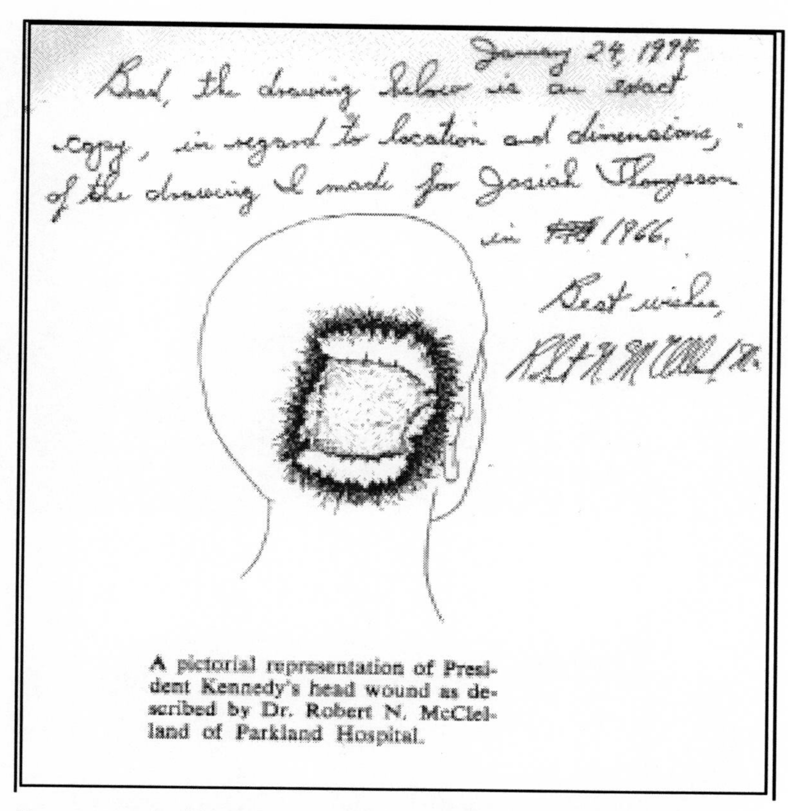

Drawing marked by Dr. McClelland for student Brad Parker (photo courtesy of JFK Lancer)

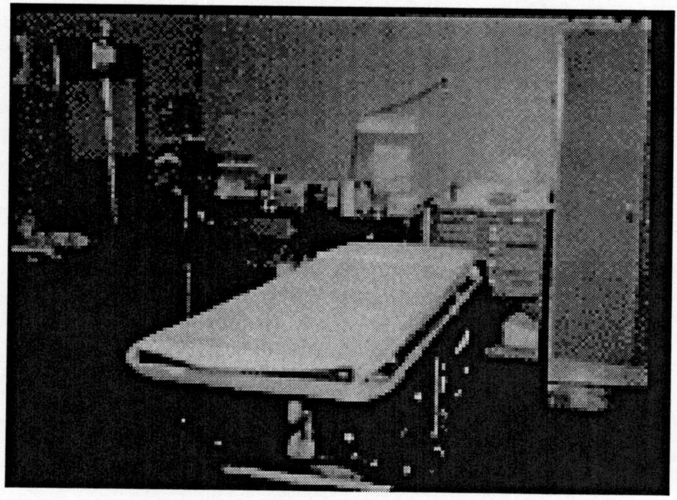

Parkland Hospital, Trauma Room One, 1963.

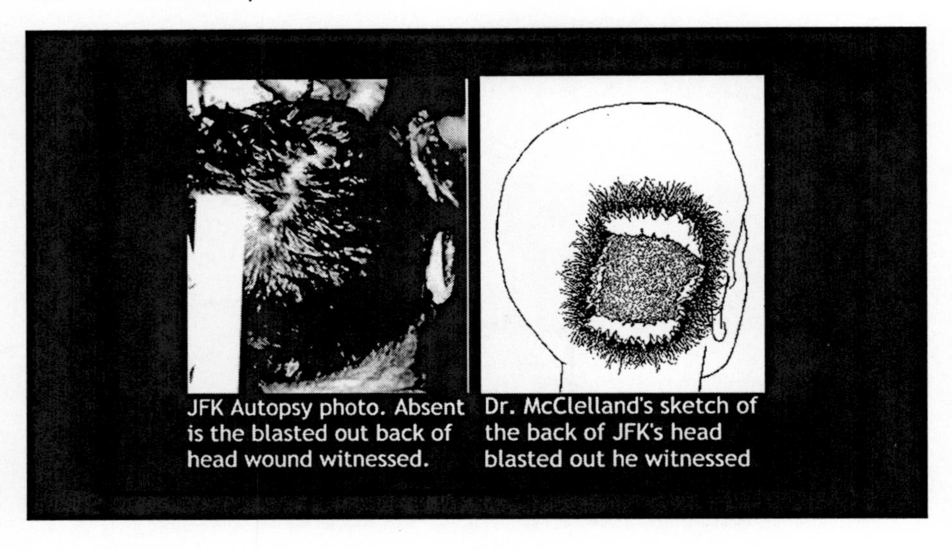

JFK Autopsy photo. Absent is the blasted out back of head wound witnessed.

Dr. McClelland's sketch of the back of JFK's head blasted out he witnessed

Dr. McClelland speaks out about his experience. He's holding his bloody dress shirt from November 22, 1963.

CHAPTER 5

JAMES TAGUE: THE MAN RESPONSIBLE FOR THE MAGIC BULLET

"It's time the American people knew the truth. I'm probably, and I hope I'm not boasting, but I'm probably the only person as close to everything that was going on as anybody. And that's being there in Dealey Plaza, testimony in front of the Warren Commission. As a matter of fact they had to re-do the whole Warren Commission after my testimony."

James Tague

The Warren Commission was assembled by the American government in 1964 to investigate the Kennedy assassination, and was about to release its findings to the press. The Warren Commission was about to say that there were three empty bullet shells found in the snipers nest on the sixth floor of the Texas School Book Depository, where they believed the purported assassin, Lee Harvey Oswald, had fired all three shots. Therefore, the three bullets, three shots and three wounds were all originating from above and behind the president, and all fired by a single assassin, Lee Harvey Oswald. According to the Warren Commission's *first* report:

- The first shot hit Kennedy in the back between the shoulder blades. As Kennedy fell to the side, he exposed Governor Connally, who was sitting on the limousine's jump seat directly in front of the president.

- The second shot hit Connally from the back causing five wounds in the Governor.

- The third and final shot hit President Kennedy in the back of the head, killing him.

It would have been a nice, neat, tidy package, except for a fellow by the name of James Tague, who was also in Dealey Plaza during the assassination. Tague courageously stepped forward to ask where the president's fourth wound came from. Now the Warren Commission had a major problem. How could they possibly explain only three empty shell casings and only three bullets from Oswald's gun, yet not three but four wounds? The Warren Commission went back to the drawing board and came up with what we now know as the Magic Bullet Theory. The Commission decided that there were still only three bullets, but suddenly, the bullets had now miraculously caused four wounds.

1. The first bullet had not hit JFK at all. Instead, it now had missed President Kennedy's limousine completely and hit a curb where it ricocheted and hit James Tague, standing by the triple underpass, who was watching the motorcade.

2. The second shot, they now stated, hit Kennedy in the back between the shoulder blades, just off center to the right, 4" below the neck. Warren Commission member Gerald Ford, who was later to become President Gerald Ford, decided that in order to have the evidence coincide with the Magic Bullet Theory, he would change the location of the wound from Kennedy's back up to his neck in the report, even though the shot was really located below JFK's neck between his shoulder blades.

   This bullet entered Kennedy's back then rose upward to exit Kennedy's throat. It then went through Connally, breaking Connally's rib and wrist, finally lodging itself in Connelly's leg. Miraculously, this bullet caused seven wounds in both JFK and Connally.

   The bullet was found laying on a gurney at Parkland Hospital. It was not bent out of shape, as bullets that break bones are. Instead it was found in an almost "pristine" condition as if it had been fired into cotton or water. On top of all this, *there was no blood or tissue found on the "magic bullet."* There are more bullet fragments actually inside Governor Connally's wounds that are missing from the single bullet that they claim made all of the wounds, which is impossible. Now you know why it's called the "magic bullet."

3. The third and last bullet apparently hit Kennedy in the back of the head where, instead of exiting from the front of the head, it did an abrupt u-turn in Kennedy's head and instead blew the back of his head out and caused Kennedy to be thrown backward, not forward, and to the left.

James Tague was present in Dealey Plaza that fateful day. He stood unassumingly near the triple underpass, watching the motorcade come towards him. He had no idea that, in the next few seconds, his life would become intrinsically entwined with the JFK assassination, and he would become *the person* inadvertently responsible for the Magic Bullet Theory. What's more, along with the president and Governor Connally, Tague was also wounded by a sniper's bullet, making him the third victim in the shooting spree that took place that day. That very wound to James Tague has carried reverberations, felt to this day.

What follows, is the true, courageous story of a Dealey Plaza first-person eyewitness, James Tague. This is the story of a young 27-year-old man whose beliefs and innocence were shattered that day in Dealey Plaza.

"Do not pray for easy lives. Pray to be stronger men." President John F. Kennedy, February 7, 1963, 11th Annual Presidential Prayer Breakfast

Explanation of Dealey Plaza / the Triple Underpass

Tague: I was at work, just a dreary old day. It was trying to rain, cloudy, a dreary old day, and it finally cleared up around 10:30, 11.

Holland: What made you want to go down to Dealey Plaza November 22, 1963?

Tague: The reason I was going down to Dallas that day, was I had a lunch with a cute red head. We'd made the date the day before and I got stopped in traffic just as I was going under the triple underpass.

To orientate you as to the position of the triple underpass relative to where James was standing, take a look at the following image. Dealey Plaza forms a

Dealey Plaza 1967

triangle with Houston Street, Commerse Street and Elm Street forming the three sides.

The Dal-Tex office building is located on the corner of Houston and Elm Streets. I only mention this building as it is where shots are thought to have originated as well.

At the bottom of the image, you can see a series of train tracks that went over Commerce, Main and Elm Streets. The traffic went under, hence the name "triple underpass." The underpass, like any bridge, was supported on both ends and in the middle with concrete supports. This middle concrete support also divided the traffic which was flowing underneath. This is where James Tague was standing.

This triangle makes up Dealey Plaza. Elm Street is the street on which the president was assassinated. The motorcade traveled on Elm Street, east to west (the opposite direction of the traffic on Main Street). The northside pergola and "grassy knoll" faces Elm Street a little over half-way between the underpass and Houston Street. The Texas School Book Depository is also on Elm Street at the northwest corner of Houston and Elm Streets.

SHOTS FIRED

Holland: And what made you want to get out of the car and go and see the motorcade sir?

Tague: Traffic was stopped in front of me and I got out of the car to see what was going on – maybe there's been an automobile accident or something – a couple of cars ahead of me a guy was standing out of the car half way leaning against the car door. And I walked to – four or five steps – to the front of the triple underpass where I could see what was going on.

Holland: And what did you see there, sir?

Tague: I noticed a crowd up around the School Book Depository and at that time I remember reading about the president was going to be in town today. And at this same time I saw this car come through the crowd with flags on the fenders, which, I had remembered reading about the president being in town.

Holland: Did you see the president at all, was he waving?

Tague: From where I stood, I could not see through the windshield because the glare of the sun. All I had was a front view from where I was.

Holland: I see, sir, and what happened next?

Well, I heard what I thought was a pop of a firecracker. And I started – looked around and thought what kind of idiot would be throwing firecrackers with the president going by – and 'course a lot of people heard the same sound like a fire cracker; as a matter of fact even Jackie thought it was a motorcycle backfire. And then there was a delay and a couple – about three seconds and then the crack, crack of two rifle shots.

Holland: One right after the other?

Tague: One right after the other.

This is important because it helps prove that there was more than a single shooter. The type of rifle that Lee Harvey Oswald was alleged to have used in the assassination (a bolt action, non-automatic, Mannlicher Carcano) took more than two seconds to aim and fire for each bullet. Many witnesses state essentially the same scenario; there was a single shot, and then two shots right on top of each other, leaving no time for anyone using the Mannlicher Carcano to cycle through and put a new bullet in the chamber to fire.

We'll get into shooter locations and other ballistics in Chapter 7 "Frontal Shot 21st Century CSI & JFK For Real." We will look at evidence from senior crime scene investigator Sherry Fiester and NASA physicist G. Paul Chambers, along with scientifically guaranteed evidence that there were shots originating from in front of JFK, and thus proving a conspiracy.

THE ASSASSINATION

Holland: Could you tell at all from where the shots might be originating?

Tague: Not really...from where I stood, the line of fire, came – could of been from anywhere from where the Dal-Tex building, School Book Depository or the grassy knoll – it could have been any one of the three. There was very little difference in degrees from those points.

Holland: But nothing seemed to originate from the right of you, over your right shoulder, your right shoulder not your left shoulder, in other words from the south of Dealey Plaza the opposite side of the grassy knoll?

I was trying to see if he had a shot from where CSI Sherry Fiester had placed the sniper who shot the fatal head shot bullet that made the president's head explode.

Tague: No, there wasn't anything coming from the right. It was all straight ahead or coming from the left.

Holland: At what point did you realize ,"Oh My God they're shooting at the president?"

Tague: I did not realize they were shooting at the president. I, being a very brave person, ducked behind the protection of the cement of the triple underpass after the third shot. And the pictures that show me down there, emerging from behind that concrete and I'm standing there wondering what had happened. A man in a suit comes running up, who I later learned was Deputy sheriff Buddy Walthers, and he asked me what happened and I said, "I do not know.

And together, we walked across the infield between Commerce and Main Streets, we crossed Main and Elm to where a motorcycle policeman had stopped his motorcycle and there was a man there sobbing, "His head exploded, his head exploded!" And the motorcycle policeman asked him "Who?" and he says "The president's." And that is the first that I knew what had happened.

Holland:Many people have said there was a smell of gunpowder in the air. Did you experience anything?

Tague: Now, you gotta remember, I'm over 300 feet from the School Book Depository. I'm not close to where the people thought they saw smoke coming up behind the fence or the School Book Depository. I'm not close to that. I'm down by the triple underpass.

Holland: What was it like when you were walking across the infield with Sheriff Buddy Walthers? Was there mayhem...you had just described one person was crying...

Tague: No, no there was no mayhem. There were still people laying on the ground. People still stunned. Nobody knew what had happened except the people that had been right there beside the car, which, this gentleman that said "His head exploded, his head exploded," I forget his name for the moment, but anyway, those were the only ones that knew what had happened cause the car was gone, there was no evidence left there.

"You got blood on your face."

Holland: At what point did you realize that you were wounded also sir?

Tague: Buddy Walthers – while we were standing there – after the man that said "his head exploded" – Buddy Walthers looked up at me and he said, "You got blood on your face." And I reached up there was a couple – three drops of blood.

And I then recalled something stunned me during the crack, crack of the rifle shots. And during the emotions of that moment, I temporarily forgot that – in trying to figure out what was happening."

Holland: I see, and did you notice that you were injured on the left cheek, on the right cheek?

Tague: Well, this has been one of those things that's been wrong for years – I've been trying to correct for years. I had little scratches, almost three of them on my left cheek and a photographer took a picture of me showing just the left side of my face and that was – everybody jumped to the conclusion that's where I'd been hit.

No, I was sprayed – probably by concrete on the right cheek. Jim Bishop, in his book, ("The Day Kennedy Was Shot" 1968) was one of the first to correct that, and then Harold Weisberg (legendary JFK researcher, now deceased) got it right. And writer after writer after writer after that kept on saying the left cheek and showed pictures of the left cheek. No, I was sprayed by probably with debris – in the right check is where I was hit.

Holland: I see sir. Did you have to go to the hospital for stitches or anything of that nature?

Tague: No, it just broke the skin. Just broke the skin. It was nothing serious. It broke the skin and I reached up with my right hand and there's some blood there and I took my handkerchief and just wiped it off and that was the end of that.

Holland: Did any of the police officers take a report of your wound at all sir?

Tague: I believe one of the motorcycle policemen said, "We want you to stay around, we want to get a statement from you." And I stood there – and looking at the time table and looking back – I was there about 15 minutes, at least 15 minutes.

Now, remember my car was back in the street. And I got in it to move it and at that time, it was 15 minutes after the shooting, people from all over town was pouring down into Dealey Plaza and traffic was starting to get to be a mess. So I just drove to the police station and told them – they were in a commotion too – and told them that I'd been sent there to make a statement.

And I don't know how long – probably stayed around 30 to 40 minutes – they sent me to homicide and stood there for a few minutes. And finally, a Detective Rose, came in and started taking my statement. And as we're sitting there and I'm about to end it – all I had to say – there was little commotion at the door of homicide and two policemen brought a guy in a little bit disheleved.

And Detective Gus Rose asked the two policemen, says: "who's this?" And they say, "This is the man that killed that policeman in Oak Cliff." He says, "Oh." Later that evening on TV, I'm watching TV and I could see Lee Harvey Oswald was the one they brought into the homicide put to the office next to me.

Aftermath: A Country in Shock; 4 Dark Days

Holland: A lot of our listeners right now sir, are in their early twenties and for them the assassination is ancient history. I was wondering if you could try and describe what was going in the country, in the news media, in the hours that followed the assassination.

Tague: Well, I was back to work just in time to see my boss was locking the place up In Dallas – the whole place is locked up. There's no traffic on the streets. I think every business in town is locked up, that was Friday evening. Saturday was the same way. And on TV they were saying things, they'd have two or three hours of footage then they'd repeat the same footage over and over again for probably 24 maybe 36 hours. Nothing really new.

I remember Sunday morning – I knew there was a news stand downtown and I had my radio on and I went to get a paper. I wanted to see what the rest of the country was thinking about Dallas. I wanted to get a New York paper and a L.A. paper and as I was nearing downtown, I was listening to them transfer Oswald and that's when Ruby shot him. I was in my car and I think I forgot to get my newspaper. And, as far as Dallas – Dallas was shut down

Holland: Sir, when you heard the news that Oswald had been killed also, only two days later, what were your thoughts?

Tague: Well, now, I, I knew – see, I knew Jack Ruby. I knew that this was something that – he was one of these guys that reacted to things on the drop of a hat – and well, that's something he would do and later in talking to (Dallas Detective) Jim Leavell, who was handcuffed to him at the time – he verified my thoughts that Ruby thought he'd be a hero by killing Oswald. He thought that's something that the whole world would think that he'd done the right thing; he was a hero. But that's a different story altogether.

Holland: What were your thoughts on President Kennedy before the assassination?

Tague: I was neutral on Kennedy, I had no thoughts about him whatsoever, one way or the other. Of course the story, my story, was not really about being there, that was just about being an accident, it was that fact that the missed shot was covered up until the next June.

COVER-UP

Holland: Why was the shot covered up and how did the Warren Commission Report change come about?

Tague: Well, in June, – it was June the 5th – I'd been following the newspapers and except for a little tiny hand showing where a bullet had hit the curb on a Sunday the 24th of November, there was no news, nothing about a missed shot. And, of course, I didn`t read that I had been sprayed by debris or where it could be I`d been struck, nothing.

Then on June the 5th, 1964, I read that the Warren Commission was folding their doors and sending people home, they`re conclusion was going to be:

- the first shot hit Kennedy
- the second one Connally
- the third one Kennedy

I was talking to a man at work – and at the time I was an automobile salesman at the time – somehow a customer had brought his car in and was in the shop and I was trying to say "Hey, one shot went wild" and at this time there was very few people I'd say that to because they wouldn't believe me. He said "Yeah, Jim I know."

But anyway, he says, "You know, we got a new cub reporter on the paper. I'm going to call him and tell him about you, of course, he needs to talk to you." And then he said, "Well, wait a minute, I'm going on vacation." He says, "Here's the phone number to call him, be sure and call on him and tell him what you been telling me." I did, it was Jim Lehrer, same Jim Lehrer on Lehrer Report (PBS News Show).

He came out – this was early in the morning – I was telling him just what I was telling you and I said "Do not use my name" and he said, "No, I won't." Because at that time, or anytime I told somebody what had happened, it was not a believable story because there hadn't been anything in the papers.

Jim put the story on the wire services and had no more than done that and he called me back and he said, "Jim" he says, "they're calling me from Washington and every place else and they're wanting to know who you are." He says then, "What am I apt to tell them?." I said, "Well Jim, that's fine – just don't use my name in the local paper." The local paper had not come out yet. He didn't.

Looking back in history in documents, the FBI was in Jim Lehrer's office at 4 that afternoon, interviewing him about me. And that was the first when it started to – I don't know what the word would be... to deflate what I had to say.

Holland: Discredit, sir?

Tague: Discredit is the word. J. Lee Rankin was chief counsel for the Warren Commission – did pick up on it and it was two assistant US attorneys here in Dallas that had known about the missed shot and wondering themselves why the Warren Commission hadn't gone into it. And that's where they got the pictures that were sent to Rankin at the Warren Commission, where the bullet hit the curb. People had seen debris fly and sparks fly and there were pictures taken. All that came out and I was called to testify on the 23rd of July 1964.

The most important part of the story that one must know is that Rankin asked Hoover – J. Edgar Hoover of the FBI – twice during that period between June the 5th and July the 23rd – to go find where that bullet had hit the curb. Hoover reported back two times to the Warren Commission they could not find it.

Now we have in our possession, I have in my possession, where he had sent a memo to the Dallas office on the 5th, that same day, to go get the pictures that were taken of the curb. So they knew that he was denying it to the Warren Commission.

I testified on the 23rd, Buddy Walthers testified, a couple of others and the pictures were there and sure enough there was hard, solid heaps of evidence there was a missed shot. And then, the next day, the 24th, the FBI says "Oh, we found where that bullet hit the curb."

Now, that's pretty much how it came out. Now the history, of going back on the 15th of December, the FBI had interviewed me, that's in '63, and this interview was forwarded by the FBI to the Warren Commission.

You've got to remember the main workers of the Warren Commission were the fifteen lawyers, not the seven figure heads. The fifteen lawyers did not really start doing any work until after the Jack Ruby trial which ended the end of February 1964. A lot of people think they were already working, they weren't. But, the real work by the Warren Commission started at the end of February and was only given 90 days, which had to be extended, to finish their work which they couldn't do.

But anyway, in that interim, the seven men who were the figure heads, I'm talking about (future President Gerald) Ford and (ex-DCIA fired by JFK Allen) Dulles and that bunch, Earl Warren, they did do some interviewing. Like Jackie Kennedy.

Earl Warren went to Jackie Kennedy's house with a stenographer and took her testimony. Anyway, this FBI interview was in the possession of the seven at that time. One of them asked the Secret Service, Agent Sorrels, what he knew about a missed shot. Sorrels reported back, that he asked around some of the Secret Service agents, whether they knew a missed shot and none of them knew anything. Sorrels reported back to the Warren Commission and the FBI statement that I'd made in mid December, was shoved aside. The information had been there but then was shoved aside. And it's made me think since then – I wonder how much information was handled in such a way and just put aside and never really looked at.

Holland: Sir, were you ever threatened because you came forward or have you been subsequently threatened?

Tague: No, I was never threatened. I know when I testified, right in the middle of the testimony – Liebeler was the attorney that took my testimony – he asked me right in the middle of my testimony, he says, "I understand that you went back there [to Dealey Plaza] and took pictures" I said "Huh!?"

He repeated and said "I understand you were back there and took pictures." I said I didn't know anybody knew anything about that. And I had. I'd went down there, and I was going to the Indy 500, my parents lived near the Indy 500, and I took some pictures to show my parents. There was really nothing to it, but, I had not been to their house. I had not seen them since May of, uh, '64. No, I'd not been to it."

Holland: Sir, how old were you in 1963?

Tague: I'd just turned 27.

Holland: Just a young man. Now you had mentioned the FBI, can we talk about the FBI interview?

Tague: The FBI interviewed me mid December '63. And after I'd talked to Lehrer, they interviewed Lehrer. That was June of 1964.

It's time the American people knew the truth. I'm probably, and I hope I'm not boasting, but I'm probably the only person as close to everything that was going on as anybody. And that's being there in Dealey Plaza, testimony in front of the Warren Commission. As a matter of fact they had to re-do the whole Warren Commission [conclusions]after my testimony.

The FBI Investigation & JFK Assassination

The assassination took place in the city of Dallas, and therefore, by law, the murder investigation, even that of a national figure, was to be handled by local law enforcement. Dallas Police Department (DPD) initiated their investigation immediately following the assassination. However, behind the scenes, in the most obtrusive way, FBI director J. Edgar Hoover was throwing his weight around.

> Hoover wanted "in" on the investigation, I think for a whole bunch of reasons, but primarily for his own ego. Here it was, the crime of the century, and he'd be damned if his mighty FBI and his own egocentricity would be left out. Think of General Patton played by George C. Scott in the film "Patton." When in a rage against the possibility that he might be relieved of his command, he blares something to the effect of: "I can't be sent home, this is the greatest war the world has ever seen, I will not allow God to do this to me!" As if his own self-created destiny must be fulfilled and screw everyone who opposes him, even the Almighty, to achieve his self-concocted legend.

It's my opinion that Hoover wanted to be immortalized, like he tried to be in March of 1932 when he sought to solve the Lindberg baby kidnapping. Charles Lindbergh, the aviator who flew solo from North America to Paris, had a 20-month-old son who was kidnapped from the family home right out of his crib. Hoover wanted to make a splash in the press and with the public for himself and his Bureau Of Investigations (it would later become the Federal Bureau of Investigation in 1935). Once again, the kidnapping was not a federal crime, but J. Edgar being J. Edgar, he managed to work his way into the investigation anyway.

Unfortunately it did no good. Two months later in May 1932, the child's body was discovered by accident when a delivery truck driver stopped by the side of the road. The body was only 4.5 miles from the Lindbergh family home, badly decomposed, with the skull caved in. Obviously he had been murdered. So, by solving the Kennedy assassination with breakneck speed, Hoover would emerge the people's hero.

Ego in concert with power can be dangerous, very, very dangerous.

Under the orders of Hoover, the FBI started its own investigation at the same time as the DPD, stepping all over their feet. Even Johnson negated the DPD investigation by the rash of phone calls between he and Hoover from the day of the assassination on Friday, November 22 until Saturday, November 23. All the while, the investigation was supposed to be in the DPD's hands. Because of this, many researcher believe that Hoover and Johnson were involved in the assassination and wanted to take control in order to cover up a government coup d'état. I do not agree.

It is said that Hoover had "dirt" on everyone. It has long been known that Hoover had confronted President Kennedy with White House telephone numbers and times of calls between Kennedy and one of his female "acquaintances." After the confrontation, the president must have stopped using the documented White House telephone system for his female "acquaintances" calls, because they abruptly stopped. My point is, Hoover, as FBI director, wielded an inappropriate weight of power in Washington, far beyond the reach of today's FBI director. Politicians feared him and stayed under his radar, or simply appeased him.

Then, suddenly, as if scripted, on Sunday, November 24, 1963, Jack Ruby entered the DPD basement and murdered Lee Harvey Oswald in cold blood, in front of 70 Dallas police officers. Hoover must have been elated when President Johnson called him and officially asked him to take over the investigation (See "Breach of Trust," pages 22-23).

> *"It's not just about doing tricks. It's about taking people so they can suspend their disbelief."* David Copperfield

What follows is a brief "who's who" list of all those who did not believe the Magic Bullet Theory.

Georgia Senator Richard Russell was a member of the Warren Commission. When the Commission was about to release its conclusion, Senator Russell refused to sign the report, stating that he simply did not believe in the so-called "single bullet theory." President Johnson, somewhat dismayed that a member of his handpicked blue-ribbon Warren Commission would dissent, decided to give Senator Russell a phone call (September 18, 1964). Senator Russell was adamant and firmly stated to Johnson, "I don't believe it!" The most explosive part was Johnson's own admission about his personal thoughts on the theory. "Neither do I!" he thundered.

As it turned out, Senator Russell was not the only member of the Warren Commission that did not believe in the Magic Bullet Theory (See McKnight's "Breach of Trust," page 283). Warren Commission members Congressman Hale Boggs of Louisiana and Senator John Cooper of Kentucky also dissented. To solve the problem, eventually some new wording was invented by McCloy. The final section of the report was changed to a very absurd and self-contradicting:

> *"Although it is not necessary to any essential findings of the Commission to determine just which shot hit Governor Connally..."*

> **Of course it's essential to find out what shot(s) hit Governor Connally so that all shots and bullets can be accounted for! This was an absolutely bizarre conclusion to the official government investigation of the assassination of a president.**

Hoover signed off on the FBI's official report sent to the Warren Commission that stated there were only three shots.

1. The first hit Kennedy in the back.

2. The second hit Governor Connally sitting directly in front of President Kennedy.

3. The third and final shot hit President Kennedy's head.

They ignored the bullet that hit the curb causing Tague to be wounded. (Unfortunately for the Warren Commission, James Tague stepped forward.) The Secret Service also believed the same scenario as the FBI (See "Breach of Trust," page 18, FBI supplimental Report).

Texas Governor John Connally, who sat on the passenger-side jump seat directly in front of Kennedy and directly beside his wife, testified to the Warren Commission that he was NOT hit by the same bullet as JFK, but by the bullet fired from the second shot.

> Governor Connally: "I heard the shot, and I say shot, because I immediately thought it was a shot. I immediately thought it was a rifle shot. Fear just swept through me and I...I turned thinking that the shot had come from back over my right shoulder. So I tuned and I obviously saw nothing but a tremendous crowd of people, where we had just come.

> And I saw nothing unusual. Nothing out of the way except people also had startled looks on their faces, they were turning, they were looking and…and I didn't catch him (meaning President Kennedy) in the corner of my eye.
>
> So, I was in the process of turning to my left and that's when I felt the impact of the bullet that hit me. Went in my back shoulder and came out my chest right here. I felt as if someone had just hit me in the back, a sharp blow with a doubled up fist. More or less knocked me over, at least enough to where I looked down and of course I was covered with blood and frankly thought that I had been fatally hit.
>
> I never lost consciousness and I was lying there and heard the third shot. I heard the third shot very distinctly. I heard it hit. I assumed that it hit the president. It obviously did. The evidence was splattered all over the car and all over my clothes and all over Nellie. It was a time of just unbelievable stark tragedy." Dallas KRLD-TV interview June 22, 1964.

Governor Connally stood fast and never wavered from his testimony of being hit by a second bullet and not the "magic bullet." He died prematurely due to the scar tissue inflicted by that second bullet to his lung (See "From Love Field" pages 07-08).

Mrs. Nellie Connally, sitting on the driver's-side jump seat directly in front of Mrs. Kennedy and directly beside her husband, said in her own words:

> I heard a loud terrifying noise. It came from the back. I turned and looked toward the president just in time to see his hands fly up to his neck and see him sink down in the seat. He made no sound, no cry, nothing. His expression hadn't changed, no grimace, no sign of pain, but the eyes were full of surprise. From the corner of my eye I saw my husband John turn clockwise in his seat. But the car door prevented him from seeing clearly so he twisted the other way toward me. "No, no, no," he cried out. Then a second shot. My husband spun in his seat. He had been hit in the back by the second bullet. "My god," he blurted, "they're going to kill us all!

Presidential aide Dave Powers was in the Secret Service follow-up car directly behind JFK's limousine and, as stated previously in the chapter "Seven Smoking Guns," saw the shots from the grassy knoll. He emphasized that "the same bullet that hit JFK did *not* hit John Connally."

FBI Agents James Sibert and Frank O'Neil were assigned to take notes and cover the JFK autopsy at Bethesda Naval Hospital the night of the assassination. The two FBI agents who witnessed the complete autopsy and all the wounds on Kennedy's body are quoted here about the "magic bullet."

> FBI Agent James Sibert: "There's no way that bullet could go that low, then come up, raise up and come out the front of the neck, zigzag and hit Connally and then end up in pristine condition over there in Dallas!"
>
> FBI Agent Frank O'Neil: "Absolutely, not! It did not happen!" (Legacy of Secrecy, page 187)

Senior crime scene investigator Sherry Fiester and NASA physicist Chambers also commented.

> Sherry Feister: Well, absolutely, the "magic bullet" is ridiculous. Bullets do not behave the way that they're saying, that they want it to behave. And of course, the "magic bullet" came up because there was a mis-shot; James Tague was injured.
>
> NASA physicist G. Paul Chambers: And the problem is the bullet hits Kennedy in the back in a downward angle, and we all know if it does that, it's going to come out his chest. Okay, so we know also that the lungs were damaged because that was included on the official autopsy with a contusion to the lung which is consistent with the – Dallas doctors indicated they couldn't maintain the integrity of the respiratory system.
>
> So the bullet comes in your back at a downward angle, hits your lung, how does it get to the trachea? How does it do that? It's got to deflect back and upwards, right? In order to do that, it's got to deflect off soft tissue.
>
> Soft tissue has a density about one gram per CC. The bullet has a density of about 8 to 10 grams per CC. The copper jacket is about 9 grams. So you're going to have a very dense bullet traveling faster than the speed of sound, 2000 feet per second. And all of a sudden that bullet deflects by his lung, not even by his rib cage, but by his lung, somehow upward to his trachea. And then it re-deflects back down again so it can hit Connally at a downward angle. So the physics of that is just absolutely impossible.

If you find yourself among this list of people who did not believe in a "magic bullet," you are a member of the vast majority who knows this theory is "Hokum" (thank you Sheldon Cooper from "Big Bang Theory" for a great word).

"I was sprayed, probably with debris. In the right check is where I was hit." (Photo JFK Lancer 2006)

Jim Tague shows where he stood on November 22, 1963.

"Traffic was stopped in front of me and I got out of the car to see what was going on – maybe there's been an automobile accident or something. A couple of cars ahead of me, a guy was standing out of the car, half way leaning against the car door. And I walked – four or five steps – to the front of the triple underpass where I could see what was going on." (Photo JFK Lancer 2006)

The triple underpass in Dealey Plaza

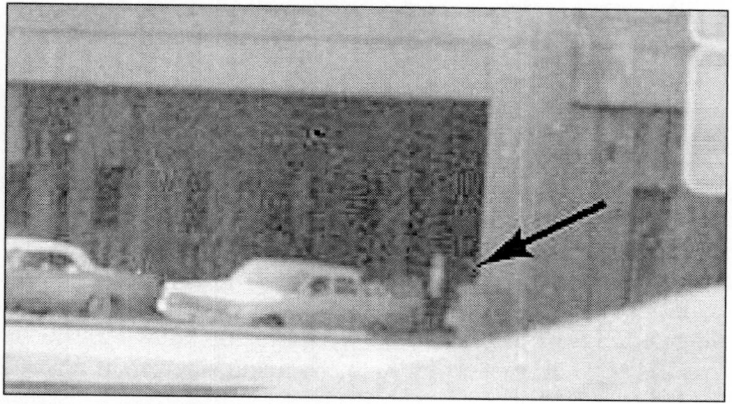

Jim Tague waiting by his car on November 22, 1963

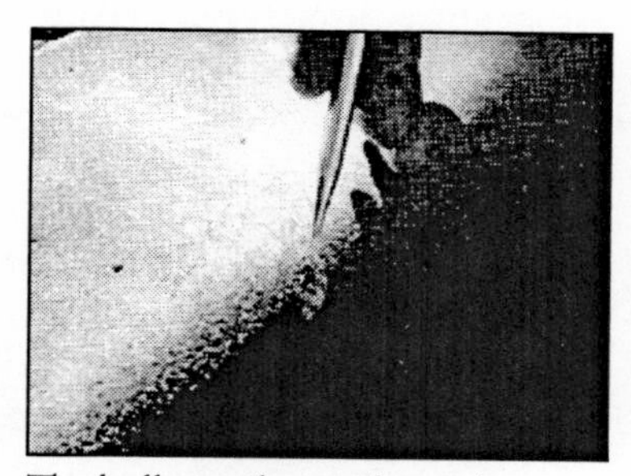

The bullet strike on the curb

CHAPTER 6

Beverly Oliver, "Bubushka Lady"

Beverly Oliver was only 17 years old on November 22, 1963. Little did she know that while standing in Dealey Plaza only feet from President Kennedy in his limousine, the next second would change her life forever.

Most people have seen the Zapruder film, the most famous film of the assassination. In the film, during the assassination sequence, you can see a young teenage girl with a scarf over her head (who became known as the "Babushka Lady"), standing frozen, witnessing Kennedy being killed right before her eyes.

Bev filmed the assassination in its entirety that day with a handheld movie camera. Shortly after the assassination, both the camera and the film were confiscated by the FBI. Beverly's vantage point, and close proximity to the president, indicate that she captured both the limousine with JFK's head exploding and the entire picket fence on the grassy knoll. This would mean that she just may have caught the grassy knoll shooter on film. Neither the film nor the camera have ever resurfaced, and their whereabouts remain unknown.

Beverly was terrified she would be killed if she came forward, so she stayed out of the limelight until the 1970s. During this period, researchers would refer to the unidentified woman wearing a head scarf in all the assassination films as the "Babushka Lady."

> **Bev worked in a club, and during breaks she would come over to the Carousel Club. She liked the buzz. She liked the action. She liked the night life. She was a young teenager and didn't we all.**

Beverly knew Jack Ruby personally. Ruby was the Mafia-linked man who killed purported JFK assassin Lee Harvey Oswald. Days before the assassination, Beverly witnessed Lee Harvey Oswald and JFK assassination suspect and Mafia/CIA operative David Ferrie together at the Carousel Club. This is important because the Warren Commission clearly stated that when Ruby murdered Oswald, there was no connection whatsoever between the two. This was a deliberate attempt on their part to make it seem that there were no accomplices or conspiracy in the JFK assassination and that Oswald had acted alone. A Mafia-connected Jack Ruby silencing the assassin gangland style would render the Warren Commission's lone gunman scenario dubious at best.

Beverly was portrayed in Oliver Stone's masterpiece film "JFK" by Canadian actress Lolita Davidovich. To this day Beverly is subject to threats due to what she laid witness to in Dallas all those years ago.

> **Beverly Oliver's story is nothing but inspiring. She had gone through the depths of hell in her younger years, found Christ, and has emerged triumphant.**

Dallas 1963 and Jack Ruby

Holland: Bev how did you come to meet Jack Ruby?

Oliver: Well, I was working at the Colony Club, which was separated only by a parking lot from Jack Ruby's club, the Carousel Club, and I started working down there at a very young age, very underage and of course I lied about my age. But, anyway, I would catch the bus from Golinda, Texas and ride it by myself to downtown Dallas, work at the Colony Club, go back home on the twelve thirty bus.

And one night I was walking down Acrid Street, which is no longer a street if you have been to Dallas recently and the Baker Hotel drugstore opened up on to Acrid and this man stepped out of the doorway and scared the mud out of me, and it was Jack Ruby. And he introduced himself to me, and of course he could tell that I was too young to be out that time of night by myself, and from that day forward Jack Ruby walked me to the bus station every Friday and Saturday night.

Holland: So, on the one hand you've got Jack Ruby as a gentleman and kind of took you under his wing didn't he?

Oliver: Yes he did – he was a rough guy when it came to men, you know, in handling arguments amongst the customers between men, but I never, ever knew Jack to be disrespectful to a female, not ever…I mean, he would be foolish to. I have heard people say that he beat his women – that would be stupid, they got up at night and took their clothes off – are you going to pay to see a bruised up, battered up women on stage? Of course not. He didn't beat his women.

Holland: What was his character like? There have been reports flying around for years that Jack and Lee Harvey Oswald, for example, were bed partners, perhaps he was Gay, …?

Oliver: Well, I really don't know – he never tried anything with me – but I was jail bait. I never saw any of those type of tendencies with Jack. However back in the 60's, you have to understand, people didn't wear labels like they do now – everybody was just kinky. It was a kinky society in the 60's.

Holland: He was running a club, the Carousel Club, and he had dancing girls, but the club was not a "strip club" per say, there were also magicians performing…

Oliver: Yes, it was a burlesque show. But all burlesque shows, like, I didn't take my clothes off either. But it was a strip club. But back then, when you talk about strip clubs, they were burlesque shows, which is different than the strip clubs are today. You see more on the beach now than you saw on the stage back on in the 60's. And they all had an act and it was, men brought their wives, it was entertainment.

Holland: Was he a fan of JFK?

Oliver: He hated John Kennedy and he hated Bobby Kennedy. That's what I found so absurd about the news reports after he killed Lee Harvey Oswald, that he did it because he loved the Kennedy's. Now he did admire and respect Jackie Kennedy, he thought she was a lady of class.

Holland: Jack came from Chicago, was there ever any mention of the Mafia, or the connection – was he ever displaying a nervousness around you like, "Oh my God, Bev, this is going to happen."

Oliver: Yes, but he never really talked about anything like that. It's just that you have to understand Dallas in '63, everybody was in the mob, and we – the showgirls I mean – we just thought it was the movie – or I did. Let me rephrase that, I just thought these things happen in movies, it's just not real life, because we lived in our own little world that wasn't the real world, it was not the real world.

And so I just never gave the mob a second thought, I mean there was always men coming in both clubs, all three clubs, the Theater Lounge, the Colony Club and the Carousel Club with bulges in their coats and pockets – you knew guns were always being thrown under the table when the vice squad came in.

The Movie Camera

Holland: Bev, how did you get the camera that you filmed the assassination with?

Oliver: I was dating a man who managed the Kodak store in Six Flags over in Texas. He actually came down from Rochester, New York to manage the Kodak store at Six Flags, and he went back up to Rochester, New York in like September – I think it was September – and he brought me an experimental camera back.

It was a Yashika experimental camera, it was a prototype, and he had brought me 12 magazines. It was a magazine loaded camera. He gave me 12 reams of film. He said that should last me 'till the camera comes out in two years. He told me it would be out in two years. I had envelopes that I had to put these in and mail them to Rochester. You couldn't even get them sent off locally. You know kids don't understand – because all they understand is video now days – but we couldn't even drop it off like at the corner drug store and pick it up the next week, I had to send it to Rochester and that was my first cassette of film, that I had used, so I hadn't sent anything off yet.

Holland: Was there any inclination that Jack wanted you to film the Kennedy motorcade?

Oliver: Oh no! Jack didn't want me to film the assassination at all! The biggest fight we ever got into was the night before – and I went to a party with Jack at the Cabana Hotel – it was I think Pepsi Cola (the Pepsi Cola company held a meeting in Dallas the week of the president's visit) – it had nothing to do with anybody connected with the clubs or with the assassination at all.

We just went there for a little while and he knew that I was going to Fort Worth that night and not to the Cellar Club. But, it was another private party. He asked, "Well, what are you wearing, you're going to see the president?" – but he didn't call him "the president." I said, "Yes, I am" And he asked, "What are you wearing? And I said, "Well Jack, I am going to wear what I have on!" He demanded, "You're not wearing that dress I gave you to see that..." And so we got into it, and yeah, I still wore it.

Bev Witnesses Lee Harvey Oswald and David Ferrie

Holland: How did you come to meet Lee Harvey Oswald, how were you introduced to him, and David Ferrie?

Oliver: A couple of – three weeks prior to the assassination, I had gone over to the club. All three clubs that I mentioned before – staggered our shows so that the cliental could make all three clubs – and the Carousel had the last show at night. And I was supposed to go to a club that night that was open late, called Alabave Club, to a party with Jada, who was the headline dancer for Jack.

I went over to tell her I had a migraine and I wasn't going to go. When I walked into the club I saw Jada – there was a table at the end of the runway – and I saw Jada sitting at the end of the table. There was a chair and then Jack Ruby and then a dark haired man. And I made my way up to the table and when I got there Jack stood up and pulled my chair out like he always did. Just as I was being seated, he very nonchalantly said "Hey, Bev, this is my friend Lee Oswald." "He's (David Ferrie) with the CIA," pointing to the man on the other side of him. Well I didn't know, at 17 I didn't know what the CIA was, at 65, I am still not sure what they are.

Holland: What type of character was Oswald...did he seem intelligent? Did he seem well dressed?...I don't know, how would you best describe him?

Oliver: I will just have to tell you what I felt at the time – okay – which I am not that way anymore – okay Brent. (Bev was only 17 years old)

I looked at this gentleman (Lee Harvey Oswald), he seemed dark, he didn't seem to have a personality, he wasn't dressed very well, he wasn't poorly dressed, but he wasn't dressed in a suit and tie, he didn't look like he had any money, so I didn't have anything to say to him.

I directed my conversation to Jada. And that wasn't the only time I saw him in the club. Though, just a couple – three nights after that – and when I say couple of three nights, don't pin me down because I don't remember the exact night, I walked in just in time to hear this same man that I had been introduced to, stand up and call Wally Weston (MC who worked at Jack Ruby's Carousel Club) a Communist. But he used a word before that and Wally said, "Excuse me, what did you say!?" He said, "I think you're an f'ing Communist!" And Wally just laid the mic down, hopped off the runway and walked over there, and cold cocked him right in the mouth.

And Jack Ruby came forward – came and grabbed him by his neck and he said, "I told you not to come back in this club again!" and pushed him out the door. I did not realize that Wally had ever told anybody about that until I did the "Geraldo Show" many years ago. And he played that segment – when he had interviewed Wally – and Wally told him about hitting Lee Oswald in the mouth.

First-Person Witness To The JFK Assassination

Holland: Dealey Plaza, November 22nd 1963, the motorcade is about to turn the corner and come down Elm Street, in seconds JFK will be shot, can you walk us through that, in all its gore and awfulness. Because I want people to know – that's why. You know as we move away from that moment, things are going to be glossed over more and more and I want people to know exactly what happened, what took place, to the best of your recollection.

Oliver: That I recall very vividly. I still have nightmares about it. When I got down to the Plaza – there was such an electricity – unless you were there – there was no way to explain it. But have you ever been in a situation where the hair stood up on the back of your neck? That's the way it was that day. The air was just full of excitement and static electricity. And I got my camera out to make sure it was working. I took pictures of the crowd, the buildings, just to make sure it was in working order, because I did not want to miss one second of my president.

And you could tell as he got closer, because the crowd got louder and louder – and he turned on to Houston Street, and the crowd just went crazy! And then they turned, and as soon as they started to turn on to Elm Street – left on to Elm Street – I started filming.

And shortly after the car got all the way on to Elm Street, there was a noise that went bang bang, bang!

I thought it was those things that we used to have when we were children that when you threw on the sidewalk and they popped, you didn't have to light them or anything and I remember thinking, "why would somebody let their children bring something like that down to a place like this?" And I just no more got that thought out and as I am filming the motorcade, no more than got that out of my mind, when this "BABOOM" happened. And when the baboom happened, it looked like the whole back of his head just blew off, it looked like a bucket of blood was thrown out the back of the car, over the trunk, it was the most horrific thing I have ever seen in my life...

There are no amount of movies that could every portray what really happened down there that day, and the awfulness of it, and oh, the... and I was absolutely frozen in shock, there's some pictures of me, there's some in my book, of everybody on the ground around me, but I am standing there with my camera up to my chest, I couldn't move, I was so shocked, I could not move and..."

Holland: What was the reason you picked that specific spot?

Oliver: Well, I walked from my parking lot where I parked my car and all the way up Commerce as it were. I didn't intend to go to Dealey Plaza. I kept looking up the side streets where I could get close enough to the curb to take a film – and there just wasn't any place – and I kept walking, and kept walking and kept walking until it led me down to what I called the "grassy place" back then. I just walked across Houston Street and then across Commerce and Main Streets and to the edge of Elm Street where there was very few people standing and so I could get right there to the curb to take my pictures, take my film.

Holland: Just prior to the shots, the fatal shot, when you were, when you started to film him, did you see him grab his throat, what did his face look like?

Oliver: You know, I don't remember that, I think there's a lot of things that I have actually blocked out of my memory because they are so hurtful, they are so...like I said, I still have nightmares and its 48 years later, I still have nightmares.

Holland: Just a horrible, horrible thing to happen, especially to a young 17 year old girl like that. What happened inside the car? I am just trying to get as much detail as possible just so folks know.

Oliver: Brent, I was close enough to that car when it happened, that I heard what she said and I [recounted it] way back in 1969. You know, somebody said that he (JFK) went violently forward but the only time he went violently forward was after the big baboom.

She (Jackie Kennedy) was right in front of his face, and she said, before the baboom, she said, "Oh my God, he's been..." I couldn't tell if she said "shot" or "hit" – and the reason why I couldn't is because… now I have seen the Zapruder film, I know she pulled him down, pushed him down and crawled out on the back to get a piece of skull off the back of the car. It was horrendous, she literally, according to Clint Hill, pieced his head back together on the way to Parkland Hospital and try to hold his head together…you know it…

Holland: Let's take a minute. (Beverly breaks down and cries)

Several minutes later.

Holland: Bev, thank you for sharing that, I really appreciate it.

Holland: After Jack Ruby was arrested for the murder of Lee Harvey Oswald, did you ever have contact with him?

Oliver: No, because I woke up on Sunday morning out of a drugged sleep. The only way I could deal with this was to drug myself to sleep, and I sleep with the TV on even today. I woke up to see this friend of mine blow the man away, on national television, that he had introduced to me as his friend. (Jack Ruby murdered Lee Harvey Oswald on Sunday November 24, 1963, 2 days after the JFK assassination. It was broadcast live on television)

Holland: Let's move on. Just after the assassination, a big wave of people ran up the grassy knoll, as we have come to know it, you followed suit. Did you smell the gunpowder and…?

Oliver: I did not know what that odor was, until, even though I had been around guns, my brother was a hunter, I just didn't know what that odor was.

Beverly Oliver, Oliver Stone and Kevin Costner & "JFK"

As I stated, Beverly was portrayed in Oliver Stone's masterpiece film "JFK" by Canadian actress Lolita Davidovich.

Oliver: The first day that we re-enacted the murder, during the "JFK" movie, all of a sudden that smell came back and I realised what it was that I had smelled that day: It was gunpowder – and it so upset me I went to the parking lot and threw up.

And from that day forward Oliver (Stone) was kind enough to tell me if they were going to do the head shot, so that I could leave.

Holland: How did you come to meet Oliver Stone?

Oliver: He contacted me about being part of the movie, and if…asked me to work with him on the movie, and we met at the Stoneleigh Hotel to have dinner.

Oliver Stone asked me if I had ever seen any of his movies. I don't [go to] movies, and I said, "No I haven't – have you ever seen any of mine…?"

Oliver: And that's how we met. I grew very quickly to love Oliver. He's a different kind of person but what you see is what you get, like it, love it, or hate it…that's who he is, and I just happened to like him. It was the same way with Kevin Costner. He said, "Don't you know about 'Dances with Wolves' ," and I said "no… "

Oliver: One of the neat things about that time period that I remember very fondly, was I got to go see "Dances With Wolves" with Kevin Costner and that was – I think it was Lakewood Theater did a special showing – and he took me to see it. I was very thrilled, just thrilled.

And there was these little old ladies sitting in front of us – about five of them – and they kept looking around and whispering. And it was sprinkling that night so he ran out to get the van. We were in my van which he drove the whole time he was in Dallas – and he came back to pick me up. I jumped in the van and as we pulled off, I rolled the window down, and I said, "Yes ladies, it was him!"

Everybody on that set was extraordinarily professional the whole time. It was real sweet and I really enjoyed it. I can't think of anybody that I met that I didn't enjoy meeting, that I didn't just consider it very special. I even got to go to New Orleans and was actually –

Kevin actually pulled me and my husband Charles, and my youngest daughter Pebbles, and her best friend, into that little bitty courtroom. And we had to sit in the back cross-legged in those chairs, but he said, "I want you to see this, I want you in here for this, this is history." We got to sit back there and watch the closing arguments of Kevin Costner (in the movie "JFK").

Death Threats

Oliver: Charles Harrelson was involved with the mob, especially the Dixie Mafia. There's a lot of people who thinks that Charles was one of the tramps that was arrested that day. (please see Chapter 12 "Assassination Noise/The Three Tramps" for more information.)

He was in prison until he died for killing a judge, I think it was, and I know for sure that he was involved with the Dallas mob because I saw him with my first husband (George McGann also a member of "Dixie MMafia) too many times.

(Charles Voyde Harrelson – July 23, 1938 – March 15, 2007 – a member of the Dixie Mafia and served time for assassinating federal judge John H. Wood, Jr., He was also the estranged father of actor Woody Harrelson.)

Holland: The night you met Charles Harrelson, you had started talking about the assassination and I think it was several nights later you ended up in the hospital almost dead. Could you tell us a little bit about that?

Oliver: Well I, I walked in from the ladies room, as I recall and into the middle of a conversation – and it was about the assassination. Now I don't recall any specifics about the conversation, except that I made some statement like, "I was there when it happened dude, and it wasn't done by some man in the sixth floor depository..."

George McGann, my husband who was later murdered himself in a gangland slaying, pulled me up – pulled me out of the chair and took me home and told me I would never ever again bring up the subject of the assassination of Kennedy, unless I didn't want to live through the next day to talk about it.

Holland: Because of that you stayed silent right up until the House Select Committee in 1977. Have you received any threats or anything like that?

Oliver: The last threats that I received was in 1993 after I went on the "Geraldo Show" and said that I was going to write my book – and they were post marked from Houston – I still have them. And one of them said, just had "DEATH" in black boxed letters, and then the next one said, "Snitch, you're dead."

I used to get really scared because I would get these phone calls all the time. Different phone calls – threatening phone calls – where we would be off in revival, I would get phone calls that came through the church. Back then, that was before cellphones – so we would hook into the church's phone and [the calls] come through the church. They knew where I was – whoever "they" are – knew where I was.

I Love My Life

Holland: What's next for you my friend?

Oliver: Well, I don't know what tomorrow holds, I will live…and when my husband says get in the motor home we're going to another revival I get in the motor home and go to another revival (Bev's husband is Evangelist Charles Massegee), I love my life.

Beverly Oliver Massegee today. Photo courtesy Beverly Oliver

Beverly with actress Lolita Davidovich filming "JFK" Photo courtesy Beverly Oliver

Beverly at the time of the shooting in Dealey Plaza (Marie Muchmore movie frame)

CHAPTER: 7

FRONTAL SHOT: CSI & JFK

"I think that it's really important for people to understand that there were several locations that shots were being fired from. I believe that there were shots from the back of the president. I believe that there were shots from the front. I believe that there were two locations from the front, one was the grassy knoll, and the other, the location that the fatal head shot came from, which is not the grassy knoll."

Sherry Fiester senior Crime Scene Investigator

It is the nature of the beast, I suspect, being a believer in the JFK assassination conspiracy, that one is frowned upon and considered a kook. Those in the mainstream media tend to roll their eyes and readily dismiss the overwhelming conspiracy evidence as bogus.

All the while they subject you to their own pretentious ignorance of the case. After all "they" are the "serious" journalists and don't have time for such conspiracy nonsense.

I personally get this all the time: "You believe in the JFK conspiracy. What scientific proof is there?"

Below, you and I are going to be looking at that proof, indisputable scientific proof. You've all seen the rash of shows on television, CSI, CSI Miami, CSI New York, NCIS with Mark Harmon and Pauley Perrette. A show called "Bones" even did an episode on the autopsy and medical evidence of the JFK assassination. That was a pretty ballsy move, considering the outrageous grief anyone gets from the media if they challenge the Warren Commission's official conclusion. These shows look at a crime, a homicide, through the specific lens of science. That is precisely what my interviewees have done.

In the first section of this chapter, we are going to be looking at the conclusions that senior crime scene investigator Sherry Fiester has proven using 21st century forensic science. In the second part we'll see what NASA physicist G. Paul Chambers has confirmed using the undisputable laws of physics.

> *"We are not afraid to entrust the American people with unpleasant facts, foreign ideas, alien philosophies, and competitive values. For a nation that is afraid to let its people judge the truth and falsehood in an open market is a nation that is afraid of its people."*

President John F. Kennedy, February 26, 1962. Great Ideas Series.

Sherry Fiester Senior Crime Scene Investigator (CSI)

Sherry is downright plucky. She just goes for it in life. I like that. A lot. The only limitations are the ones between our ears. She is this tiny, unimposing woman. However, in a time when it was an upward battle for a woman to be a police officer, there was Sherry.

Long before it was sexy and in vogue, Sherry became a crime scene investigator and a leading expert in blood spatter analysis. Suffice it to say, her contribution to the scientific proof that there was a frontal shot and shooter in the JFK assassination, meaning at least two shooters involved in the assassination and therefore a conspiracy, is unprecedented.

Sherry is a retired senior crime scene investigator, CSI, just like you see on TV. She's put criminals behind bars using the science that she's speaking about in this chapter. To my knowledge no other modern CSI has ever looked at the crime scene evidence before now.

Holland: Let's start off a little bit about your background just to tell folks how you became a crime scene investigator when it wasn't so sexy and in vogue as it is now with so many television shows covering it. What brought you to that occupation, that vocation?

Fiester: In 1982 I was working as a police officer on the street. Believe it or not, I wore a uniform with a gun, yes.

Holland: Don't mess with her.

Fiester: I had the squad car with the lights and everything. Then there was an opening in the forensic unit and they asked me if I would apply. At first I said no. I felt the last thing I want to do is deal with dead bodies. They kept coming back to me and finally the lieutenant of the unit said, "I just want you to look at this one book." I looked at the book and just became enthralled with what forensics could really do for homicide investigations and I accepted the position.

Holland: For you, what is that?

Fiester: I think forensics gives you, well, it's specialized training, of course, that allows you to look at physical evidence and first recognize it – because if you don't know its evidence – you're not going to do anything with it. You won't collect it, you won't photograph it; you won't know how to process it. So, there's a lot of training.

I received over 3600 real time hours of specialized training in just the field of forensics, and attended numerous seminars and conferences all over the country. I was tested by IAI (International Association for Identification Forensic Certifications) and that's an organization that specifically looks at different fields of investigative work – and was awarded the "Certification of Senior Crime Scene Analyst."

That was in the late 80s. I have subsequently retired and am no longer working as a crime scene analyst. However, I certainly have that background and the training. I definitely could apply the training that I had on working homicides, which was almost exclusively what I did, and translate that information to the Kennedy assassination.

Analysis of Blood Spatter Pattern

Holland: Now fast forward to the point where you started to do some crime scene investigation based on the Zapruder film. Did you just happen upon it? Was it just something you always wanted to look at? How did this come about?

Fiester: I think my sister Debra (Debra Conway, the president of JFK Lancer) asked me every time I would see her, "When are you going to do something with the Kennedy assassination?" And I always said to her, "surely everything that has to be done has been done. This is old. This is not new. Forensic people have looked at it. If there was something new, it would be announced."

JFK Lancer Productions & Publications, started in 1995 as an historical research company specializing in the administration and assassination of President John F. Kennedy. They are dedicated to helping researchers and the general public by making research materials concerning Kennedy's assassination easily available to everyone. Their prime concerns are the accuracy of history, understanding the political era from Kennedy's inauguration to his death, understanding his particular stance on political issues, and researching the truth of his death. Thousands of related documents have been released through the JFK Act of 1992. Lancer was responsible for obtaining many of those and providing them free of charge to researchers and authors. JFK Lancer organizes the premier international conference on President Kennedy's assassination each year in Dallas, Texas, coinciding with the date of the assassination. Researchers and experts attend from all over the world and provide in-depth presentations. Sherry plays a big part in the organizing of this conference each year.

Fiester: A day came that Debra was looking at some photographs. I believe it was in David Lifton's book, "Best Evidence" that had a picture of frame 313 with the blood spatter.

Z313, each frame of the Zapruder film was given a number for reference purposes for investigations; the kill shot, also known as the head shot, is frame number 313. Z stands for Zapruder.

Fiester: And Debra said, "Well, they have this – it looks like this is blood in the air." Well that caught my ear. You know, "blood in the air"? I was a blood spatter expert. Analyzing blood stains on crime scenes is where I really excel. For her to say that was absolutely intriguing.

I walked over and just looked at it and said, "Okay, that's back spatter." She said, "What's back spatter?" I said, "That's blood that comes from the entry wound, but it's projected back towards the direction the force was traveling from." In other words, it goes back towards the shooter."

Oh, my gosh, Debra became so animated, saying, "Nobody knows this Sherry! Nobody knows this!" And she wanted to know everything. "Tell me how you know this." And so I had to give her a mini course in blood spatter.

Holland: Why the direction of this shot is important is because the Warren Commission, a government sanctioned commission organized in 1964 to investigate the JFK assassination, came up with the conclusion that JFK's fatal head shot was shot from the back. Actually they said all the shots originated from the back.

> **With CSI techniques of today, we can clearly see that the Warren Commission was wrong. The blood spatter patterns seen in the film are caused by a bullet coming in from the front. This is incredibly significant. This solidifies the difference between back or front entry wounds.**

Fiester: When Debra heard what I had to say about that and the Zapruder film, she asked me about when this type of forensic tool was originated and had actually been used before the death of President Kennedy. I told her that it didn't originate until the early 1970s. And she replied, "Well, then maybe this was painted in," – because people thought the Zapruder film was perhaps faked. I explained it may have been altered or faked, but the blood pattern in this particular point of time in the Zapruder film (frame Z313, the head shot) could not have been altered because the expertise necessary to make that contribution of knowledge was not there. It didn't exist for another seven years, so there was no one to tell alterationists what it should look like, how big it should be, how dense it should be, how long it should be visible in the Zapruder film itself - how many frames.

Holland: Once again folks, the main essential point here is the fact that there was a frontal shot which the Warren Commission and the history books say never happened.

Why Kennedy's Head Exploded

Fiester: I would really like to talk about cavitations. It has to do with when the bullet goes through the head. A bullet goes through the head in different stages, but it's happening so fast, it looks like it's going through all at once. But, it's really in stages. So, the bullet strikes the skull and creates an entrance hole. And as it goes in, it immediately starts creating cavitations.

And that cavitation is that pressure that pushes the blood back out of the entry hole as back spatter and what you see in the Zapruder film, that red mist in front of President Kennedy`s head, in fact it kind of obscures his face in frame 313 of the Zapruder film.

Fiester: Then the bullet continues forward and it can fragment or tumble or expand as it continues to pass forward. At the same time it's creating a permanent cavity which is the hole that the actual solid projectile is creating while it drills through the brain. But also, a temporary expanding cavity is created. It is temporary because it expands out and it comes back in.

You know the balloons that are long and skinny? And you can blow those up? That's what it looks like. It's around the bullet as the bullet travels. Like when you blow up that balloon it kind of goes down into itself? Well that's what cavitation does. It follows the bullet and it starts to expand following the bullet.

Holland: That's a great analogy by the way.

Fiester: Can you tell I've had to testify a few times? We need for a jury to understand and we need for your audience to understand. When you do research, or when you do analysis, the idea is that you should be able to explain it so that the person listening comes, on their own, to the same conclusions you have. That's what I want. I don't want you to believe just because you think I'm good at what I do. I don't want you to believe me personally. I don't want you to just trust because I have a background in criminal forensics and I know what I'm doing. I want you to understand [the science] and say "I understand it and I think the same thing."

So, as this bullet is passing through – at the same time we have the skull that is fragmented – just like a cracked egg. And we have this pressure that's building up.

Imagine if that balloon was inside that egg. When it started to blow up, it would push some of that eggshell off and some of the egg would come out. And that's what happens with the blood and the tissue. Because the brain cannot be compressed. You cannot compress water.

So when the cavity expands out, it is compressing the brain, which has a lot of liquid in it – it cannot be compressed – so it has to go somewhere. Well, if there's an opening it's pushed out very forcefully out of that opening and if not, then – if there's a crack in the skull, it'll push it open so that it can escape.

And that's how the bone flap, or the pink blob, over the president's right ear, that's how it was created."

Holland: That explains everything you see in the Zapruder film right down to the bone flap.

Fiester: When a bullet strikes the body, the idea is that the energy is transmitted to the tissue. When people create bullets they talk about "take down power" or "kill power" – that's what they're looking for.

The temporary cavity is much *more damaging* than the size of the bullet going through. It's the damage *within* the cavitation. So, if you don't have cavitation, then it's just an in and out wound and not a lot of damage.

That's why someone can be shot in say – the shoulder – so it goes in and out. Or the thigh or whatever – not that they're not injured, but, that energy has a place to go. But if it's in the enclosed head, then the damage is much more severe.

Holland: It's like a minor explosion inside the head.

Fiester: Exactly. But it's not that it's an exploding bullet – because some people say "oh, it was an exploding bullet..." No, it doesn't have to be an exploding bullet. It just has to be a regular bullet.

All of this happens in about 5 milliseconds. That's why it looks like it's immediate. And tissue that is as far away as 40 times the diameter of the bullet are stretched and torn and just sheered. So you have this little bitty bullet that causes 40 times the diameter of the bullet – in 360 degrees – in every direction. It's more than 360 ,it's the center of that balloon that's opening and going down. So it's in front of it, it's behind it, it's on every side.

Holland: So it's just expanding all the way along that route.

Fiester: Exactly. So, when you really think about what has to happen and then you think about what's documented by the medical personnel, what's visible in the Zapruder film and other photographs it all falls into place.

THE LOCATION OF THE "KILL SHOT SNIPER" IN DEALEY PLAZA IN FRONT OF JFK

Fiester: I think that it's really important for people to understand that there were several locations that shots were being fired from. I believe that there were shots from behind the president. I believe that there were shots from the front. I believe that there were two locations from the front, one was the grassy knoll, and the other, the location that the fatal head shot came from, which is not the grassy knoll.

Holland: How many shots were there? The official Warren Commission report states very clearly there were only three shots. And, of course, that includes this wonderful, implausible "magic bullet."

Fiester: Absolutely, the Magic Bullet Theory is ridiculous. Bullets do not behave the way [the Warren Commission] claimed, that they want it to behave. And, of course, the magic bullet was invented because there was a mis-shot. James Tague was injured. (Please see Chapter 5 "James Tague: The Man responsible for the Magic Bullet" for more information).

The Warren Commission had to say something and so they came up with the "magic bullet." And of course the person saying that was an attorney (Arlen Specter), had no forensic training, had absolutely no idea how bullets react, and hoped that the general public, that also had no training, would just accept that. Of course we know that it didn't. Why?

I think people are a lot smarter, sometimes, than politicians give them credit for, then and now. I think that there were a lot of shots. And I don't know exactly how many. There have been acoustical tests. The problem is they didn't test from all areas of the plaza, so we don't really know. We have witnesses that have given different numbers, so you know, it's really difficult to say.

Fiester: I think that we definitely have enough shots to show that there's a conspiracy and that there were probably at least three shooters in the plaza that day firing shots.

21st Century Crime Scene Science Proves Shot From Front

Fiester: The area of my expertise that I really want to talk about, and if you don't mind, I want for people to have an understanding of why I'm saying that the shot came from somewhere besides the grassy knoll.

And what I have done in my presentations, and even with just speaking with people over the phone or away and just out at a friend's house and they ask me about this, I just get a piece of paper. I start out by drawing what would be an overhead of a skull if you were looking down on a head. I just draw an oval. But you just take that oval and you divide it into four parts by drawing a cross and then the lengthwise of the head. And that gives you four quadrants.

Now if you look at the medical evidence, almost exclusively, everyone says and believes that the *entry* wound is to the *front right quadrant*. They're not saying that there's a particular point. They're saying it's somewhere in the right front quadrant. And they believe that the *exit* is somewhere in the *right rear quadrant*. That's the exit points.

Normally when you do trajectory analysis to determine where the shot came from, you would start with the entry point because you're at an autopsy. There's an X-ray. Here's a hole, there's a hole. You line the two holes up. Or the pathologist puts a dowel during the autopsy through the head. They can measure that exact angle as it's traveling through the head. And that gives them a trajectory.

Then you place the victim back in the scene – and you can do that with blood spatter or however – then you use that trajectory angle that has been created at autopsy, and it goes back to a particular point, and that's where the shooter was located.

It's a little geometry and that's all it is, a little geometry. But the problem is we don't have a specific point. We don't have an autopsy with a little dowel measuring the angle of impact. What we have is a big area in the front and a big area in the back. And so what I did is I made that entire front quadrant the entry and the entire rear quadrant the exit.

The autopsy of President Kennedy was an absolute disaster. It raised more questions than it answered. It was part of the overall purposeful cover-up to confirm a single shooter.

Sherry's point is that it is common practice, in any autopsy involving gunshot wounds, to track the bullet holes and cavities, to determine entrance and exit wounds and the angles and paths that the bullets traveled through the body. This allows them to assess damage to internal organs and tissue. This simply was not done.

Fiester: Now I want you to imagine that you're going to go to the extreme if you were facing that head and you were all the way to the right – the most angled shot that you could make and still enter just to the left of center as you're looking at your victim – and then still exit in the back right behind the ear. If you were to draw that line: that's one possible trajectory line.

So imagine that it's coming *in* just to the side on the forehead, as you're looking down right here, okay, and that it's traveling back to *come out* right behind the ear. That would give you one trajectory line.

Now as you move from in front, and then you moved across, every one of those locations is going to be another trajectory line until you finally are over here where it would just come in, in *front* of the ear and *exit* at midline in the back. What you've created is a large area called the *trajectory cone*. And the shooter is somewhere in that cone.

Holland: In that cone area.

Fiester: The next step is that you would take the president as he is in the limousine.

In Dealey Plaza, they had Thomas Canning who was a NASA scientist. The Warren Commission asked him to provide measurements on the location of President Kennedy's head, and he did so. There's another person that's done that. His name is Dale Myers.

Now these two men are very close, *very* close in their computations. They measured:

- How much is the head tilted down?
- How much is the head tilted to the side?
- How much is the head turned from profile as reference to Zapruder? So if Zapruder is at a 90-degree angle, he is turned beyond the 90-degree angle a certain degree.

Now both of these men came up with 26 degrees. So, if you take a compass, a protractor, you can put this down on a map of Dealey Plaza. You can measure that angle at 90 degrees plus another 26 degrees. And you have now indicated on your graphic the direction the president is facing.

If you were to straighten him up, he would be looking 26 degrees from profile to Zapruder. Now 26 degrees beyond Zapruder makes him looking at the *south* corner of the triple underpass.

Now that angle of possible trajectories that you create by looking at the most extreme from each direction, that trajectory cone can then be placed within Dealey Plaza to determine where the shooter could be.

Now beyond that, you're going to have injury to the other quadrants of the head.

Holland: Yeah, and we know that never took place. There were no other quadrants injured on JFK's head.

Fiester: So we know that we're restricted to that field, that angle, those trajectories. So, you limit yourself mathematically to a certain range that the shooter can be within. And if you step outside of it, then you're going to have injury to another part of the head. So, I did that and the grassy knoll is not within that area. So that eliminates the grassy knoll as being the originator of the fatal head shot.

Holland: Wow, there it is folks, the science, the proof, by a senior Crime Scene Investigator.

Fiester: You know, this is something that anybody can do. A lot of it is just common sense. You can take a ninth grader who has had geometry and they can figure this out for you.

But you know, the thing that bothers me about it – coming from the grassy knoll – because some people say, "I still think it came from the grassy knoll." Well you're going to have to have entry to the side of the head, one point on the side of the head.

So, you get to choose:

- Do I want it to be damage to the *right front quadrant* or do I want the damage to be the *right rear,* because you *don't* have projectiles that go in and make a 90-degree turn so that both quadrants can be damaged, number one.

- Secondly, you have a projectile that's coming in at over 2000 feet per second. It's going to impact a piece of bone that's less than two tenths of an inch thick. Then it's going to have to penetrate less than three inches in order for it to come from the grassy knoll. I just don't think that that's likely.

Holland: How do we get "back into the left" and not "back to the right"?

Fiester: But here's why a shot from the front is going to create a back and to the left. It doesn't have to be straight on to push it that way. Have you ever played pool? Play snooker?

Holland: Sure.

Fiester: Ever hit a pool ball and made it angle into the pocket? Because when you have a round surface and you strike that round surface, it creates a momentum that is angular. And so it goes forward or with the force – but it also angles away from the direction that the force is traveling from. So if you've ever played pool, then you already know why it went back into the left although the shot was coming almost directly straight on from the front.

Holland: That's absolutely brilliant. And here we have scientific proof once again, that there was indeed more than a single shooter and by definition that means conspiracy.

Validation of the Location By a Professional Military Sniper

Fiester: My husband had made friends with and had worked with a man who was retired as a military sniper. And, he was in our home one evening, had no idea what my background was, as far as he was concerned I was "the housewife." He started talking about his life as a sniper.

I asked him, "What if I wanted to shoot someone, but I wanted to blame it on somebody else. I don't want for them to be constantly looking for me; I want to make sure somebody else gets the blame for it?"

He said, "Well, if you're going to kill someone – if you're going to shoot them – and you want to blame it on someone else – you're going to have make some plans about when is the person accessible."

So, I said, "Oh I know I can do it outside – because I have a place where I know that they will be and I know they'll be outside."

So, he said, "Well, you would probably need *three people*. Think of it as a *triangle*. You put one person at each point:

- One point would be you *shooting* the person.
- One point would be the person you want to *blame*.
- Another point would be the *distraction*.

"Because, when you are a sniper," he said, "there are *four* really important things that you have to remember:

1. You have to do one shot / one kill.

2. You need to know that you can do the job.

3. You need to know that there is concealment or some way that you are not going to be noticed – people are not going to see you.

4. You have to be able to get away.

And the way that you can do that is you have someone that creates a distraction, everybody looks that way – and *then* you shoot – they don't see you. And in the midst of explaining all this to me, he suddenly stops and looks at me and says: "you're talking about the Kennedy assassination aren't you?"

I was shocked! Because he had been doing all the talking – not me. And suddenly he said that and I was, "how did you know?" He said, "we talk. We talk." That's the only thing he said. He never said another thing about it. Wouldn't discuss it anymore with me. I got chills from it.

Well, years later, I had an opportunity to speak with Craig Roberts. Craig Roberts wrote "Kill Zone. He was also a sniper.

Craig Roberts is a Vietnam vet. He was "in country" with the Marines from 1965 until 1968 when he was badly wounded at Da Nang and sent back home. Because of his military training in explosives and experience as a sniper, in 1971 he became part of the Tulsa Police Department's TAC squad, a predecessor to SWAT. He retired from the Tulsa PD in 1996. He has since written eight books including two specific to the JFK assassination: "John F. Kennedy: Kill Zone: A Sniper Looks at Dealey Plaza (1994)" and "JFK: The Dead Witnesses (1994)."

Fiester: The last time I spoke at a JFK Lancer Conference, Craig Roberts, of whom I am in awe, comes up to me and says: "Would you like to go to Dealey Plaza with me?" So, we go to Dealey Plaza. While we were there I stopped at a point on the north side of the plaza, up at the height of the railroad bridge and told him this is where I think the shooter was located based on my trajectory analysis.

Professional military sniper Craig Roberts stops at the exact same spot, turns and says, "If I were going to do it, this is where I would have been." Debra and I look at each other and it's like WOW! "

It was just so nice to have him validate that– that same spot. What was also really good about it was that his experience coincided with my analysis. Experience is important. Experience says it was a doable shot.

It's do-able and this is the best place. Well, if it was the best place for him, then, it was probably the best place for the shooter in 1963.

EVEN MORE VALIDATION FROM A PROFESSIONAL POLICE TACTICAL UNIT SNIPER

Brian Edwards has a master's degree in Criminal Justice and was a professional sniper with the Lawrence, Kansas Tactical Unit. He is the co-author, with Casey Quinlan, of their book "Beyond The Fence Line." It is the true story of Ed Hoffman, the only witness to see the shooter, behind the picket fence on the grassy knoll, take the shot at President Kennedy (See Chapter 1: "Seven Smoking Guns" for Brian's interview with me about first-person witness Ed Hoffman).

It was Brian's expertise and experience as a professional sniper that I sought when I interviewed him on Night Fright about the Kennedy assassination.

Holland: You were a sniper. Could Oswald have done the shooting job he did?

Edwards: You know, I get asked that question a lot.

If I was by myself, going to shoot anybody, I would not put myself in that position, up 60, 70 feet up in the air shooting at an angle. (Brian is referring to the sixth floor Texas School Book Depository where it is believed that Oswald made three shots and killed President Kennedy)

The hardest shot for a sniper – or anybody – or hunter – is to shoot from high to low. There are too many variables."

Edwards: You know, the easiest shot would have been, for the target, is coming down Houston Street right towards where you would be positioned. That's where I would have taken the shot. Why did Oswald or whoever was in the building wait until the car was going away from you?

A moving target inside a moving vehicle, 187 feet away – you know the superior shooters of today couldn't do that. I mean, I would never attempt something like that. That's the reason there were no shots taken, because it would have given the position away.

They waited until they were in a position where they could all triangulate into one spot. I mean that's a typical standard military operation, is you put people in front, people on the side and people behind so the target can't go anywhere, can't stop. It can't back up. It can't go forward. And wherever it goes, it's going to run into a – you know, the field of fire is going to be right in front of him.

Holland: If you were in charge of the shooting teams that day, where would you have placed them?

Edwards: I would put a shooter low, on a flat trajectory somewhere in front, to the side of the target, behind the grassy knoll, by the fence. You've got concealment. Nobody can see you. I mean you're behind the fence. I certainly would wear some type of disguise like a police uniform or, you know, a suit and have some type of identification. I would put another shooter in the Dal-Tex Building which is adjacent to the Texas School Book Depository, on the second floor perhaps.

Brian specifically identifies the Dal-Tex building as an ideal location to put a sniper team. This is important for several reasons:

- We now know a known Mafioso by the name of Jim Braden was questioned moments after the assassination coming out of this same Dal-Tex building.

- In 1977 a spent shell was found on top of that very building. (please see Chapter 1 Seven Smoking Guns; 5 Jim Braden. A known Mafioso who was arrested in Dealey Plaza seconds after the fatal head shot, where I cover that story in its entirety)

- The Dal-Tex building aligns perfectly with the bullet trajectory that hit the curb, splintering off and wounding bystander James Tague standing near the triple underpass. (Please see Chapter 5 "James Tague: The Man Responsible for The Magic Bullet")

Edwards: The target makes the turn. It goes down Elm Street. You simply point the barrel of the rifle towards the lane of traffic and just wait for him to show up in your crosshairs and you pull the trigger.

You've talked to Sherry Fiester. I'm in complete agreements where she puts the fatal headshot coming from: the south knoll. That's a great spot. You've got great cover and concealment. And then the final place would be, if I had multiple people at my disposal, I would put somebody at the west end of the picket fence."

Again, you've got two people in front, you got two people on the back and you've got one person on the right side. You can't put anybody on the left side, that's too far of a shot. But I'm going to put six people in there.

I'm going to put six people, one or two with a spotter and a security officer. Probably the guy on the picket fence is going to have a security person with him so he can, you know, in case he's focusing in on the target, somebody doesn't walk up behind him."

Edwards: I think you've got six or seven people out there. And not everybody had to take a shot.

Holland: Would there have been a way to coordinate the shots so they would all come in at around the same time?

Edwards: The first shot that's fired is your signal for everyone else to fire. Perfect example, a good analogy is: I'm sure you've been to a military funeral of some kind where they have seven shooters, seven military officers firing a 21-gun salute. How many sounds do you hear? You hear one, but you hear it three times. You hear three shots, three rounds fired by seven men. It sounds like one shot.

I think the people that were involved in this shooting were highly trained military people who had done this before – this wasn't thought up overnight. This was well planned out. They were professional hunters or military people.

Validation of the Crime Scene Science by Peer Review

Herbert MacDonnell is the foremost authority on the interpretation of bloodstain patterns period. His book "Blood Stain Patterns" is considered to be "the Bible" of blood spatter forensics. MacDonell has a Master's in Chemistry and a Ph.D. of Science from the University of Rhode Island.He has testified in over 100 international trials and is a leading expert in his field. (http://www.enotes.com/macdonell-herbert-leon-reference/macdonell-herbert-leon)

Fiester: Herb MacDonnell is regularly referred to as the "Grandfather of Blood Spatter Analysis" and looked at the Kennedy case. Of the spatter patterns, Herb said, "Yes, it's true. This is right! But everybody knows that. It's old hat."

So, you see, a lot of people in the forensic field think that their expertise has already been applied to the Kennedy assassination, when it really *hasn't*.

G. PAUL CHAMBERS NASA PHYSICIST

"Isaac Newton says that every action has an equal and opposite reaction. So if you're struck by an object, your body has to absorb that recoil momentum. Just if a boxer hits you in the jaw, your head would have to do something. It wouldn't just stand there and it wouldn't lean into the punch. It would go back and that's what happened to Kennedy."

Dr. G. Paul Chambers: NASA Physicist

Anybody who has seen any of the films of the assassination, like the Zapruder film, clearly sees the president's head jerk back and to the left when the fatal head shot happens (Zapruder frame 313 or Z313).

And anybody that knows about the laws of physics knows that they're universal and they haven't changed from 1963 to now. They're the same.

Paul Chambers has examined the physics behind the Kennedy assassination and where the fatal headshot originated from. The Warren Commission findings said that the JFK assassination was the result of one lone-nut assassin, by the name of Lee Harvey Oswald, that shot from above and behind the president from a building called the Texas School Book Depository, in Dealey Plaza on the sixth floor. So when you hear "the sixth floor School Book Depository," now you know what they mean.

As we're about to find out below, there was more than one shooter in Dealey Plaza that day, and more than one shooter means by definition, a conspiracy. Paul Chambers takes us through his research and findings using the undisputable laws of physics and will clearly identify the locations of the assassins and demonstrate multiple shooters with scientific certainty.

G. Paul Chambers has worked as a contractor for the "NASA Goddard Optics" branch and is currently working on the development of renewable energy sources with "Bellatrix Energy LLC." Formerly he worked as a supervisory research physicist for the "Energetic Materials and Detonation Science Department of the Naval Service Warfare Center" in Maryland and a research physicist for the "Condensed Matter and Radiation Sciences Division of the Naval Research Laboratory" in Washington.

Paul is a straight-ahead no-nonsense guy. He deplores stupidity in the face of the truth; an undisputable truth he knows can only come from the laws of science and physics.

He is a perfectionist and is angered when simple truths like 1 + 1 =2 gets referred to as "well, that's only your opinion."

"We are not here to curse the darkness, but to light a candle that can guide us through that darkness to a safe and sane future. For the world is changing. The old era is ending. The old ways will not do."

President Kennedy's July 15, 1960 Democratic Presidential Nomination acceptance speech at the LA Coliseum

Holland: Paul, what got you involved in the JFK assassination?

Chambers: A few years ago, I got a copy of a book by Vincent Bugliosi. It's almost 2000 pages long. As a scientist, I immediately jumped to the chapter he had on the physics and the Zapruder film. And I started reading it and became a little bit agitated as a lot of material in there just wasn't accurate. Then I read page 488. He says, "Well I had avoided taking physics in high school." Then it dawned on me what the problem was.

Newtonian Physics / "A" is for Apple

Holland: Paul, what were Bugliosi's conclusions and how were they inaccurate?

Chambers: Just some basic laws of physics, like Conservation Momentum for instance. He thinks that a bullet can't push a head backwards because it's too small. Well, it has nothing to do with the size. It's the combination of size and velocity that gives you momentum.

You can use that law which says the initial momentum system has got to be the same as the final momentum. So his head recoils back. That means the bullet struck him moving very, very fast and lodged inside his skull – and now his head has to absorb all that recoil momentum.

So that's a starting point to calculate how fast the bullet was going, where it came from, because momentum is a vector which means it has a magnitude and a direction. And that information is enough to back up actually *what* bullet, *what* gun was used.

Holland: Can we break that down in layman's terms so the folks can understand the principles behind the physics?

Chambers: Isaac Newton says that every action has an equal and opposite reaction. So if you're struck by an object, your body has to absorb that recoil momentum.

Just as if a boxer hits you in the jaw, your head would have to do something. It wouldn't just stand there and it wouldn't lean into the punch. It would go back and that's what happened to Kennedy. To argue that the bullet comes from behind and his head recoils backwards makes no sense whatsoever".

And there have been various ridiculous theories like "jetting". The jetting would have to be traveling faster than the speed of sound and faster than the bullet to make that work. None of those things - hypotheses work out. And you can prove them wrong with simple experiments that you can do in your home.

TRY THIS AT HOME

Holland: Simple experiments you can do in your home – what are those experiments Paul?

Chambers: One would be Conservation Momentum. You go down to your basement and check out when one pool ball contacts another. Where does it go? Well it's going to have to absorb that momentum and it will also go in the direction of the initial momentum.

Now, you could hit it at a glancing blow, but, when you *sum* the momentum of the cue ball and the object ball, they will give you a vector point of in the *direction* of that the original ball was going. An air hockey table is another good way to test that.

There are also simple experiments you can do to test human reaction times. And what you can see from the Zapruder film is that, for instance, Governor Connally is *not* reacting at all. And Kennedy has *already* got his hands to his throat. So he's already well into his reaction but Connally is sitting there completely *un-reacted.*

So to argue that the bullet struck them both would suggest that there were gross *differences* in human reaction times. And the bullet's traveling so fast and there are only three pin apart. It's *milliseconds* between them. Meanwhile, human reaction time is *over* several hundred milliseconds.

Human reaction times rule it out. And the physics of that assassination rule it out as well.

Holland: And Governor Connally was sitting directly in front of President Kennedy.

Physics and The Magic Bullet

Holland: Paul, the Warren Commission, as I stated before, said that JFK was shot from the Texas School Book Depository, which was behind President Kennedy, to his right, and from a downward position. Is there any evidence at all that a shot originated from that location?

Chambers: Well, there's one shot that struck Kennedy in the back that was noted at the official autopsy. But the bullet didn't penetrate through his body. They couldn't find a clear path through the body. Later they conjectured that "somehow" it bounced around inside the body and came out his throat and then "happened" to reposition – re-angle – itself back down again so it could go and hit Connally and create all his wounds.

Now the reason it had to do that was primarily because Oswald might have gotten off *three* shots in six seconds. He could *not* have gotten off *four* shots. And we know there's a final fatal headshot that hits Kennedy and they call it a recoil shot.

Another bullet strikes the bystander James Tague in the street. That's two. If two separate bullets hit Kennedy and Connally, I've got four shots. Even Oswald can't get off four shots in six seconds with that rifle. The best marksman was two and a half seconds to get off a shot with a Mannlicher-Carcano. So, immediately, the single bullet theory fails. You know there's a *conspiracy*. There has to be another shooter somewhere in Dealey Plaza. And that's why the Warren Commission stuck on that point.

In fact, all the Commission members did not agree with it. In the official findings, they say Governor Connally's test and other factors give rise to a difference of opinion as to the probability of the single bullet theory, none the less we all think Oswald acted alone. Well that's like saying the Epimenides Paradox. The statement below is false. And then you get down to the statement above is true. It's a paradox. It can't be one without the other. So when you have a paradox in an official government statement, you know it's *disinformation*. You know it's wrong.

Holland: I just wanted to orientate [the reader] to the car JFK was traveling in. Driving the car is Secret Service Agent Bill Greer. Next to him in the right front passenger seat is Secret Service Agent Roy Kellerman. Sitting directly behind on one of the two folding "jump seats" is Texas Governor Connally. To the left of the Governor, in the driver's-side jump-seat, is his wife Nellie Connally. Behind Mrs. Connally, in the rear left driver's-side seat, is President Kennedy's wife Jacqueline Kennedy, and of course, beside Jacqueline and behind Governor Connally is President Kennedy himself. Now we're going to discuss a little bit about James Tague and why that shot is so important. James Tague, was the third person that was wounded in Dealey Plaza that day.

President Kennedy was fatally wounded. Governor Connally was wounded, but he survived. Then along comes James Tague just as the report is being printed. It becomes public that he was hit and wounded as well. Now the Warren Commission has four wounds with only three bullets (See Chapter 5 "James Tague The Man Responsible For The Magic Bullet" on this very subject). Hence Arlen Spector (lawyer from the Warren Commission) creates this Magic Bullet Theory.

THE JUICE: PHYSICS PROVES SHOT FROM THE FRONT

Chambers: Everyone else calls it the "magic bullet." I call it an "impossible bullet." If your bullet has to violate the laws of physics, it's wrong. It can't happen.

The problem is that the bullet hits Kennedy in the back in a downward angle, and we all know if it does that, it's going to come out his chest.

Also, we know that the lungs were damaged because that information was included on the official autopsy – "with a contusion to the lung" – which is consistent with the Dallas doctors indication they couldn't maintain the integrity of the respiratory system.

So, the bullet comes in your back at a downward angle, hits your lung, how does it get to the trachea? How does it do that? It's got to deflect back and upwards, right? In order to do that, it's got to deflect off soft tissue.

Soft tissue has a density about one gram per CC. The bullet has a density of about 8 to 10 grams per CC. The copper jacket is about 9 grams. So you're going to have a very dense bullet traveling faster than the speed of sound, 2000 feet per second.

All of a sudden that bullet deflects by his lung – not even by his rib cage – but by his lung – somehow upward to his trachea. And then it re-deflects back down again so it can hit Connally at a downward angle.

So the physics of that is just absolutely impossible. The whole thing collapses like a house of cards. And as you discussed, there was only three casings found at the School Book Depository. Four shots means another shooter, and that means, as you said, a conspiracy. And just that information alone forces you to that conclusion. I'm not a conspiracy theorist. I'm a conspiracy empiricist because that's what the data forces you to conclude. There's no other possibilities consistent with the laws of physics.

Multiple Sniper Locations in Dealey Plaza

Holland: Paul, where do you think that some of the shots originated from?

Chambers: There are multiple locations in the Schoolbook Depository. Another shooter could have been at a window that was closer to the street than the (sixth floor window) of the Schoolbook Depository. So some theorize another one could have been at that location. In fact, there were multiple guns found in that book depository. There was a .22 found there, another gun found there. There was a whole bunch of guns in there and turned in at the time.

Another location was the Dal Tex building which was behind that, which would also have given a nice, clear shot. It's possible the bullet that lodged in Kennedy's back was fired from a .22 calibre, small calibre, so it wouldn't penetrate him from that location.

There's also some locations on the triple underpass. In the bridge there was a location on the far side where the shot that struck him in the neck could have come from. But the most likely shot, I think we can say with scientific *certainty*, that one shot comes from the grassy knoll. And that you were right with that conclusion, with a series of scientific records.

And they form two things:

1. One is the Zapruder film. And you can analyze that using the laws of physics. Concentration of momentum and back out where that final shot came from by just looking at the angle his head recoiled. Tracing that back along and you get a position right behind the picket fence about eight feet from the side of the fence on the grassy knoll.

2. That's the exact location that the House Select Committee came to, analyzing acoustic records on a Dictabelt recording. Now that committee was formed in the 70s in response to public outcry. The Zapruder film was shown on the "Geraldo Rivera Show" in 1975.

It was clear from what you talked about originally that that recoil looks like a shot from the front and the public outcry become enormous at the time. So the House Select Committee was called to examine not only that assassination, but others as well, like Martin Luther King and so forth. And they came across a Dallas Police Dictabelt recording that appeared to have gunfire on that tape.

There are likely more than one additional shooter. But there's at least one and as you say, once you've got two, you've got a conspiracy. The odds of two guys shooting to hit him of their own volition without prior coordination within the same six seconds is just astronomically like winning the lottery or something. So, one extra guy means conspiracy. So that means other people were involved. And because it was covered up so well for so long, it suggests it's not necessarily a small conspiracy.

The Conclusion of the House Select Committee on Assassinations: Probable Conspiracy in the JFK Assassination

From the moment President Kennedy was assassinated, there have been those who have challenged the US government's official position.

> **And with good reason; the government's case was so full of holes it could give Swiss cheese a run for its money.**

Throughout the 60's and into the middle 70's, the cry for the truth and for a new investigation into the JFK assassination built like a volcano, waiting to explode. On one fateful night, March 6, 1975, America and the world finally got to see the truth, and the volcano erupted.

There was an evening talk show in the 70's on ABC, hosted by Geraldo Rivera, called "Goodnight America." His guests that night were photography expert Robert Groden and social activist Dick Gregory (See "Chapter 11 JFK The Movie – Robert Groden – Jim DiEugenio – Jim Marrs" for more information).

They had brought a bootleg copy of the Zapruder film for Rivera to broadcast live. All who saw it that night witnessed the terrible sight of President Kennedy's head explode and then jolt back and to the left. It was obvious to all that the kill shot had come from the front of the president, not the rear, as the government had declared in its Warren Report. People realized the consequences of a frontal shot:

two shooters, and therefore a conspiracy. Their own government had covered it up and lied to the American people.

To put it mildly, there arose a storm. The American people, many of whom had served their country in wars and had lost loved ones, were furious. They had fought and died in faraway places for the truth. They were not going to be denied. Tired of being treated like little children and only months after Watergate, the House Select Committee on Assassinations was created in 1976 and ended two years later in 1978.

The House Select Committee on Assassinations' mandate was to gather all evidence, new and old, pertaining to three assassinations: President John F. Kennedy, Dr. Martin Luther King Jr. and the attempted assassination of Alabama Governor George Wallace. What they would find would unnerve even the most steadfast believer in the Warren Report. Below is the actual text of their conclusions in the JFK assassination:

> I. Findings of the Select Committee on Assassinations in the Assassination of President John F. Kennedy in Dallas, Tex., November 22, 1963
>
> "The committee believes, on the basis of the evidence available to it, that President John F. Kennedy was probably assassinated as a result of a conspiracy. The committee is unable to identify the other gunman or the extent of the conspiracy."

The House Select Committee on Assassinations never released a finding on Governor Wallace. Surprisingly, in the Dr. King assassination, they found:

> "The committee believes, on the basis of the circumstantial evidence available to it, that there is likelihood that James Earl Ray assassinated Dr. Martin Luther King as a result of a conspiracy."

Dictabelt Sound Recording Evidence

> Holland: Can you tell the folks what a Dictabelt recording is?
>
> Chambers:Well it's a primitive kind of recording device that's not as sophisticated as even a tape recorder back at that time – probably using some stylus type thing. And today it's been used so many times that the grooves have worn down and you can't even get it anymore. But tape records were made of the Dictabelt. And this was a technology the police at that time used to record conversations over walkie-talkies, etc.

And there was an *open* mic somewhere in that motorcade that was causing this recording to be made. This was found years after, locked in a safe or something.

Holland: So there is a recording of the assassination and what does that recording show?

Chambers: Well a number of experts, people who did sonar analysis, a number of firms like BBN Bolt, [Berasic and Ackensy] looked at this recording and concluded that there was a series of sounds consistent with gunfire. And the way they looked at that was to look at acoustic signatures, acoustic waves or shock waves in air when a bullet is fired.

With the speed of sound you get like a "sonic boom" effect. It's like when you crack the end of a whip – you hear that loud noise because the tip is *exceeding* the speed of sound. A fighter jet flies at the sound barrier, you hear that boom. You hear the crack of a rifle was when that bullet exceeds. And so you get a very consistent echo *pattern* because sounds are echoing off structures in Dealey Plaza. One wave is going to come quickly, but another is going to bounce off buildings and bounce off other buildings.

So what they did, ultimately, is a series of life fire tests:

- They took marksmen in Dealey Plaza
- Fired shots from the grassy knoll into sandbags
- Fired shots from the Texas School Book Depository
- Then they ring lined Dealey Plaza with microphones every 10 feet or so.

They placed a series of microphones listening to all the shots. They could match up acoustic *signatures* identically with *gunshots* in Dealey Plaza. Then they could tell exactly when they came in relation to each other and where they came from. One of the shots is a *perfect match* to a shot from the grassy knoll; in the *exact* location that you get from the Zapruder film.

Holland: You've got a whole series of witnesses seeing the shooter from the grassy knoll and now you've got the audio Dictabelt Audio Recording also giving the same results. This is explosive information folks.

Chambers: There have been peer reviewed work. There's a journal in forensics that has written and published a work on acoustics a few years ago. And then another group of scientists, some of them in IBM, others worked with a very famous Physicist at Harvard to try to quash the original acoustic data.

The National Research Council was hired by the FBI because the problem was the House Select Committee on Assassinations in '78 said, "There's a probable conspiracy based on the acoustic data and we recommend an investigation."

The FBI didn't want to redo the investigation. Government agencies are not going to spend a lot of money to embarrass themselves. If they open that investigation up with being told they have to find a conspiracy, it's not a "win" situation for them. So they hired the National Research Council to cast doubt on the original data – which they did. But even they *admitted* they were being pretty picky about how statistical analysis was done and some other issues as well.

Then another fellow who came out years later – works at the Department of Agriculture – and he wrote a very nice paper and published it in the "Journal of Forensics" and said, "Look, I did the acoustic analysis and I get a higher probability of a gunshot from the grassy knoll. I get *96%*. The original guys did it wrong."

Then in 2005, the famous scientist Norman Ransom, published a paper in the same journal and said, "No, this guy was wrong too. We read your analysis and here's why." Blah, blah, blah.

The key that you know its *right* is that it *matches* up so well with the other piece of data that you have. That's why you want multiple independent instrumented records, because if they don't match up, you know, something's glitched up. But if they're matching up perfectly and this matches up – the shots going along the microphones in the recreation *match* up the speed of the motorcade exactly. That will *not* happen by accident.

You can go shot by shot from the Zapruder film and you get a perfect match all the way around. Again, none of that's going to happen by accident. And I calculated the odds of all that just happening randomly are like winning the lottery twice in a row.

If you can do that, then you can discredit the acoustic analysis. If you cannot, then you got to believe it because those are the kind of odds you're facing. So you know some physical phenomena is causing both instruments to record and that's how you get a confidence in science. And that's why I say with scientific certainty because this is the same technique I would use to study a transitive earthquake.

GUN SMOKE ON THE GRASSY KNOLL

Holland: There was also smoke seen from the grassy knoll. SM Holland, who was again on that triple underpass, a whole bunch of his crew – he's a railway guy – saw smoke coming from the knoll. One of the arguments says new bullets don't give out any smoke. Well, that isn't entirely true is it?

Chambers: No. Any kind of explosive will never react 100%. That no smoke would be a 100% reaction. In other words, you've got a solid material called a nitrocellulose compound that will react. And when it does that, it will produce gasses. And those gasses are very hot and expand very rapidly. That's what propels the bullet down the gun. But if they reacted completely so that you got perfect gas formation, you wouldn't have any particulates, which means no smoke. But that's not a reality. That never happens in reality.

Any gun *will* give off some smoke. In this particular gun, it was a custom round because we know it's a "frangible round." We know that from the medical evidence, X-rays, etc., and Dr. Cyril Wecht, if I could name drop, he was a Forensic Expert on the medical data and he wrote letters to the House Select Committee on Assassinations and explained it must have been a "frangible round" that impacted and shattered the inside of his skull to produce the X-ray patterns that they saw.

I've been going around this a lot, but the round was a "custom round" which meant you could have put potentially *black powder* in there which would *produce* copious smoke. Now I wouldn't put that in my hunting rifle, but it would have been used at that time.

So there are conceivable explanations for lots of smoke. And in fact, a lot of witnesses saw smoke. There are *15* witnesses if you count them all, who either saw a shooter, heard the shots, or saw smoke at the location of the grassy knoll. So it's overwhelming.

Holland: This knowledge about Physics has been around since 1963. It makes me wonder why the Warren Commission never instituted somebody to examine this the way you have.

Chambers: That's an interesting question because no one on the Warren Commission had a background in science. When you try and explain the science to them, they said, "Science doesn't matter. All that matters is what I can prove to a jury. And if you put your expert on and he starts talking science, by God, I'll get another expert and he'll talk other science and they'll cancel each other out, so it doesn't matter."

The truth *isn't* what you can prove to a *jury* – if it was, NASA would be using juries to decide the Space Shuttle missions– I guarantee.

Corrupted Data

Chambers: Once the data is corrupted or altered, you can't base your model on it. This is the flaw and failing in the Warren Commission. They're basing their model on corrupted data. Someone's distorted the data and monkeyed around with it and so forth. And as a scientist, you immediately dismiss corrupted data if you know someone's been tampering with it. You immediately throw it out and redo the experiment. Unfortunately, in the paradigm of the lawyers, "Oh we can use the corrupted data," and so forth. Sorry, it didn't work that way. People are going to get the wrong answer.

The other thing the Warren Commission did do, by the way, was alter the data. Gerald Ford wasn't happy that Kennedy was shot in the back so he decided, "Well I'm going to fudge it a little bit. We'll move that one to his neck. Okay, now it works out. Shoot him in the back of the neck. Okay, it'll come out his throat. Everything works out well."

When you corrupt data, two ways to absolutely get the wrong answer: base your model on corrupted data, alter the data yourself, guarantee you'll get it wrong every time. Those are the things that the Warren Commission did, and one of the reasons among others that they completely got it wrong."

Holland: And that's a true story. That is President Gerald Ford, before he was president, he was indeed a member of that Warren Commission. And Kennedy was shot midway in the back, six inches below the neck. Ford wrote a memo that moved the wound up so it would be in the back of JFK's neck. He didn't physically move up the shot, but he moved up the location in the report. And he admitted to that later on. The other thing Gerald Ford was doing at the time was feeding information on the Warren Commission to the FBI so they could adjust the FBI's information back into the Warren Commission.

"The human mind is our fundamental resource."

JFK

I know what you're thinking: "Holland's trying to pull a fast one here. In the first section of this chapter, Sherry Fiester says that the kill shot came from the opposite of side Dealey Plaza, and now, in this section with Paul Chambers, Chambers states that, no, the kill shot came from the grassy knoll." I pride myself on transparency with the assassination, so I put that very question to Sherry Fiester herself.

Holland: Sherry, Paul Chambers was here several weeks ago. He's done impeccable work. He's a physicist, and was saying because JFK's head goes back and to the left, that means the shot that entered his head and caused that momentum - that movement - had to have come from the grassy knoll. You dispute that.

Fiester: I do. Paul and I went to Dealey Plaza. It was his first trip there. And I believe that what Paul has done is correct. And I think he has used his expertise, but he didn't have all the information that he may have needed because, like most people, when you think about the shots from the right and from the front, what's the front? Where's the front? The front of the president at the time of the head shot is not the grassy knoll. So if you don't know where the front is, then you don't know where the shot came from.

Paul had never been to Dealey Plaza. So, he used information that he had, and I think he did an outstanding job. Actually, we don't conflict on anything except where the shot came from. I really believe that had Paul and I collaborated prior to him doing his book, that it would have made a difference.

Holland: But you're not saying that a shot did not originate from the grassy knoll. You're just saying that the kill shot, the one seen in Zapruder 313, is not from the grassy knoll.

Fiester: Yes. And you know, I don't expect him to say that. I'm happy if he never does. What I'm really thrilled about is that someone who is an expert in their field has taken the techniques that they work with every day and applied it to the Kennedy assassination, because this is just like going to trial.

My job when I'm at a trial and I'm on the witness stand as an expert is to educate the jury, give them the information that I have and let them come to a conclusion. I tell them my expert conclusion. They can disagree or they can agree. It is up to them. And if I want them to agree, then I need to give them a persuasive argument with a clear understanding of how I've reached my decision. And so that is all I can hope to do.

It's okay if people disagree with me. I have no problem with that. I'm happy that anyone brings any kind of focus to this because I think that the people that hear the contradictory information, they're going to want to find out for themselves. "Why are these two experts not agreeing?"

Entry and exit blood spatter patterns show blood going out the wound, back to the source, and exiting with the bullet.

Crime Scene Expert Sherry Fiester

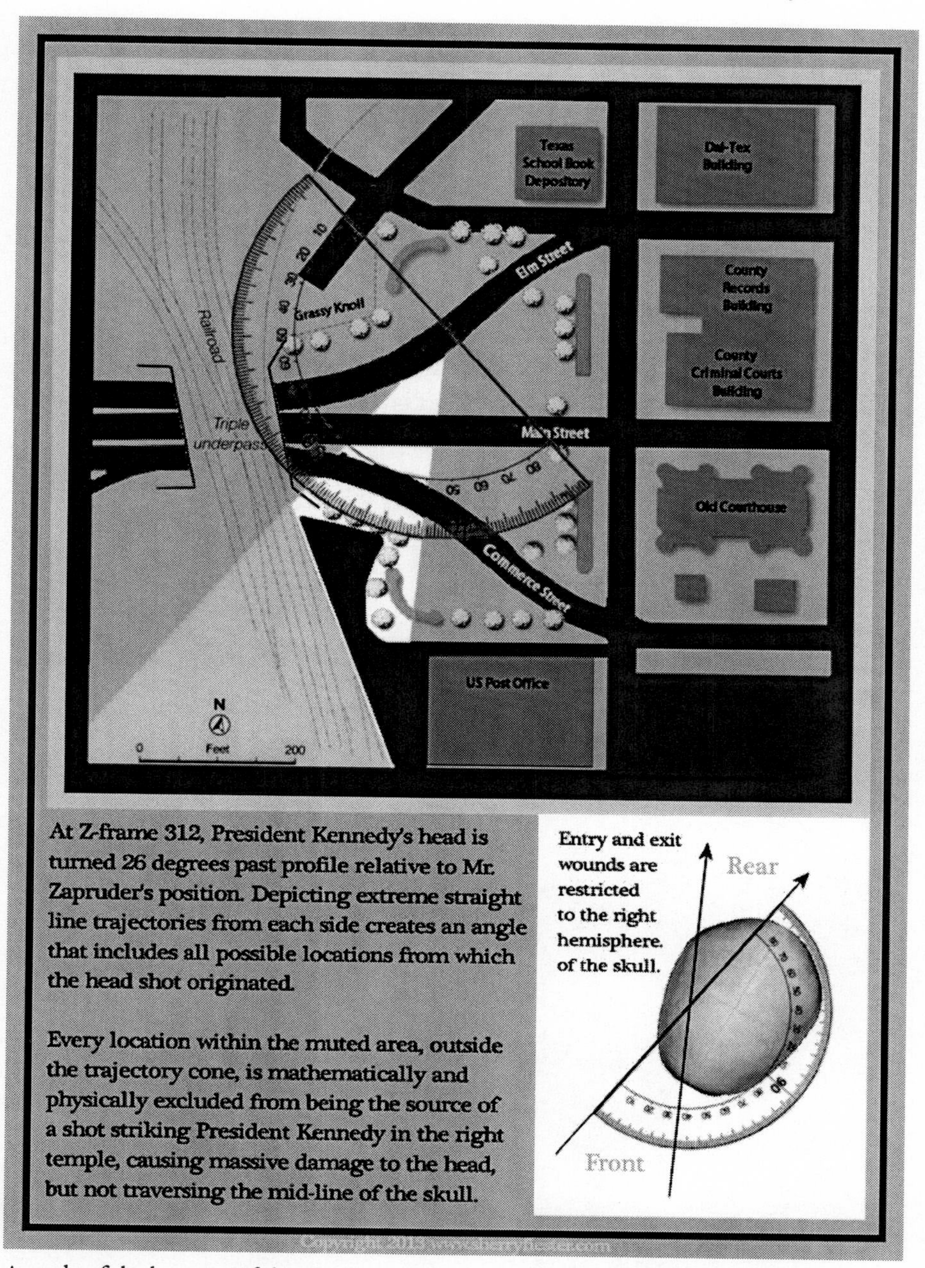

A study of the location of the south knoll shooting locations by Sherry Fiester (used with permission)

G. Paul Chambers on "Night Fright Radio Show

A Warren Commission study to recreate shots from the sixth floor of the Texas School Book Depository with the Dealey Plaza in the background

CHAPTER 8

THE CIA: GUILTY AS CHARGED

"This Nation was founded by men of many nations and backgrounds. It was founded on the principle that all men are created equal, and that the rights of every man are diminished when the rights of one man are threatened. Now the time has come for this Nation to fulfill its promise."

President John F. Kennedy, Civil Rights Address June 11, 1963

Mark Lane is a lion. He is Sean Connery as King Arthur. He is the elder statesman that all turn to. And he was there when the world needed him most. When the disadvantaged needed justice in sweltering Harlem, lawyer Mark Lane was there. When JFK needed help in New York to get elected, campaign manager Mark Lane was there. When Dr. King cried out that freedom could wait no longer, civil rights advocate Mark Lane was there. When the American government lied about the murder of President Kennedy, Mark Lane stood firm against the storm and dared to challenge. When The American Indian movement was attacked, Mark Lane defended. When Segregation reared its ugly head across the South, Freedom Rider Mark Lane put his life on the line and faced it down.

> **There is no doubt that America has benefited from the tireless work of Mark Lane. With my show, "Night Fright," I consistently state that one person can change the world, then I always point to Mark Lane. It was both a privilege and an honor to have Mark come on my show and give willingly to inspire a new generation.**

Mark Lane worked hand-in-hand with John Kennedy, Bobby Kennedy, Dr. Martin Luther King, and the American Indian movement. He survived the night of Kool-Aid poisoning in Jones Town. He was the first to challenge the Warren Commission with his groundbreaking, bestselling book "Rush To Judgment." His documentary, by the same name, remains the benchmark for all researchers. He represented Lee Harvey Oswald's interests and testified in front of the Warren Commission. He wrote the screenplay for the Hollywood film "Executive Action," starring Burt Lancaster, which convincingly portrayed the assassination of JFK as a conspiracy, and virtually shook the foundations of the establishment in Washington. With his exhaustive efforts he brought "the House Select Committee On Assassinations" into being. He continues.

Lane with Candidate Kennedy

JFK's New York City Campaign Manager

Holland: Let's jump in right away shall we? Let's start off with JFK. You first met him in 1960. There's a great picture in "Plausible Denial," your book, of you and JFK. ("Plausible Denial," Mark Lane, 1991)

Lane: I was actually a Candidate for the New York State Legislature. He was a Candidate for president of the United States. They asked me to meet with him and later to become one of the two Campaign Managers for him for New York City in his presidential campaign.

And Kennedy was running for president and wanted to have everybody in the Democratic Party support him – so they had the regular organization appoint one person be his Campaign Manager, co-Campaign Manager for New York City. Then I was chosen by the Reform Movement to represent Eleanor Roosevelt and Governor Lehman and others in our movement.

So I met with him. He endorsed me. I supported him – he supported me. We were both elected. His election was revolutionary and was measured in terms of what was to take place. And then three years later he was assassinated. When he was, J. Edgar Hoover, the Director of the FBI, on the *very* day of the assassination said that Lee Harvey Oswald was the *lone* assassin. He acted alone. There was *no* conspiracy.

CIA And JFK

Lane: Just before the investigation began and the FBI issued a report saying basically that, the new president, Lyndon Johnston, appointed a commission led by Earl Warren, who was the Chief Justice of the United States; but he wasn't the most active member. The most active member of the Warren Commission was Allen Dulles.

Allen Dulles had been the Director of the Central Intelligence Agency who was fired by John Kennedy for lying to him about the Bay of Pigs invasion series of events which took place. And so Kennedy fired Dulles.

Now, when President Kennedy was killed, Dulles basically ran the Warren Commission to investigate the murder of President Kennedy - was put in the key position because the CIA had actually killed President Kennedy – and his role was to cover that up. And he did that really well.

CENSORSHIP AND THE JFK ASSASSINATION

Lane: From the time of the arrest of Lee Harvey Oswald, for more than a year and a half not one single newspaper, not one single radio or TV station permitted one word of dissent in America; not one word of dissent in America from the official version. You couldn't get on the air and talk about it.

I did reach people on local radio stations in the United States. And the only way I reached people in more than one city - at one time - was when I went to *Canada* and was involved in radio broadcast, CBC and other Canadian radio stations - which of course came into border cities -certainly like Detroit and many other cities in the United States. That was the only way I could reach people in America, and one city at a time, was by *broadcasting from Canada.*

The Warren Commission Report was released in 1964 to the absolute support of everybody. Everyone in the news media - New York Times, CBS, NBC, - *everyone* of the news media in America said it was the greatest thing that happened - was considered to be the *greatest* investigation in the history of America etcetera. The only problem was that I knew it was *not true.*

So, I conducted my own investigation. I took key witnesses, went down to Dallas, etcetera, and I wrote a book which not one publisher in America would publish. *Not one.*

I went to every publisher. It was called "Rush to Judgement." I ended up in London talking to an old conservative firm there, the "Bodley Head"; they're about 100 years old. And they agreed to publish it.

And when they did, one American company said they would publish it. And it became the number one bestselling book, according to the "New York Times," that year when it was published; number one bestselling book in America for 1966. It came out in paperback the next year, number one bestselling book in America in paperback, and then in 23 other countries as well.

It's a book which shattered the secrecy surrounding the assassination of President Kennedy. Lots of new theories, no speculation, merely compared the *facts* to the conclusions reached by the Warren Commission. I never thought it would be a bestselling book. Almost like a law book, just comparing what the Warren Commission said to what the facts were.

Something Not Right With The JFK Assassination

Holland: What didn't smell right to you, right off at the beginning?

Lane: Well, Ruby played a big part. It was a live murder on television. Ruby came out and fired a shot and killed Lee Harvey Oswald. As he was handcuffed and the two police officers – in the basement of Dallas Police and Courts Building - Jack Ruby walked up with a gun and – the building was "allegedly" sealed off – he walked up with a gun and fired a shot and killed Oswald.

Ruby actually worked for the Federal Bureau of Investigation (FBI) and Ruby was also on the staff as investigator for Richard Nixon (before he was president), who at that point was a member of Congress for the House on American Activities Committee; Ruby worked for him. All of these documents came out many, many years later. But they're official documents and there's no question that these things are so.

But I guess the killing of Oswald and seeing Oswald originally when he was being questioned by the authorities as they moved him from one room to another, short little glimpses of him, he said "I don't know what they're talking about. Will some lawyer come forward and give me representation? I didn't do anything. I don't know what they're talking about." Then of course there was no trial because he was killed.

Of all of the evidence being covered up - most of it was by the government at that point – the single most obvious fact of the disruption of evidence of the murder of Lee Harvey Oswald. If Oswald had not been murdered he would have been tried, presumably since they said he did it. And there was not one shred of evidence – *not one* shred of evidence – which moved in the direction of showing that Oswald had been involved in any shooting at all that day.

In fact, the president was killed by a rifle shot and a paraffin cast test taken by the Dallas police showed that there was no nitrates in suspension on his face or on the one hand, meaning that he could *not* have fired the rifle. Remember that he was arrested right after the assassination and even washing would not have removed those traces. So the evidence was only, that Oswald could not have killed the president, and yet there was such a resistance in the United States. No one would talk about it.

LEE HARVEY OSWALD EXPLAINED

Lee Harvey Oswald (October 18, 1939 – November 24, 1963) is the purported assassin of President John F. Kennedy. Oswald was raised by a single mother, Marguerite, and had a "troubled" childhood. On one occasion he was admitted to a juvenile home and was assessed by psychiatrist Dr. Renatus Hartogs, who just "happened" to be working on mind control techniques for the CIA (See Chapter 13 "Montréal and the Assassinations of JFK, MLK, RFK" for more information).

At the age of 17, Oswald entered the Marine Corps and was then stationed at Atsugi Airforce base in Japan, where U2 spy planes flights would originate. It was the U2's task to fly over the Soviet Union and secretly photograph Soviet military movements. It is believed that this was his introduction to the secret world of US intelligence. Oswald was given Russian language tests by the US military, which seemed strange as he would have no need for the Russian language in his current role in the Marines, unless he was to go undercover into Russia.

As if on cue, Oswald left the Marines and "defected" to Russia. At the American Embassy, before officially entering Russia, Oswald boasts that he is going to tell the Soviets all his "top secret" information from the Marines.

It is well worth noting that the Office of Naval Intelligence (ONI) had a program at this very time, where they recruited young men in their twenties. On the surface, they all seemed to be disenchanted with America, "malcontents" and all with "Communist tendencies." The ONI would then have them defect to Eastern Europe or directly into the Soviet Union. After a year or so, the ONI would bring them back, some married, as Oswald did, to wives from the countries they were in. ("JFK and the Unspeakable" by James W. Douglass, 2011, Pg. 40)

True to form, Oswald returned from Russia with his wife, Marina, and baby daughter. But, instead of being arrested as a traitor, he is allowed back into the country without reprimand. It is commonly believed that this was for two reasons:

- US intelligence wanted any and all of the intel he had gathered and brought back from Russia.
- US intelligence was going to use Oswald as a "dangle," (think of a "dangle" as bait on a fish hook waiting for someone to take hold of and bite). They would wait and see if the Soviet Intelligence Services would try to contact Oswald to spy for them on the US. If that were to

happen, the US intelligence service could then feed false information back to the Soviets through Oswald.

"Sheep Dipping" Lee Harvey Oswald

It is my belief that, now that Oswald was back in the States, US intelligence was going to engage him once again and attempt to send him into the heart of Castro's Cuba on a mission similar to what he had so successfully done in Russia. This would mean setting up Oswald's character and actions to resemble that of a pro-Castro, Cuban Revolution activist, anti-American Capitalist.

This process is called "sheep dipping" and is commonly used in intel circles. The term comes from dipping a live sheep in a chemical solution that kills bugs nested in their wool. Sheep dipping an intel asset gets rid of the person's identity and makes it easier for a fake character to emerge to the public. That is exactly what we can see taking place.

In October 1962, Oswald miraculously manages to get a job at Jaggars-Chiles-Stovall Co. in Dallas, Texas. This is a high-tech photographic company that examines the very same top secret U2 spy photos mentioned above. With such a strategically placed job, it is hoped that the Soviets might reach out to him at this juncture to spy for them.

> **By the way, Oswald gets the job within days before the Cuban Missile Crisis photos are examined by the very same company. There is no way a real defector, just returning from the Soviet Union, would be given clearance to work in a company with top secret US military work going on. At any rate, the Soviets didn't "bite," and shortly thereafter, Oswald left the company.**

The Backyard Photos

On March 31, 1963, while still living in Dallas, Oswald's wife, Marinna, takes the famous "backyard photos" of Oswald holding a rifle and wearing a pistol and belt around his waist. He is also holding two "leftists" magazines in his hand. Many researchers argue whether the photos were faked with Oswald's face "cropped" in. In a scene in the movie "JFK," the argument is made that the shadows from the sun don't align correctly and that there is a "crop" mark on the chin of Oswald's face.

Rick Nelson, who was the first curator of the JFK Assassination Museum in Dallas, is personal friends with Marina and rented a room from her and her husband while he was in Dallas, running the museum for a year. They would spend countless hours speaking at Marina's kitchen table. One of the subjects that came up was the "backyard photos." She told him she remembered Oswald insisting she take the photos, and she finally complied.

> **I believe it. Those photos could then be used to contribute to the ongoing sheep dipping of Oswald as being pro-Castro and pro-Marxists.**

It is worth noting that the two "leftist" magazines that Oswald held in his hand in that photograph were at odds with one another. It is improbable that a real pro-Marxist "in the know" would buy both magazines. A more logical scenario is that Oswald held the magazines, believing it would add to the sheep dipping ruse that he was an extreme pro-Marxist, when in reality he was unaware that each magazine represented polar views.

THE ATTEMPTED ASSASSINATION OF GENERAL WALKER

Only a few days later, on April 10, 1963, Oswald makes a phony assassination attempt on General Edwin Walker (November 10, 1909 – October 31, 1993), with a single shot through a window into Walker's residence in Dallas. Walker was in a different room at the time and was not injured.

Walker had been a General in West Berlin when JFK "fired" him for insubordination. It seems Walker was illegally ordering his troops on how to vote. Walker was a right-wing fanatic and bigot who rallied protesters in an attempt to stop Black student James Meredith from entering the University of Mississippi in 1962. Bobby Kennedy, the US attorney general, thought Walker to be so mentally unstable that he had him committed for psychiatric evaluation. Walker was released on a technicality five days later.

Many researchers argue whether Oswald actually took the shot at Walker or if it was a setup. Once again, I turn to Rick Nelson and what Marina told him; indeed Oswald took the shot.

> **Giving Oswald credit for the Walker assassination attempt would give continued credence to his sheep dipping. IE, he took a shot at a right-wing raging anti-Communist like General Walker.**

DAVID FERRIE, GUY BANISTER AND OSWALD

Only two weeks later, on April 24, 1963, Oswald drives from Dallas to New Orleans. It is commonly believed by most researchers that he then became involved with Guy Banister and David Ferrie, both of whom were involved with Operation Mongoose. It was an operation that had military intelligence, the CIA, the Mafia and anti-Castro cuban exiles all working together for the same common goal: to overthrow Castro and return to Cuba. At first glance this may seem at odds with Oswald's sheep dipping. However, on May 26, 1963, Oswald officially opens the New Orleans chapter of the pro-Castro "Fair Play for Cuba Committee" whose headquarters are in New York City.

The committee office, as it turns out, is in the same building as anti-Castro Guy Banister. What's more, Oswald was the New Orleans chapter's only member. Coincidence?

PRO-CASTRO LEAFLETS

On August 9, 1963, Oswald is arrested for getting into a fist fight with Carlos Bringuier. Bringuier was the New Orleans head of an anti-Castro Cuban group called DRE. Oswald had gone to meet Bringuier the day before the fight and the arrest. The next day Oswald was on a New Orleans street handing out pro-Castro leaflets to passersby. Bringuier miraculously showed up and a fight ensues. The police said the whole incident looked "staged."

Next, Bringuier challenged Oswald to a live broadcast debate, the auspices being Bringuier representing the anti-Castro perspective and Oswald representing the pro-Castro perspective. The debate was broadcast live on WDSU Radio, August 21, 1963 on a show called "Latin Listening Post." Any pro-Castro spies or informants living in New Orleans would most certainly tune in to this show to keep abreast of the pulse of the Cuban community in New Orleans. They would most certainly make note of the name and pro-Castro views of one Lee Harvey Oswald and pass his name along. US intel would know this as well. Once again, this incident is just more fodder for the sheep dipping, which is almost complete.

TRIP TO MEXICO

Next, on September 23, 1963, was a trip to the Cuban Embassy in Mexico where Oswald would attempt to get a visa to allow him into Cuba. Again, there are various perspectives from researchers as to whether this trip actually took place and if the person representing Oswald at the Cuban Embassy was an imposter. Either way, the trip was unsuccessful, and no visa was issued.

My guess is that Oswald made the trip and returned back to Dallas very frustrated, having spent close to a year playing the part of a pro-Castro / pro-Cuban revolution activist. Perhaps, and this is only my own speculation, in the minds of Oswald and US intelligence, it would take one last defining stunt to salvage all the work they had done

and finally get Oswald pronounced a true pro-Castro Marxist and be accepted into Cuba. It was into this scenario that President Kennedy's Dallas trip was announced.

THE JFK ASSASSINATION AND LEE HARVEY OSWALD

In another miraculous turn of events, Oswald gets a job at Dallas' Texas School Book Depository (TSBD)in Dealey Plaza, which is perhaps the best spot for a sniper in Kennedy's entire Dallas motorcade route. He had applied to all kinds of places along the motorcade route for weeks. Marina had been staying with their children at her new friend Ruth Paine's house. Oswald was alone renting a room in a rooming house closer to work. It was Ruth Paine who got him this job at the TSBD. Paine's sister Sylvia Hyde Hoke was employed by the CIA. Paine's mother also had a connection to DCIA Allen Dulles. I don't think that Oswald got the best spot along the motorcade route for an assassin by coincidence.

On November 21, 1963, Oswald spent his last night with his family. He opted not to stay at his rooming house that night, and instead went to stay with Marina and his two children. He told Marina he wanted to pick up curtains from her for his room at the rooming house. In the morning, he rose before Marina. He left $170 (around$1,000 today) and his wedding ring on the bureau. He asked a neighbor, Buell Wesley Frazier, who also worked at the Texas School Book Depository, for a lift to work. Frazier noticed a brown paper package under Oswald's arm which Oswald told him contained curtain rods.

On November 22, 1963, in Dealey Plaza, at 12:30 PM, JFK's limousine had just made that awkward turn onto Elm Street. The president was obviously relaxed and happy, smiling and waving to the well wishers that lined the sidewalk. Shots rang out and shattered the scene. In six seconds, the future of the world changed. The president is mortally wounded.

Dallas Police Officer Marion Baker rushes through the front door of the TSBD and encounters manger Roy Truly. Baker believed that the shots had come from the grassy knoll, but since he was in closer proximity to the TSBD, he decided to check there. Both Officer Baker and manager Truly ascended the stairs to find Lee Harvey Oswald alone in the second-floor lunch room "calmly" drinking a Coke. They both stated that no more than 90 seconds had passed since the last shot. Most researchers are adamant that, if Oswald was on the sixth floor, 90 seconds would not have been enough time to hide a rifle and then bolt down four flights of stairs to the second-floor lunch room. I disagree.

Author's Dissention

First off, I do not now, nor have I ever believed Oswald shot JFK or even targeted him. Is it possible that Oswald was asked to take a shot that day but purposely missed the car? Perhaps the bullet that missed and caused the wound in James Tague was from Oswald's gun. Maybe. (See "Chapter 5, James Tague, the man responsible for the Magic Bullet" for more information.)

It is my opinion that Oswald was supposed to disappear out of Dallas and hopefully into Cuba, having been given the credit as the person who shot at JFK, just like he had done with Walker. Or, maybe, Oswald was told to target Connolly for the same reason. There is simply no way of knowing.

> **I differ with most researchers on the next point as well, and I am certain to catch hell for it, but here goes anyway.**

I do believe Oswald was in the sixth floor window that day with a rifle. In my opinion, getting down the stairs into the second-floor lunch room and having a Coke is possible in the time frame allotted. However, I think Oswald was stunned and dismayed when he saw Kennedy's head come apart. I believe he had no idea there were other shooters in Dealey Plaza that day to actually assassinate the president. Hence, when he later stated to the press that he was just a "patsy," I think he was telling the truth.

He didn't know which way to play it, still trying to hold on to his cover that he had worked so long with US intel to set up, trying to figure out what the hell was going on. Perhaps US intel was unaware of the other shooters as well. And maybe the anti-Castro Cubans, rogue CIA members, or Mafia got wind of the Oswald scenario and took advantage of it. Maybe.

At any rate, Oswald calmly walked out the front door of the TSBD and took a bus back to his rooming house. This is an important point. It would seem to me that if someone was planning to kill the president of the United States, he would most certainly have a competent exit plan that would not include a public bus. A more likely scenario is that Oswald was in a fog as to what just happened. He exited the TSBD not knowing which way to turn or exactly what to do; his world had just been turned upside down. The bus appeared and he took it. However, I also believe that there was a plan in place for Oswald to connect with an intel agent in the Texas Movie Theatre after the shooting, which is what kept Oswald moving and not freezing up. And that is exactly where Oswald was headed.

THE TIPPIT ASSASSINATION

Upon returning to his rooming house, Oswald grabed his coat and his hand gun. If he did not have a prior rendezvous with someone in the Texas Movie Theatre, Oswald probably would have stayed right there. While he was in the room, a police car pulled up to the door and honked its horn, obviously a signal for Oswald to take notice. Whether or not this was a prearranged signal or a contingency plan is uncertain. The police car left slowly. Oswald left the rooming house and started walking, perhaps thinking that he would be given a lift and/or instructions by whomever was in the police car. Uncertain what was happening, he had to make his prearranged rendezvous at the Texas Movie Theatre.

Along the route, it is alleged that around 1:15PM Oswald was questioned by Dallas Police officer JD Tippit (September 18, 1924 – November 22, 1963) who had spotted a man who resembled a description given out over the police radio of a possible suspect in the JFK shooting. It is widely speculated that it may have been Tippet who honked his police car horn to signal Oswald. Whomever Tippit has stopped to question shoots and kills him.

Around 1:30 PM, Oswald arrives at the Texas Movie Theatre. A shoe salesman, Johnny Brewer, notifies the police that he has seen a suspicious man entering the theatre. Oswald was arrested by Dallas Police, but not before pulling his pistol and trying to shoot the arresting officer. Many people believe this to be a defining moment that solidifies Oswald's guilt as the assassin of JFK in a last ditch attempt to get away.

> **Personally, I think he just "snapped" at that moment at the prospect of getting arrested and his entire year spent sheep dipping unraveling. Oswald simply lost it and lashed out. It's important to remember that Oswald had just turned 24. He was a young man. A misnomer in this story is that Oswald was arrested for killing JFK when in fact the arrest was for the killing of Dallas Police Officer JD Tippit.**

It is also worth noting that Oswald was found with a cereal box top ripped in half. It was very common for those in the clandestine business to rip dollar bills in half. One connection would get one half and the other unknown connection the other. If dollar bills weren't available they use other things like cereal box tops. This method was used to give two "unknowns" confirmation that they were meeting with the correct person. At Oswald's rooming house room, many ripped dollar bills are also found. Obviously Oswald had a prearranged rendezvous with an unknown connection at the Texas Movie Theatre, perhaps the person that would take him to Cuba.

At the Dallas Police Station, Oswald later composed himself while being interrogated and put on view for the media. It was in front of the media where he calmly asked for legal assistance and stated crisply that he was just a "patsy."

Jack Ruby Murders Lee Harvey Oswald

It may be surprising to learn that the very Dallas Police Headquarters where Oswald was being held, was in Dealey Plaza across the street from the Texas School Book Depository. The murder onslaught in Dealey Plaza was not quite yet over.

On Sunday, November 24, 1963, at11:21 AM, Oswald was to be transferred to a more secure location and was brought out through the Dealey Plaza police station basement to an awaiting car. He was securely handcuffed to two Dallas homicide detectives: Jim Levelle on his right and L. C. Graves on his left. As they were moving Oswald, Jack Ruby lunged forward, and with a single shot to Oswald's abdomen from his .38 pistol, silenced Oswald forever. He was sent to the grave, taking his secrets about the details of November 22, 1963 with him.

The whole scene was captured live on television, reminicent of the barbaric horror of people leaping out of the windows of the Twin Towers live on television. (See Chapter 4 "Dr Robert McClelland" for more information.)

Ruby claimed that he murdered Oswald to protect Jacqueline Kennedy from having to go through a trial concerning the murder of her husband. Both Ruby and the Warren Commission declared that there was never any connection between Ruby and Oswald. Immediately, researchers found alarming connections between Ruby, Oswald, and the Mob, indicating a "Mob hit" to silence the assassin and a government cover-up of the truth. Red Flag.

How The Grassy Knoll Got Its Name

> Lane: I wrote an article about the Kennedy assassination. I interviewed a couple of witnesses by telephone. Jean Hill, she was there; you can see pictures of the Zapruder film. You can see her there. I read her name in the New York Times and I called her up, told her I was looking into this.
>
> She said "Well do you know what Dealey Plaza looks like?" I said "No, I've never been to Dallas." She said "Well, I'll explain it to you." And then set it up and the shots came from a grassy knoll, which was on the president's right side. And I said, "Can I tape this?" and she

said "Of course." And I did and I released that information to some of the newspapers.

That's how that little piece, that little green hill, got the name "grassy knoll." She didn't even know that she had named it. She was just describing it to me. I met her many years later and said, "Do you know that you're the one who named it the grassy knoll?" And she said "I didn't know that until I read your book 'Citizens Assembly.' You said it, but I didn't know that I was the one who named it."

Mark Lane Takes On The Warren Commission

Holland: Marguerite Oswald, folks, who was Lee Harvey Oswald's mom, approached Mark Lane to represent Lee Harvey Oswald after he was killed. Can you tell a little bit about how that came about?

Lane: I got a lot of information and wrote an article. I got a phone call from Marguerite Oswald. It seems that a woman named Shirley Martin in Harmony, Oklahoma – I didn't know her – I didn't even know there was a city called Harmony, Oklahoma – She read it and sent it to Marguerite Oswald. She didn't know Marguerite either but she just said "This is something you ought to read."

And so Marguerite Oswald called me to be look after her son's interests for the Warren Commission. I said, "It's hard to be council to someone who is not alive and I can't talk to him and find out what his position is. But what I will do is I'll conduct an independent inquiry if you like. But whatever the facts show, even if it shows your son was guilty, I'm going to have to release it – because it's not an attorney-client matter – because I'm not going to be representing him." She said "That's all right. I'm sure he's innocent."

So I went back, called the Warren Commission, wrote to the Commission and said "I'd like to appear" and I told the purpose. And they said: "No. We will have closed hearings. Everything's Top Secret and nothing will be revealed and you cannot be present" – except – they called me twice as a witness. I'm the only critic of the Warren Commission who ever actually testified before the Warren Commission.

And I released a documentary film called "Rush to Judgement," which has the actual voices and pictures of interviews with people who were eyewitnesses to the assassination, witnesses to how Ruby got into the basement, all that kind of stuff which has been covered up.

That's the history of how I got involved. I never planned it to be something which would dominant so much of my life."

Holland: Essentially, the Warren Commission at that time, they came out and said that it was Lee Harvey Oswald alone. Do you think Johnson was behind that and set it up that way?

Lane: I don't know the answer to that question. I can tell you why the Warren Commission reached that conclusion. The Commission started this investigation; they brought in lawyers from various places around the country. They wanted to bring in a really good lawyer from Philadelphia, Pennsylvania; he was the District Attorney there, very talented, intelligent lad.

But he wasn't going to do that, he had his job. He said "I can send you the young man, the Assistant here named *Arlen Specter*. He sent Arlen Specter and Specter, together with David Belin, invented the Magic Bullet Theory. This one bullet did the most astonishing things in an *acrobatic* sequence.

Arlen Specter (February 12, 1930 – October 14, 2012) then became the United States Senator for all of these years, just recently deceased. And I'll tell you why they did it though – I know why they did it. I didn't know it at that time; I know it now because I've seen all of these documents which we've gotten under the "Freedom of Information Act."

The CIA met with Earl Warren and gave him a briefing. And this is what the CIA said, this is the legend they gave him: "In September of 1963 Lee Harvey Oswald went to Mexico City. He went to the Cuban Embassy and we have absolute proof of that. Then he went to the Soviet Embassy and we have proof of that. We have photographs of him and we have a tape recording of him when he called the Soviet Embassy from Mexico City. It was right there. He called them and he said he wanted to see Kostikov "Is he in? This is Lee Harvey Oswald calling." In other words, the tape recording showed that Oswald had a relationship with Kostikov.

Valeriy Vladimirovich Kostikov – the following quote is from the CIA directly to The Warren Commission: "Kostikov is believed to work for Department Thirteen of the First Chief Directorate of the KGB. It is the Department responsible for executive action, including sabotage and assassination." (see www.maryferrell.org)

Lane: Kostikov, and this I think is accurate, although he was called the Secretary, Deputy Secretary, something of the Embassy, was the KGB agent for the Soviet Union in charge of assassinations in the Western hemisphere. And there's Oswald meeting with him in September 1963, two months before. According to the CIA, he went back to the United States and killed the president.

And Warren is listening to this briefing and the CIA continues, "We have conducted a thorough investigation. We are convinced, without any question, Lee Harvey Oswald was the assassin and that he acted alone. But if this information comes out about his going to Mexico City, meeting with the Cubans and the Russians, including the KGB guy in charge of assassinations in the Western hemisphere, and then coming back to the United States and killing the president, no one will believe there was no conspiracy involving the Russians and the Cubans.

The whole idea was that, according to the CIA, Oswald was going to kill the president and then he was going to go back to Mexico City and from there fly off to Cuba."

Kostikov was an expert in assassinations, according to the CIA. Of course, you can see Warren – the blood draining out of his face as he hears this. They said "It's the only way to save America because if this comes out, what will happen is the American people will believe that the Russians were involved, the Cubans were involved, demand war, 100 million Americans could be killed in a war, 40 million could be killed in a war. You have to do what will save America now.

Warren went out, and we have the minutes of the first meeting of January '64 where he talks to the staff, the lawyers, where he says basically "Truth is no longer our objective. We cannot have 40 million Americans die because of our investigations." And there's a record of this. I have those minutes. It was top secret at the time, I have them now. And he's talking about 40 million Americans. He didn't say why, but how were 40 million Americans going to die?

But he knew the story. And few other people who knew Warren knew the story because Warren no doubt told them "I have no choice. I have to do this to save the country." Why Warren issued the report and of course it was led by Allen Dulles, former Director of the CIA.

If you read the 26 volumes of evidence filed by the Commission – the first 15 of the testimony – and if you read those you'll see that Dulles was *always* there and always playing a major part. Read the minutes of the Warren Commission meetings, you see he plays a major part – much more active than Warren and much more active than anybody else. And he had been the Director of CIA, as I said, had been *fired* by John Kennedy for lying.

Holland: Mark, I just want to mention to the folks too, that Bobby Kennedy, upon learning about his brother's assassination - the first thing he did was call John McCone and asked him: "did the CIA kill my brother?" John McCone, by the way folks, was the head of the CIA in 1963, handpicked by President Kennedy. But he was out of the loop. A lot of the stuff that was going on in the CIA, the CIA was not telling the head of the CIA. Can you believe that? Bobby Kennedy's first reaction was the CIA had killed his brother.

And let's not forget folks, October 1962, just a little over a year before that, everybody went through that horrible time of the Cuban Missile Crisis. Do you think a lot of that residue and a fear of perhaps a nuclear war was getting the best of their judgement?

Lane: I'm not sure about that, but I do know that they were very concerned. Of course that was a year before, but they were very concerned about the fact that the year after that, actually September of '63, John Kennedy withdrew one thousand, they called them "advisors" from Vietnam. So publicly we had 18 thousand there and he withdrew one thousand of them. They were the Green Beret Special Forces teams there, called "advisors."

And he said "Well they'll be out by the end of next year." And then in November he withdrew another one thousand, down to *16* thousand, saying "They'll all be home before the end of next year." Then he was killed and we had *500* thousand take their place after Lyndon Johnson became president.

Holland: In Oliver Stone's film "JFK," he attributes that particular war to the death of Kennedy. Do you believe in that thesis?

Lane: I think that played a major part, yes.

MARK LANE AND ABRAHAM BOLDEN

Lane: I know Abe Bolden (first African American Secret Service agent to work the presidential detail; hand-picked by JFK; not on duty November 22, 1963; please see Chapter 10 "Secret Service Abraham Bolden, A Real American Hero" for more information). I interviewed him when he was in prison. I knew that it was outrageous. And he talks about this in his book, "Echo from Dealey Plaza."

When I heard that he was sent to this penitentiary where part of the prison is a mental ward, I was very concerned – I told him that they might try to put him in this mental ward and claim that he was insane.

Of course what he had to say was, he was a member of the Secret Service as you know, he was the first Black person ever on the White House Detail of the Secret Service, personally selected by John Kennedy to protect him.

Holland: He's an American hero folks, a true American hero.

Lane: He got there (guarding President Kennedy) and fellow Secret Service Agents, a number of them, said "We will never put our body in front of the president if they try to kill him. He's a "nigger lover!" He's destroyed America and if he gets killed that's fine. We will never do anything to protect him!"

If you look at the Zapruder film, that's an 8 mm film, Bell and Howell camera, taken by Abraham Zapruder who was up there on the grassy knoll filming the assassination. He thought he was going to film the president going by in a motorcade in a parade; instead he filmed the assassination of the president.

The car slowed down almost to a stop. And, of course, the first training of the Secret Service is, if there's any danger, if you hear a shot or anything like that, step on the gas, get out of there.

Instead they did just the reverse. The car was driven by a Secret Service Agent (Bill Greer). The right front of the car, the passenger-side of the front seat, was another Secret Service Agent (Roy Kellerman). His job was to leap over the seat and knock the president down and cover him with his body. He had 5.6 seconds, which is an eternity after a shot is fired at the president, and he never moved.

If he had knocked the president down after the first bullet hit the president in the back, Kennedy would have survived. But he took no position at all. He just stayed perfectly still as the car almost came to a stop and then the president was assassinated.

Bolden then provided information. He wanted to tell the Warren Commission that the Secret Service had in fact said in essence that's what they would do. If there was an attempt to kill the president they would not protect him. When he was trying to contact the Warren Commission, instead he was arrested and framed and sent to prison. And then they were going to send him to a mental institution, but I had warned him that the prison he was going to had a mental ward.

And they had to go through a whole big procedure to move someone from the prison part to the mental ward part, which they didn't do. They just put him in that mental ward, violating all of their own regulations, and they started giving him these mind-altering drugs. This is no question. He writes about it and it's really clear and there's a lawsuit about it.

At that point he wrote a letter to his wife. Since he knew that this was a possibility, they had discussed it, he wrote a letter to his wife, and they had a "code" – because he knew everything would be read. And the code was that "If you see an 'i' which has a circle dot," I think that's what it was – a circle dot on it – instead of just a point – just a little circle around it – "that means: contact a lawyer and get someone down here at once." She got that letter, got the lawyer down there. They found that he was in a mental ward; they got him out immediately into the prison facility. But that's how that was thwarted. Anyway, he is an American hero.

WHY JFK WAS KILLED

Holland: Why was JFK killed?

Lane: I wrote the legislation which set up the "House Select Committee on Assassinations." That's a committee of the United States House of Representatives. And I traveled around the country - spoke at 180 colleges and universities and law schools – formed "Citizens Commissions of Inquiry" at each of them – and together all of us got more than a million letters and telegrams to members of Congress demanding that there be an investigation. And so they formed the "House Select Committee on Assassinations." (See Chapter 7 "Frontal Shot: CSI & JFK" for more information.)

The last official government position on the question was the "House Select Committee on Assassinations" which said in all probability there had been a conspiracy to kill President Kennedy, and in all probability there had been a conspiracy to kill Martin Luther King Jr. So that's the official position of the United States government now, which a lot of people missed.

THE CIA ON TRIAL FOR THE ASSASSINATION OF JFK: GUILTY AS CHARGED

Lane: John Kennedy was about to dissolve the Central Intelligence Agency because he knew that they had deliberately misled him on any number of matters. He was about to end the war in Vietnam, which the CIA at that time said "It may be a dirty little war but it's the only one we have." It was a war basically run in large measure by the Central Intelligence Agency. We did have a trial on this question and most people don't know about this. And that's the book "Plausible Denial," that you made reference to, Brent.

E. Howard Hunt, the Watergate Burglar who was a convict – was named in a very Right Wing newspaper called "The Spotlight" in an article by Victor Marchetti - who had been an officer of the CIA - who had left that organization and said that: "Hunt was involved with the CIA and the assassination of President Kennedy."

Hunt came out of prison and sued the newspaper and won. And they awarded him $650 thousand for his "good" reputation – although he just got *out of prison* after some years for trying to destroy American democracy and Watergate. In any event, he filed a lawsuit and he won. But an *error* was made by the judge and instructions to the jury were sent back for a new trial.

Then the newspaper asked me to represent them. I had never heard about the newspaper; I didn't know about the story at all. But they then asked me to represent them, I did and we *won* the case. And what was our defense? That the article was *correct*; not basically absence of malice or something, those technical defenses.

I said to the jury "The CIA killed your president and we're going to prove it to you at this trial." And the forewoman came out - we won the case unanimously. The forewoman came out and said "When we started this case I believed in mom, apple pie and the American justice system. Now I believe in mom and apple pie.

She said "There's no doubt in my mind, we are convinced that the CIA killed our president. So we have a jury verdict, the only jury verdict on the question."

This was a jury chosen by both sides to be impartial and fair – a very fair judge at the trial that allowed just relevant evidence in. They heard the evidence and that was their conclusion. So we have the Committee of the Congress and we have the jury verdict.

Marita Lorenz

Lane: Marita Lorenz was a witness to a number of things. She had worked for the CIA for some time. She had a romantic relationship with Fidel Castro. It's a long, interesting story, but I'm not sure we have time for it, but I'll try to do it in a sentence or two.

Her father was a Captain of a German luxury liner which was in Havana on January 1, 1959 when Fidel Castro's revolution was successful. And Castro came into Havana, saw the beautiful boat and went on board - not long after he'd won the revolution - and he met this extremely beautiful, very young woman, the daughter of the Captain. They liked each other and he said "Would you like me to show you what Cuba looks like in my Jeep?" And they went and they were together for some time.

When she came back to the US, the CIA recruited her in an effort to have her go back and kill Castro. That's one of those many attempts that the Church Committee (set up in 1975 to investigate any wrong doings by the CIA in the Watergate scandal), the United States Senate, uncovered of the CIA trying to assassinate Fidel Castro. She was involved with them in a number of acts of getting weapons and sending them to Cuba to overthrow Castro because of personal problems that developed between her and Fidel. We don't have time for that now.

She was then recruited by Frank Sturgis (who was also a Watergate burglar and CIA Agent and close associate of CIA Agent E. Howard Hunt), who was a CIA operative. And a lot of this isn't known about him for some reason.

His name was Frank Fiorini, but he used the name "Frank Sturgis." He ran the Cuban Air Force under Castro *and* he was working with the CIA at that time. He's the one that told Marita that "Fidel's going to kill you. You better get out of here." That's why she was so upset with him.

Anyway, now she's working with him. He's a CIA operative out of Miami and he said "This is the big one coming up." It was November 1963. And they got into some cars with some Cubans, two of the Novo brothers and they drove to Dallas and checked into a motel.

"Eduardo" she said, was the person who was the paymaster for the operation. This was her testament, which means it was under *oath* – in the trial in the United States District Court in Florida – in the case of E. Howard Hunt against the Liberty Lobby and the newspaper "The Spotlight."

And she gave specific information – she was cross examined – the jury heard all of it. She said "We went there and "Eduardo" was there and "Eduardo" was the paymaster running the operation." "Eduardo" was *E. Howard Hunt* and that was his CIA *codename*, 'Eduardo'." Not much of a codename, but that's been documented and Hunt actually *admitted* that.

So let me just jump forward for one second. I had recently been talking to St. John Hunt, who is E. Howard Hunt's son. He wrote and said I could use this publicly.

When E. Howard Hunt filed his lawsuit against the newspaper he said "I was at home with my children and my wife for 72 hours after Kennedy was killed. I heard about the president being shot - went to the car - drove back home outside of Washington and stayed there with my wife and my children." St. John Hunt said:

1. He was there; that is St. John Hunt was there with his siblings and with his mother and with an aunt. E. Howard Hunt was not present however, at all.

2. His mother said to him that his father had been in Dallas.

3. St. John Hunt said, "When my father was dying he said to me 'Mark Lane was right. I and the CIA were involved in the assassination. I have to tell you that now.' It wasn't exactly those many words; just said that I was correct and he had played a part. St. John Hunt said that to me in writing actually."

CIA Hit Man Admits Being Part Of JFK Assassination

Lane: He also said that Gerry Patrick Hemming was part of it. He also was a CIA killer – we know that.

I was in Miami and I called Hemming at his number and said "I was wondering if I could talk to you about Marita Lorenz's testimony." I said "My name is Mark Lane."

He said "I know who you are!" I said "Okay, you want to be that way." I was in a big hotel. I said "When can you do it?" He said "I can do it now. I could be there in an hour." I said "Okay" and I gave him the hotel. And I said "I'll meet you in the *lobby.*"

Holland: Smart move.

Lane: "Just call me up from the lobby." He said "Okay, that's what I'll do Mr. Lane." I called down to the desk and said "If anybody comes looking for me - asking my room, don't give it." "We never give room numbers." I said "Okay, especially don't give this room number to anybody now." They said "Okay."

15 minutes later there was a knock on my door. And I open it up and it's Gerry Patrick Hemming. We were not in the lobby and he walked into the room. And I don't know if he was armed or not, but he was about 6'6" and weighed about 290 pounds or something. He could have thrown me out of the window if he wanted to I guess.

Anyway, he came in and he said "Okay I want to talk to you about Marita. I said "Listen, it's such a "beautiful day." Why don't we go for a walk?" He said "Okay." So we went for a walk on the grounds, which made me feel a little better. I told him exactly what Marita Lorenz had said:

- It was a two-car caravan
- Sturgis was there
- She was there
- The Novo brothers were there
- Other Cubans were there
- Went to Dallas and
- In Dallas, Eduardo, who is E. Howard Hunt, paid Sturgis off for the operation.

He said "All right, so what's the question?" I said "Is that true?" He said "No." He said "It was a three-car caravan. Everything else is true." So that was Hemming's statement to me."

Holland: You mentioned that E. Howard Hunt paid everybody. Where did the money come from? Where was it financed out of?

Lane: Well, they assumed since Hunt was CIA and they were all working for CIA, they just presumed it was made available by the Central Intelligence Agency.

Holland: Any speculation Mafia dollars may have been involved?

Lane: Well, I don't see any indication to that at all. You've got to remember, at that time the Mafia and CIA were working together in planning the assassination of Fidel Castro and various things.

Holland:That's right, Operation Mongoose (CIA, Mafia, anti-Castro Cubans, US intel, all working together to get rid of Castro and return to Cuba)

Lane: So it's possible there was interlinking - because they worked together on other projects. But everything I've seen:

- Sturgis was CIA,
- Hemming was CIA,
- The Novo brothers were CIA;

They weren't arrested, the Novo brothers.

Do you remember the killing of Orlando Letelier in Washington, DC after Allende had been overthrown by the CIA in Chile? He came to the United States and he was working with an American woman named Ronni Moffitt, and they were in Washington DC and they were murdered. It was a big, big story at the time because it was a murder right in Washington of a guy who was a diplomat and an American woman who was working with him.

The Novo brothers, who were in the caravan to kill Kennedy, were *both* convicted of murder of Letelier and Moffitt. They had been arrested in 1963, based upon what Marita was trying to tell the government.

Holland: Was there anybody beyond E. Howard Hunt, above him, pulling the strings and who?

Lane: Well, I don't know the answer. I don't know that. I presume of course, because he was not a policymaker.

Holland: With all that has been exposed, how come no disclosure at this point?

Lane: The last I heard the government was saying that Oswald was the lone assassin. They take that position still - obviously not the Congress because they've issued a report - they've investigated it. But the FBI, which is a branch of the investigatory part of the Department of Justice, takes that position. So far as I know, it's still their position.

Holland: Why should students today care that Kennedy was assassinated and the government was involved and it's been covered up all these years?

You know if you kill the president of the most powerful country in the world during a nuclear age, you've taken a step which imperils everybody on the planet. And when the government not only did that but then prevented the facts from being known, it means that they have a license, it's a "007" almost, to do what they feel is appropriate in the future without fear of being prosecuted for a crime.

Executive Action: Hollywood Feature Film That Rocked The World

Lane: That's the film that I wrote with Donald Freed. A good friend of mine was (Canadian actor) Donald Sutherland and he was going to produce it. It was so clear what that film said.

The film said, basically, the CIA killed President Kennedy. I wrote it with Donald Freed, as I said, and then Donald was unable to raise funds for it so he sold it to a guy named Ed Lewis and Ed Lewis brought in someone to rewrite it. Dalton Trumbo is a good writer actually. Donald Sutherland was so committed to this project – Donald's a very, very bright person I think – a wonderful actor. He's Canadian – you know that.

Holland: Yes, absolutely. And his son is Kiefer Sutherland, by the way, folks, the TV show "24."

Lane: And we called it "Executive Action" – which is the "phrase" used by the CIA, meaning the "Killing of the Head of State." Donald loved the title - but Donald was very clever too and he said "I think" which is cool "that Executive Action done on all the movie marquees around the country – we'll put the words: "Conspiracy In America." But the first letter of each word will be red, the rest will be black"; in other words, C-I-A.

But he couldn't get the funds for it, so he gave it to Lewis. Lewis then had it rewritten and only one group is exonerated in the entire film. I think that's when Will Geer is asked, by Burt Lancaster– Burt Lancaster was a friend of mine too and we had discussions about this – but he is asked "Are you saying the CIA was involved?" And the answer was "Absolutely not." So from the film which said the CIA did "it," we had a film which only cleared one organization in the entire country, and that was the CIA. That's the way the "Executive Action" was changed.

Donald Sutherland, Robert Ryan's last film I believe, and Will Geer. It did focus a lot of attention on the matter. In fact it was really extremely successful. It was a low-budget film. As I recall, it was $600 thousand (3.6 million dollars today), of course things are more expensive now; but even then that was a very low budget for these kinds of folks they had in it. And it made $18 million (110 million today) in the first few months and was wildly successful. Now it's out I think in video.

Holland: It also showed two teams in the field practicing triangulated fire. When you just transpose that as a template right over to Dealey Plaza, you can see how it all comes together.

Lane: Yeah, that's something that we actually did write that stayed in, right. It was a groundbreaking film actually because it's not only about the Kennedy assassination but about secret government operations.

WITNESSES TO THE ASSASSINATION

Lane: Several shots were fired but the bullet which hit him in the head came from his right front. Because:

1. First of all, you see the effect on the president; he is driven backward and to the left suddenly, number one.

2. Number two; there was a police officer on a motorbike behind him who said he was almost knocked off his motorbike by brain and skull material which hit him. (Motorcycle Patrolman Bobby Hargis who was at the left rear of the limousine) That was to the left rear of the president. There's no question the shot which killed the president came from the right front.

3. And there were eyewitnesses like Charles Brehm and others who saw the same thing. They were standing right there, just a few feet away.

There may have been shots from other areas and maybe that's what the investigation shows, but there's no question the bullet which killed the president came from the right front.

4. And everybody on the railroad overpass, a lot of them are in our film (Rush To Judgement) that we interviewed, S.M. Holland, there were various folks who worked for the Union Terminal Railroad up there watching. They not only heard the shot but the guys on the railroad, which ran behind the wooden fence, because they *saw* puffs of smoke come from there. So there's no question that the shot came from there. That was the shot that killed him I believe.

Holland: Do you believe Lee Harvey Oswald fired a rifle that day, at President Kennedy?

Lane: No. I think he had nothing to do with the Kennedy assassination.

Lee Harvey Oswald with Dallas Police after capture.

Lane with Mrs. Marguerite Oswald

Lawyer Urges Defense for Oswald at Inquiry

Ex-State Assemblyman Files Brief With Warren Unit

He Charges Many Gaps Exist in Data on Assassination

By PETER KIHSS

A former New York Assemblyman has urged Chief Justice Earl Warren's investigating commission to appoint a defense counsel for Lee H. Oswald in its inquiry into the assassination of President Kennedy.

Mark Lane, who has frequently been a defense counsel in civil rights and murder cases, submitted a 10,000-word brief to the Warren commission by mail Tuesday night.

The brief is being reprinted in full in today's issue of The National Guardian, which calls itself a "progressive newsweekly." Yesterday, Mr. Lane said in response to a question that he would be willing to take on such a defense role, but was "not offering" to do so.

On one hand, his brief analyzed and attempted to rebut points made by Henry Wade, Dallas District Attorney, and on the other offered what

The New York Times

Mark Lane

throat injury was an "entry through the throat" and obviously therefore altered the bullet hole.

In rebuttal to District At-

the tests found no gunpowder traces on Oswald's face, such as might have come from a rifle.

¶There are questions whether Oswald would have been permitted to leave the building after 500 policemen surrounded it within moments after the shooting, or whether he would have stopped first for a soda in the lunchroom.

¶After taking a bus for six blocks, Oswald allegedly hailed a taxicab driven by William Whaley, whose log says this was at 12:30 P.M. The President was shot at 12:31 P.M.

Potential Questions

Mr. Lane set forth potential questions on whether Oswald actually ever had the alleged assassination rifle, on varying accounts of the murder of a policeman, and on conflicting statements about Oswald's presence in a movie theater and attempted firing at another policeman.

As to motive, Mr. Lane asked, "If Oswald were a leftist, pro-

The National Guardian published Mark Lane's legal brief on behalf of Lee Oswald on December 18, 1963, and The New York Times published a summary that same day.

Watergate Burgler, CIA Operative and admitted JFK conspirator E. Howard Hunt

Marita Lorenz with Fidel Castro

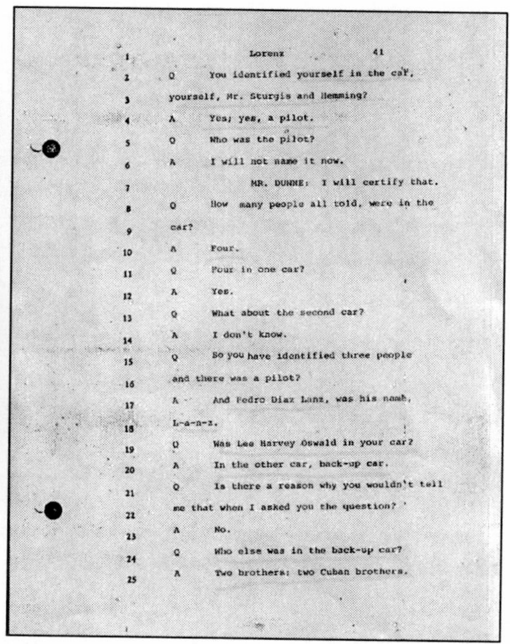

Lorenz 41

1
2 Q You identified yourself in the car,
3 yourself, Mr. Sturgis and Hemming?
4 A Yes; yes, a pilot.
5 Q Who was the pilot?
6 A I will not name it now.
7 MR. DUNNE: I will certify that.
8 Q How many people all told, were in the
9 car?
10 A Four.
11 Q Four in one car?
12 A Yes.
13 Q What about the second car?
14 A I don't know.
15 Q So you have identified three people
16 and there was a pilot?
17 A And Pedro Diaz Lanz, was his name,
18 L-a-n-z.
19 Q Was Lee Harvey Oswald in your car?
20 A In the other car, back-up car.
21 Q Is there a reason why you wouldn't tell
22 me that when I asked you the question?
23 A No.
24 Q Who else was in the back-up car?
25 A Two brothers; two Cuban brothers.

Marita Lorenz deposition for the Hunt v. Liberty Lobby trial

CHAPTER 9

THE MAFIA'S ROLE: LAMAR WALDRON AND "LEGACY OF SECRECY"

"The Mafia tried to kill JFK first in Chicago, motorcade cancelled, Tampa, motorcade went ahead but the godfather there found out that authorities knew, so the hit was cancelled. Succeeded in Dallas, the phony evidence pointing to Fidel's, believed by many. Mafia got away with murder, but now, as people can read, I mean, Marcello eventually, once he was finally in prison, he just admitted, "I had the SOB killed and I would do it again. He was a thorn in my side. I wish I could have done it myself."

Lamar Waldron

PREFACE

Author and researcher Lamar Waldron has been digging through JFK-related files with his co-author Thom Hartman for the better part of 25 years. Together they have unearthed an enormous amount of previously hidden information.

Lamar believes that a "Palace Coup" (a situation in which a leader is removed from power by the people who have worked with him or her) was planned to take over Cuba and overthrow Castro on December 1, 1963. The third highest ranking Cuban official at the time, Commander Juan Almeida, in charge of the Cuban Army, would spearhead the coup.

The United States wouldn't back the coup *overtly*, but they would be the first to officially recognize the new Cuban Government under the leadership of Commander Almeida. This would create a government that was democratically friendly to the US and oust the dictator, Castro, and his Communist Soviet-backed regime. Most importantly, it would finally allow UN weapons inspectors into Cuba to verify that all nuclear missiles placed there during the Cuban Missile Crisis had been removed.

The plan was thwarted and did not proceed on December 1, 1963 because JFK had been assassinated only eight days before on November 22, 1963 (See my own assessment "My Opinion On The Palace Coup Lead By Commander Almedia"). Lamar has uncovered documents reporting that when Mafia Don of New Orleans, Carlos Marcello, was in prison in the 1980s, law enforcement sent an undercover officer under the guise of a fellow inmate, as is often done with high-profile prisoners, to see what Marcello would unknowingly offer up about his lengthly criminal career. What they got was unexpected. Marcello confessed to ordering the hit on Kennedy.

Lamar and Hartman's book "Legacy Of Secrecy" is being turned into a feature film produced by Leonardo Dicaprio starring Dicaprio himself and Robert DeNiro. In the book they discuss the probability of Mafia involvement in the JFK assassination, which was the primary focus of our interview together on "Night Fright."

> *"First, were we truly men of courage, with the courage to stand up to one's enemies, and the courage to stand up, when necessary, to one's associates, the courage to resist public pressure as well as private greed?"*
>
> *John F. Kennedy January 9, 1961, Massachusetts State Legislature address*

New Ideas and New Directions on the Assassination

Waldron: Thom and I, back on the 25th anniversary of JFK's murder, 1988, for two or three years, we looked at every theory, and I mean *every* theory. You know, did the secret service driver shoot JFK? Was it LBJ? Was it Hoover? Was it the CIA? Was it the military industrial complex? We looked at every theory and came up to the same dead ends and lack of evidence everybody does when they go down those roads.

It sounds good in theory, but there's no evidence. And so that's what we decided. We need to talk to people who were very close to John and Robert Kennedy, who might know things that they never said or that they couldn't even testify about. Dave Powers was the second of the Kennedy aides, associates that we talked to. The first was JFK's Secretary of State, Dean Rusk.

SECRETARY OF STATE, DEAN RUSK

As Lamar stated, Dean Rusk (February 9, 1909 - December 20, 1994) was Kennedy's Secretary of State and stayed on at Vice President Johnson's urging after the assassination of JFK. He played a significant role during the Cuban Missile Crisis in October 1962, during which he adopted a diplomatic solution to the crisis, as opposed to the those posturing invasion.

During that same crisis, when the Soviets suddenly stopped and turned their ships around when faced with the Cuban blockade, it was Secretary of State Dean Rusk that turned to National Security Advisor McGeorge "Mac" Bundy (March 30, 1919 – September 16, 1996) and said, "we're eyeball to eyeball and the other fellow just blinked."

A POSSIBLE PALACE COUP PLANNED FOR CUBA, DECEMBER 1, 1963

Waldron: I did the interview with Dean Rusk and then filled Thom in. I was pretty shocked. I was doing the interview for a Georgia public television show about Rusk's reminiscences. Thom and I wanted to know what Rusk might know about the Kennedy assassination and Cuba, because we did keep feeling there was some Cuban connection to this. We didn't know why. So I was pretty stunned when Secretary of the State Dean Rusk told me, "You know, the Cuban missile crisis never really ended. We were preparing a second invasion of Cuba at the time JFK was killed."

I told the former Secretary of State, "Well surely, you must be mistaken." And he responded, "Look my boy, I was the Secretary of State. I know these things. I was in the secret Cabinet meeting." The Cuban Missile Crisis it never really ended, here's why:

The head of Russia and JFK reached a deal to end the crisis. It called for missiles in Turkey to be removed and a non-invasion pledge against

Cuba. But Fidel Castro had to allow UN inspections for weapons of mass destruction in Cuba to verify that all the missiles were gone.

Otherwise, how could we know they weren't hidden in caves or something? JFK first used that term: UN weapons inspections for "Weapons of Mass Destruction" (WMD). Well, how do you think Fidel Castro felt about that? He wasn't part of the deal. He wasn't consulted.

Khrushchev said, "Look, I struck this deal with Kennedy." Fidel Castro said, "No, I'm not going to allow those inspections." This is straight from Rusk, and backed up by documentation, not just in "Legacy of Secrecy." You can find it in other places too, like the National Security Archival, a good private, liberal, non-profit group in Washington. Fidel wouldn't allow the inspection, so there was no non-invasion pledge.

Now, if the US had tried to openly invade Cuba again in 1963 (like The Bay of Pigs failed invasion in 1961), it would have no doubt triggered World War III. But, the 1964 election was coming up. What was JFK going to do? His potential challenge was Goldwater, Nixon, Rockefeller.

They were beating up on JFK in the press, claiming missiles were still in Cuba. JFK had tried to get those UN weapons inspections. Fidel would not allow them. JFK was going through the UN. What was he going to do? There was no way to prove that there were no missiles without doing inspections.

This was the height of the Cold War. People should know, both the US and Russia were armed to the teeth, and at that time could have destroyed each country several times over. It literally would have been World War III.

JFK tried to find a secret peace accommodation with Fidel, which has been known for a few decades now. But that wasn't producing solid results. The whole thing became a political football game, with the Republican candidates in America, each trying to outdo each other, wanting to invade Cuba.

JFK already has his hands full with Vietnam. 100 people had died in Vietnam at that point. He had no combat troops there. So, put yourself in JFK's position. What do you do? Well here's what happened.

THE VIETNAM WAR EXPLAINED; WHAT IT DID TO AMERICA'S YOUTH & THEIR PARENTS

The Vietnam War was fought from 1955 to 1975. It has been called "Kennedy's War," which is a misnomer. It was under Eisenhower in the 1950s, before Kennedy was president, that the US first sent military advisors.

Most of the leaders of the West had fought against Hitler's Nazi Juggernaut between 1939 until 1945. They saw how the West had tried to appease Hitler; allowing him to take country after country, making "Puppet States" out of them. Like a marionette puppeteer remains hidden and pulls on the strings, Hitler could get the "puppets" to do exactly what he wanted.

Hitler had even signed a "Peace Treaty" with British Prime Minister Neville Chamberlain, then ignored it and invaded Poland. He has suckered the West into believing he wanted peace in order to buy himself time to increase his army, keeping the West off guard until it was too late to retaliate. It might have worked if not for the defiance of the British people and her allies, led by Sir Winston Churchill.

Eisenhower led the allied forces as the General in charge during World War II. In 1952, seven years after the end of the German war, he was voted president of the United States. The West saw another Hitler-type tyrant, Joseph Stalin, leading the Soviet Union. Stalin was as ruthless as Hitler. Eisenhower, as the president and leader of the free world, believed Stalin was trying to slowly take over the world under his Soviet system of Communism. Indeed, they already controlled most of Eastern Europe at the time, and they were perceived as now spreading their Communism to Indochina and to South and Central America.

It was in this Soviet-backed expansionist "mode" into Indochina that brought Vietnam into focus. Eisenhower wanted to stop the Communist expansion into Vietnam and "drew a line in the sand." In reality, Vietnam was going through a civil war, divided between North Vietnam and South Vietnam.

In the North, their leader, Ho Chi Min, was a devout Communist. Seeing a possible opportunity to make North Vietnam into a puppet regime, the Soviets decided to send arms and Soviet "advisors" (which were military officials sent to train the North Vietnamese army) into North Vietnam.

In the South was a quasi-dictator by the name of Ngo Dinh Diem, who postured that he wanted South Vietnam to be free of Communism and claimed he wanted Democracy for his people. In truth, his regime was elitist and corrupt. In reality, he was soliciting US military support in order to retain his own power and the wealth that accompanied it.

With Eisenhower's "line drawn in the sand," the US tried to bolster the Diem regime by doing the same thing as the Soviets: supplying armaments and US military advisors. When the US military advisors realized that the South Vietnamese army was woefully inadequate to fight a war against a much larger North Vietnamese army, they began requesting additional American troops to fight directly against the advancing North Vietnamese. The US military thought that professionally trained US combat soldiers, in fewer numbers in the field, would quickly overpower and win any confrontation by the North Vietnamese army.

> **Let's not forget, when JFK became president he inherited Vietnam. As in all wars and conflicts people died and died and died. JFK wanted out of Vietnam.**

It remains uncertain what course JFK would have taken had he lived. Kennedy ordered all military personnel in Vietnam out by the end of 1965. However, only two weeks before his own assassination, the South Vietnam military led a coup to take over South Vietnam and murdered its leader Diem. Kennedy was visibly shaken by this. I believe he still would have pulled the military out, opting to stay in the peripherals. Perhaps he would have reached out for a dialogue, for which he was known, and would have brokered a solution for all.

The Vietnam War ushered war into the modern age.

- The US military used napalm bombs with a gasoline derivative that would stick to the skin.

- Agent orange, a chemical used to kill the thick jungle brush where the North Vietnamese were hiding, caused unintended horrors, giving cancer to American soldiers and Vietnamese innocent civilians alike.

- Barbaric interrogation techniques were used. Prisoners Of War were thrown out of helicopters while in mid air. All this and more reveals why we should never entertain war as anything but a last resort.

At home, during the 1960s, the war was ripping the country apart. The average age of a soldier being sent to Vietnam was only 19, as opposed to World War II where it was 26. The youth didn't see the Vietnam War as America's war; North Vietnam was not a direct threat against America, and they didn't want to be forced to go, and possibly die, for something they did not believe in. The draft was in effect for anyone not enrolled in school. Consequently, the vast majority of those forced to go and fight were the poor who couldn't afford a college or university education.

The parents of the draftees, many of whom had fought the Nazis, saw Vietnam, much like those in government did, as a war against tyranny, not an isolated civil war. They viewed their children's hostility toward the war as unpatriotic. The parents had grown up in an era when they believed that whatever the government said was gospel.

The Kennedy assassination changed all that. The youth of that era, the baby boomers, demanded answers. They not only questioned everything, they demanded the truth. If the government was not going to reveal it, they would get it themselves. The streets were flooded with young people, protesting and demanding change.

If JFK had lived, they would have had a leader that understood their desires, a leader that was in tune with inevitable change for the better, a leader with a vision of serving America and mankind through the Peace Corps. The Peace Corps was pure inspiration.

> **Why not send out Americans, not to kill people in war, but to give of themselves in countries around the world? JFK's vision of an "army" of volunteers living, teaching and being of assistance in countries around the world, was unprecedented. Bobby Kennedy was just such a visionary. President Johnson and President Nixon were not.**

THE CUBAN LED PALACE COUP TAKES FORM

Waldron: In May of 1963, the number three man in Cuba, the head of the Cuban army, the founder of the Cuban army, much more powerful and well known in Cuba than Ché Guevara, was Commander Juan Almeida. He was more popular and powerful than anybody, except for Fidel and Raoul, because he commanded the army. He was the highest Black official in Cuba, 70% of which is of African descent.

Commander Juan Almeida was not a Communist. People also don't realize that Fidel didn't liberate Cuba on his own. There were many people to help him, Commander Almeida, Ché, and many others. One by one they had been pushed out of the government, exiled, in some cases killed.

Commander Almeida could see the writing on the wall in May of 1963. He saw that Fidel was becoming just another dictator. They'd fought a revolution to throw out a dictator, Batista. Almeida knew he might remain a figurehead for a year or six months, but Fidel was slowly taking the power. He contacted the highest Cuban exile aide, a personal friend of Robert Kennedy, and said, "Look, I will stage a Palace Coup against Fidel." The indication was that Raoul would be killed as well as Fidel. But Almeida would not take the blame for killing Fidel because Fidel was very popular in Cuba.

Holland: Raoul, by the way folks, is Fidel Castro's brother.

Waldron: He is currently ruling Cuba, since Fidel is rather ill. And so, there were still 8000 or 9000 Russians in Cuba, not combat troops, but "advisors" like we had "advisors" in Vietnam. How do you neutralize them? If Fidel dies, maybe they'll just try to take over Cuba for Russia. Well, he had a brilliant plan.

According to people who worked with Almeida, and declassified CIA files that most people have overlooked for years, if Fidel's death were blamed on a Russian or a "Russian Sympathizer"– a Fair Play for Cuba member from the US. (Waldron is making reference to Lee Harvey Oswald here – please see "Chapter 8 The CIA: Guilty As Charged / David Ferrie, Guy Banister and Oswald," for more information).

Almeida would say, "These dastardly Russians, they have killed our beloved Fidel. The Russians are going to try to take over." Then Almeida could actually ask for help from the United States, and from Cuban exiles who were trained and ready and respected in Cuba, to prevent a Soviet takeover.

To the world it would look like Fidel had suddenly been killed on December 1st, 1963 by some dastardly Russian or Russian sympathizer, maybe someone who lived in Russia for a time. Almeida had taken the brains of government, this popular figure, and controlled the army. He also controlled the media. He could set up a patsy, no problem. Then Almeida would say, "Look, we need US assistance so the Russians. Hey they killed Fidel. Who's to say they're not going to kill…"

Flash ahead to 1963. You have these secret plans being made. I was shocked when Dean Rusk told me he didn't know these plans were real until after JFK died. How can you make plans without knowing all about Commander Almeida?

As Rusk explained, one reason the Bay of Pigs failed, aside from treachery by the CIA, was it was an "open secret." Fidel knew that there was going to be an exile invasion. Newspapers knew it. He arrested a lot of the Cuban resistance before the Bay of Pigs. It was an open secret because so many Washington officials knew. Their assistants, aides and under secretaries knew. There was no way to keep it a secret because, remember this Brent, this is very important, if the coup had occurred and had been successful, it was never supposed to have been known that JFK and Almeida had worked together on this Palace Coup.

Bobby Kennedy wound up with the crucial evidence that could have proved conspiracy, like JFK's brain. Bobby Kennedy didn't kill his brother, but he was part of the cover-up. It was, however, for the best reasons, to prevent World War III.

PREVENTING A PERCEIVED WORLD WAR III NUCLEAR HOLOCAUST

Holland: Lamar, this begs many, many questions. Did Vice President Johnson know about the coup that was about to take place?

Waldron: No, because Bobby and Johnson hated each other. So, you're the vice president; you become president; the next day you're learning we were poised and ready to invade Cuba. You're learning that your hated enemy, Bobby Kennedy, still Attorney General, was partially in charge of those plans. You learn that JFK had delegated most of that planning to Bobby. You're starting to get reports that there's some sort of "official" Cuban-Castro-Cuban connection to JFK's murder. And you know that if this reaches the public, or the conservative, hawkish members of congress, they're going to call for an invasion of Cuba. If you invade Cuba under these circumstances, you are triggering World War III.

So, if you're Lyndon Johnson, what do you do? Remember, those shots had flown over Lyndon Johnson's head, for people that think he was involved. If someone had knocked the rifleman, Lyndon would have been splattered. Johnson knew he must cut off any public or thorough investigation of the assassination, or it would lead to World War III.

People should know too, Lyndon Johnson did not want the Warren Commission. J. Edgar Hoover (head of the FBI at the time) did not want the Warren Commission (the official government investigation into the Kennedy assassination whose conclusion was that JFK was killed by one lone-nut assassin, Lee Harvey Oswald).

Hoover and LBJ were friends. They wanted to do the investigation themselves. You know who wanted the Warren Commission? Bobby Kennedy's associates. So many people think, "Yeah, Lyndon had JFK killed." Here's the other incredible thing Lyndon is learning the day after JFK's assassination in Dallas: JFK was almost killed four days earlier in Tampa, Florida in a motorcade under circumstances that would have been almost identical to Dallas.

Evidence of Multiple Attempts to Assassinate JFK

Most folks are unaware that JFK was being hunted in November of 1963, and had been marked for assassination prior to November 22, 1963 in Dallas. In fact there had been three previous attempts, all with the same plan and template that was used in Dallas.

Chicago Plot

Abraham Bolden was the first African American Secret Service agent handpicked by JFK. On November 2, 1963, Mr. Bolden was working in the Chicago Secret Service office. In Washington DC, President Kennedy was just getting ready to board Airforce One for the flight to Chicago, where he was due to arrive for a speech. Suddenly, the trip was cancelled. The following interview is the true, historical account of why that trip was cancelled, from none other than Mr. Bolden himself.

After the JFK assassination, the FBI took over the investigation into the Chicago assassination attempt and, offering no reasons, dropped the case. Sadly, in the 1990s, the Secret Service destroyed files relating to JFK's November 1963 travels, after specifically being ordered not to destroy any files. One can only speculate why a governmental body would purposely disobey a presidential order.

> Holland: Can you talk about the investigation and the threat against President Kennedy two weeks before his Dallas trip?
>
> Bolden: There were a couple of investigations that were happening a couple of weeks before his assassination, in Dallas, Texas. One of them involved a Cuban named Echevarria who told a Secret Service informant that the president was about to be assassinated. (Homer Echevarria was an anti-Castro Cuban exile working for a group who wanted to violently overthrow Castro.)
>
> This happened in the last week of October (1963). The Secret Service had an agent next to Echevarria who verified that these words were, in fact, spoken. He said that the president was going to be assassinated because he was withholding his support from the exiled Cubans in Miami, Florida. We already had foreknowledge of an assassination plan against the president that emanated in Miami during a telephone conversation between a couple of suspects.
>
> The president was supposed to come to Chicago on November 1st. We got a call at the Secret Service office from the FBI, who said that

they had an informant, a lady, who had seen rifles and the route that President Kennedy was supposed to take when he arrived in Chicago. He was going to Soldier Field for the Army / Navy football game.

The Secret Service here in Chicago talked with the informant and set up a surveillance on these men. They were alleged to have been two Cubans who were being visited by European gentlemen. But that investigation fell through. The Echevarria investigation was turned over to the FBI after the president was assassinated. We didn't hear anything else from that Echevarria investigation. We were told to "tear up all the notes that we had concerning that Echevarria investigation" and, "as far as we were concerned, the Echevarria investigation did not exist."

Since they took such great pains in covering it up, I'm of the opinion that the Echevarria investigation, and the investigation of the Cubans who had the rifles in the rooming house, were the same investigation. And that Echevarria was indeed mixed up with these people. Although, the Secret Service never brought that out, and the Warren Commission was never advised of those facts, to my knowledge.

Holland: Can you speculate as to why it was covered up?

Bolden: I think that it involved the CIA echelon and members of the CIA and the FBI. Also, the investigation that the Secret Service had done in reference to these suspected assassins was terrible. It would have not only been embarrassing, but it would have looked to the American people as if it was planned by these organizations.

There's no question that the FBI and the Secret Service were involved in the Echevarria investigation. I think that after the president was assassinated, the US government wanted to assure the American people that Oswald was the lone assassin. In order to sell that "bill of goods" to the American people, they covered up everything that could point in another direction. They did it in hopes that the American people would buy the thing they were calling the truth, but it was absolutely falsehood.

CHICAGO PLOT CONTINUED...

Jim DiEugenio may be the most knowledgeable person on the planet when it comes to the JFK assassination. Even Oliver Stone asked Jim to contribute his research to the DVD version of his film "JFK." I asked Jim, in one of our many "Night Fright" interviews, about the Chicago Plot.

DiEugenio: The Chicago plot occurred in the very late part of October, early part of November (1963). It was immediately hushed up by the powers that be in the Secret Service, the Treasury Department, the FBI, and probably the CIA also. No one ever really heard about it because the guy who first talked about it, Abraham Bolden, was framed on these phony charges and was sent to Springfield Prison. (See Chapter 10 "Secret Service Abraham Bolden A Real American Hero.")

In fact, I don't think the Chicago plot is even mentioned at all in the Warren Commission volumes. Then, in 1975, a very famous investigative reporter named Edwin Black, out of Chicago, apparently discovered what had happened. He wrote a very interesting article called "The Plot that Killed JFK in Chicago" for an independent alternative magazine called "The Chicago Independent."

There are very few articles from the decade of the '70s that I think are better than Edwin Black's piece on the Chicago plot. He dug into this thing for a period of eight months, did dozens of interviews, went to four different cities, and combed through all kinds of articles and archives. His house was broken into. He was trailed by a DIA agent, but he finally got this thing out.

Right-winged radical and Kennedy hater, Thomas Vallee, was arrested prior to JFK's arrival with an M1 rifle, a handgun, and 3,000 rounds of ammo. Additionally, a motel manager called federal agents after seeing in a room rented by two Cuban nationals, several automatic rifles with telescopic sights, with an outline of the route the president would take in Chicago bringing him past that building.

The amazing thing about the Chicago plot is that the guy who was framed to be the patsy very much resembles Lee Harvey Oswald:

- He has three names: *Thomas Arthur Vallee.*

- He was a former Marine.

- He was stationed in Japan.

- He had been associated with anti-Castro Cuban exiles. He had been training them for the CIA. In this case, it was Long Island, New York.

- And, like Oswald, he was leaving from the place where he was associated with the anti-Castro Cuban Exiles and moving back to his hometown.Oswald had been associated with the anti-Castro Cuban

Exiles in New Orleans in the summer of 1963 and was moving back to his hometown in Texas.

- They were going to frame Vallee for shooting at Kennedy from an upper story building as Kennedy's motorcade was coming off an expressway. This was almost the exact same tactic as would happen in Dallas.

- Vallee was supposed to have worked at the print shop on the third floor of a building that overlooked the street where Kennedy's motorcade was going to be entering this expressway.

- The actual assassins would be a four-man hit team with high-powered rifles along the expressway route.

It looks like it's almost the same operation that took place in Dallas. Now, here comes something even more interesting. Why didn't it succeed? The FBI got a tip from an informant whose code name was Lee!

Holland: I wonder who that was.

James DiEugenio: When the tip came in, the FBI basically handed off the case to the Secret Service. They got a second tip from a landlady who had four guys with rifles move into an apartment. She also saw a map of JFK's motorcade route.

Then the Secret Service springs into action. They manage to get two of the hit men. They arrest Vallee on a pretext, like not using his turn signal on a freeway ramp, so they can get him off the streets. They can't find the other two guys, so Kennedy decides to go ahead and call off his trip to Chicago. The pretext was the overthrow of the Diem regime in Vietnam, but it was probably because of this threat to his life in Chicago. That is interesting in and of itself, but what is even more interesting is what happens to Abraham Bolden (see "Chapter 10 Secret Service Abraham Bolden A Real American Hero" for more information).

Bolden noted that it was being hushed up. He went home and told his wife, "You know something, I have a really funny feeling about what's going to happen to President Kennedy." Sure enough, Kennedy is killed in Dallas, with almost the same tactical operation as was used in Chicago, and they framed it on Oswald, who resembles the profile of Thomas Arthur Vallee.

MIAMI PLOT

Joseph Milteer was a white supremacist and a member of the radical extremists "The White Citizen's Council Of Atlanta." On November 9, 1963, a mere 13 days before Kennedy would be assassinated in Dallas, Joseph Milteer described a plan that was in operation to assassinate President Kennedy, presumably in Miami. Milteer's plan was an exact template that would be used successfully in the assassination of JFK on November 22, 1963, in Dallas.

Undercover Miami police informant, William Somersett, had the wherewithal to place a tape recorder in the room where he and Milteer had a conversation. Milteer had no idea he was being recorded and thought Somersett to be a like-minded ally. What was taped is chilling:

MIAMI, NOVEMBER 9, 1963

> Somersett (undercover): How do you figure the best way would be to get him (meaning JFK)?
>
> Milteer (supremacist): From an office building with a high powered rifle
>
> Somersett: Think he (meaning JFK) knows he's a marked man?
>
> Milteer: Sure he does.
>
> Somersett: They gonna really try to kill him?
>
> Milteer: Oh yeah, it's in the works. They'll pick up somebody within an hour of that. (note: Lee Harvey Oswald was arrested approximately 1hour and 15 minutes after JFK was shot.)

After JFK was assassinated, Somersett and Milteer spoke again. Milteer was still unaware Somersett was an undercover Miami police informant. Milteer boasted about his accuracy foretelling of the deed.

> Milteer: Everything ran true to form. I guess you thought I was kidding you when I said he would be killed from a window with a high-powered rifle.

Asked whether he was guessing when he made the original remark, Milteer replied, "I don't do any guessing."

Tampa Plot

Tampa Police Chief J.P. Mullins confirmed that on November 18, 1963, only five days before Kennedy was assassinated in Dallas, yet another plot was discovered to assassinate JFK. This time, it was in Tampa.

Once again, the similarities between the Tampa plot and the events in Dallas are unnerving. In Tampa authorities had been told to be on the lookout for "a person of interest" by the name of Gilberto Policarpo Lopez.

Lopez resembled Lee Harvey Oswald, not only physically, but in his character and actions. Like Oswald, Lopez had made a trip to Mexico in an attempt to get into Cuba. He had recently separated from his wife and had gotten into a fist fight for handing out pro-Castro leaflets. Documents stated that Lopez was on a secret mission for US intelligence and, therefore, should not be investigated.

The Mafia In The JFK Assassination: Mafia Dons Sam Giancana, Johnny Roselli, Santos Traficante, Carlos Marcello

Lamar Waldron: The three Mafia bosses who confessed their roles in JFK's murder were –

1. Carlos Marcello of Louisiana, Texas

2. Santos Trafficante, the godfather of Tampa, where JFK was almost killed four days before his trip to Dallas

3. And Don Johnny Roselli of the Chicago mafia of Vegas and Hollywood

They used people like CIA agent and long time Mafia hoodlum, Bernard Barker. They also used Barker's Associates and David Morales, a very high ranking CIA officer who headed operations at the world's second largest CIA station down in Miami (code named JMWAVE). Barker worked for Trafficante for years. Morales was close personal friends with Chicago Mafia Don Johnny Roselli.

Barker and Morales both helped to plant phony evidence ahead of time, pointing to Fidel, and plant more afterwards. Phony evidence went up to Lyndon Johnson and the head of the CIA (John McCone). They thought, "Fidel did it. We're poised to invade, but if we do, it's World War III, so we just have to cover all this up and keep it out of the press."

> So, why is the Mafia after Kennedy? The Mob basically ran most of America because the vice president, Richard Nixon, was essentially supported by the Mob from his start in politics.

Nixon was vice president during the Eisenhower administration from 1953 to 1961. He would later become president from 1969 to 1974, when he would resign over the Watergate scandal, which included E. Howard Hunt Frank Sturgis and Bernard Barker.

> Waldron: People like Godfather Carlos Marcello and Roselli were not even citizens. It was known that Marcello was not a citizen. He should have been deported. But of course, when you give a lot of "support" to people like Richard Nixon, you can just openly flout the law.
>
> The Mafia was starting to try to take over labor unions, like the "Teamsters" (headed by Jimmy Hoffa). Senator John F. Kennedy and his Chief Council, his brother Bobby, spearheaded crime hearings in the Senate, our upper House of Congress, in the late 1950s.
>
> They specifically went after Carlos Marcello, who was dragged in front of a committee, and Santo Trafficante, who hid out in Cuba. Members of the Chicago Mafia, like Roselli's boss Sam Giancana, were dragged in front of the committee. There is great footage of him "sparring" with Bobby Kennedy. They just hated each other.
>
> They went after the guy who was funneling a lot of money to the mafia, Jimmy Hoffa (president of the Teamsters Union), who shared a lawyer with Trafficante. He was very close to Trafficante and Marcello.
>
> The Kennedy's went after the Mob. That's how JFK made his name. He pledged, in that 1960 campaign, that he was going to go after the Mob if he was elected. The Mafia "loves to win" no matter what. They played both sides. They gave a little support to JFK. They gave the vast majority of their support to their man Richard Nixon. Via Frank Sinatra, JFK got a little Mob support through his father who had connections.
>
> I can tell you, Richard Nixon got far, far more support from the Mafia than JFK did, because the Mafia wanted Nixon to win. That's one reason Nixon could not contest that close race, because he had taken so much Mafia support.
>
> JFK was elected and did something rare for any politician. He kept his promise. He waged the biggest war against the Mafia America had ever seen, and has ever seen to this day. He made his brother the

Attorney General, and they went after the Mob hard. Now, did JFK have any Mob connections after that? Well, he had a "weakness for women."

JFK AND MARYLYN MONROE, FRANK SINATRA, JUDY CAMPBELL

Holland: I was just about to ask you about Marilyn Monroe.

Waldron: Marilyn Monroe was certainly "friends" with Frank Sinatra and "close" to Johnny Roselli and to Sam Giancana. Judith Exner was very, very "close" to Sam Giancana and Johnny Roselli. The Mob tried to get to JFK and convince him to back off, but he wouldn't do it. He broke off relationships with both women. Marilyn may have died because she would not compromise.

Holland: Oh, can you tell us about that?

Waldron: There have been many stories about what happened the night Marilyn died. It's hard to sort out because so many stories have been told for money. People overlook the fact that she spent the weekend before she died with Sam Giancana, Roselli's boss, and Frank Sinatra, at a gambling casino up in Reno called Cal Neva Lodge.

They got "compromised." Basically, it was like a drunken, drugged orgy, with very compromising photos of Marilyn Monroe that would have shocked America to see. This was at a time when they were actually plotting to kill Bobby Kennedy. They were either going to blackmail Bobby or kill him. Imagine if Bobby had been killed at Marilyn Monroe's. The cover-up it would have triggered probably would have brought down the JFK Presidency.

Apparently Marilyn would not "play ball." Either she was killed, or she had a potential reason to commit suicide.

A month after her death, Hoffa wanted to kill Bobby. Giancana wanted to kill Bobby. Carlos Marcello, much more powerful than Sam Giancana said, "Look, if we kill Bobby Kennedy, JFK is just going to send the Army in to get me."

He was speaking from experience. When Marcello and Trafficante had murdered the Attorney General elect of the state of Alabama in 1954, President Eisenhower had actually declared Martial Rule and sent the Army into this little city called Phoenix City. They never went after Marcello or Trafficante for it because Nixon got "support" from them and their associates.

Marcello said, "Everybody knows Bobby and LBJ hate each other." In the 1960 campaign, JFK ran against LBJ for the nomination. JFK got the nomination, and LBJ agreed to be vice president. But Bobby and Lyndon never mended fences. "Look, if I kill JFK, Bobby's power is over once Lyndon becomes president."

Marcello and Trafficante told a different FBI informant that they were going to kill JFK. They had a whole year to plan, to carefully groom their patsy. Remember, their main plan to kill JFK in Chicago had a backup plan in Tampa. Dallas was the backup plan for Tampa. There were also backup patsies.

Why Did The Mafia Assassinate JFK?

Waldron: So why did the Mafia kill JFK? Well, this big war was being waged against them. You can look in the newspapers from the fall of '63. Bobby leaked a series of articles saying he was going to send his own Justice Department people into Las Vegas to run out the Mafia.

The Mafia cannot go back to Cuba, so their backs are against the wall. The Mafia clearly wants to get away with murder. In Chicago alone they've gotten away with 1000 murders. Marcello and Trafficante had ordered numerous hits. They were never prosecuted, never convicted. Certainly the hit man was not prosecuted, let alone the people who ordered the hit. But you know this is higher stakes, killing the president. How do you commit a murder of that magnitude and get away with it?

Remember, how I said Nixon and the Mafia were close? Well, Nixon had the CIA hire the Mafia to kill Fidel right before the 1960 election. Nixon thought that would get him elected. It didn't happen. (Nixon lost the presidential election to JFK.)

Only a dozen US officials knew about Commander Alameida. Secretary of Defense (Robert McNamara) didn't know. Secretary of State (Dean Rusk) didn't know. Powers, O'Donnell (Council and friends to JFK) didn't know. Secretary of the Army, Cyrus Vance, knew and reported directly, in this case, to Bobby Kennedy. Bobby knew. Bobby's own Cuban exile, Hanes, knew.

It was a very tightly held secret. However, as I said, E. Howard Hunt was the CIA liaison to Bobby's aides dealing with Almeida. Hunt's assistant was Bernard Barker, operative for Santos Trafficante.

Barker was involved in all of the sensitive information with the coup plan. He was telling Trafficante everything: from to the bullet found in Oswald's rifle, to the way the JFK was killed, which was the way Fidel was going to be killed by Almeida.

The Mob made sure that a clear signal was sent. They wanted it to look like Fidel must have found out and used the plan that was going to kill him to kill JFK. The hope of the Mafia was that the invasion would go forward. Nobody would ever find out they were behind it because it would trigger World War III. The Mafia got much of what they expected.

Oswald Incapable of Assassination Plotting

Waldron: The Naval intelligence here in America did a secret investigation. I talked to two different people involved with that investigation who concluded that Oswald was incapable of doing the actual shooting or of masterminding the assassination. Oswald was a low-level CIA asset.

From the time he was in the US Marines, the Warren Commission said he was a "teenage Communist." How many teenage Communists join the United States Marines in the Cold War, McCarthy 1950s!? None. Oswald did, and he tried to join before he was old enough. He joined the Civil Air Patrol first. Both of his brothers were in the military. One was in an intelligence service. Neither were Communist. Oswald's favorite TV show was "I Led Three Lives," one of many shows and books about people who went deep under cover, pretending to be Communists but actually were working for US intelligence.

I'll just say, Oswald, though he was defecting to Cuba as one of the low level assets for some upcoming act, he didn't know about the coup. He knew "something" was coming up. That's what he thought he was going to be doing that day.

Jack Ruby worked for Carlos Marcello. Ruby owed an impossible amount of money to the IRS and to Marcello, so he had to take care of killing the patsy (Lee Harvey Oswald).

THE MAFIA TAKES CREDIT FOR THE JFK ASSASSINATION

> Waldron: The Mafia tried to kill JFK, (1) first in Chicago, where the motorcade was cancelled, (2) again in Tampa, where the motorcade went ahead, but the Godfather there found out that authorities knew, so the hit was cancelled. (3) They succeeded in Dallas, with the phony evidence, many believed pointed to Fidel. The Mafia got away with murder, but now, as people can read, I mean, once Marcello was finally in prison, he just admitted, "I had the SOB killed and I would do it again. He was a thorn in my side. I wish I could have done it myself."

AUTHOR'S OPINION ON THE PALACE COUP

> **Lamar is my friend, and what his research has uncovered is unparalleled. However, I remain personally undecided on the "Cuban Palace Coup" Lamar has described above. Do I believe that President Kennedy could have been entertaining a plan for a coup and an uprising of the Cuban people? Yes. My problem is whether it was ever given the "go ahead" to proceed or was just a "contingency plan," another option. Ted Sorensen told me that, after the Bay of Pigs, Kennedy wanted as many options for solutions as possible.**

Lamar's thesis is that the Mafia ordered the assassination of JFK, or, at the very least, played a major role in the plot. I completely agree with this. Let's not forget that the Mafia had been running all the casinos in Cuba, earning enormous profits. Then, along came Castro, who kicked the Mafia out of Cuba, and shut down their casinos, and revenues. The Mafia was pissed and wanted Castro dead, so that they could return to Cuba and reinstate themselves in the casinos, thus reclaiming the vast amounts of money they had been making.

It would seem to me that the best course of action for the Mafia was not to kill Kennedy, but to return to Cuba and allow the Palace Coup, led by Almedia, to take place. This would allow "someone else" to finally get rid of Castro for them. This would provide a very real possibility of returning to Cuba and ushering themselves back into the lucrative casino business.

If they killed Kennedy before the coup, which both Lamar and I believe they did, the Mafia would have realized that the planned Palace Coup set for December 1, 1963, would not take place and would be cancelled. Therefore, Kennedy's assassination would prevent the Mafia from ever returning to their casinos in Cuba. In my opinion, the Mafia did kill Kennedy, so, it cannot be one or the other. Therefore, I don't believe that the Palace Coup plan was scheduled to "proceed," but was just a "contingency plan" drawn up on paper.

Another glaring problem I have with Kennedy going ahead with the Palace Coup is this: the Kennedy administration principals didn't know about it, specifically the Secretary of Defense Robert McNamara and Counsel Ted Sorensen. Kennedy, only months before, had almost entirely relied on both men, along with Bobby, to solve the Cuban Missile Crisis peacefully. After speaking with Ted Sorensen for many hours, I don't believe JFK would have excluded them in something that could generate another national security crisis and nuclear standoff.

The Cuban Missile Crisis had happened only one year earlier. All of the Kennedy Administration thought the world was doomed to a nuclear holocaust. We were so close that Jackie Kennedy had called the president saying she wanted to return home to the White House with Caroline and John Jr. so they could all die together. Now, imagine Mrs. Obama calling her husband from Chicago and saying that, because of a North Korean nuclear escalation, she was bringing their two daughters home so that they could all die together. Close your eyes and ponder that right now. That's exactly how close we were!

> **One of the reasons Lamar believes that Kennedy would back the coup was to finally remove the nuclear missiles that were still there, never removed from Cuba by the Soviets. It is my own belief that some of those very same nuclear missiles remain in Cuba to today. Please see "Chapter 13 My own Perspective" for more on my thesis.**

However, Kennedy refused to invade Cuba in October of 1962, precisely because he feared that Cuba would launch the nuclear missiles in retaliation. In fact, Castro had asked the Soviets for permission to do just that, and knowingly destroy both America and Cuba. Then the US would retaliate with their own nuclear missiles at Cuba. Castro had no problem with that scenario. Thank goodness Khrushchev did, and negotiated a peaceful settlement with Kennedy.

Even if the Palace Coup was successful, there was still a very real chance that Castro, being the loose cannon he was, would have suspected the US behind the coup as it was unfolding and launched those very same missiles at the US.

> **I just don't believe JFK or any other of the administration would have rolled the dice again...ever. In fact, JFK had just given his outstanding American University speech on June 10, 1963, where he reached out to the Soviets. He wanted to stop nuclear weapon testing.**

The very moment JFK was killed in Dallas, a US emissary was in a meeting with Castro to discuss a possible normalization of relations between the United States and Cuba. Castro's response to the assassination of JFK was one of mortification, saying, "this is bad – this is very bad." Castro saw Kennedy as the best president with which to conduct dialogue and come to a mutual understanding.

For Kennedy to intentionally throw in a monkey wrench and ignite another nuclear confrontation seems too far off of Kennedy's vision for mankind.

Chairman Khrushchev (head of the Soviet Union), Prime Minister Macmillan (Prime Minister of Great Britain), and I have agreed that high-level discussions will shortly begin in Moscow, looking toward early agreement on a comprehensive test ban treaty. Our hopes must be tempered with the caution of history – but with our hopes go the hopes of all mankind.

The United States, as the world knows, will never start a war. We do not want a war. We do not now expect a war. This generation of Americans has already had enough – more than enough – of war and hate and oppression. We shall be prepared if others wish it. We shall be alert to try to stop it. But we shall also do our part to build a world of peace where the weak are safe and the strong are just. We are not helpless before that task or hopeless of its success. Confident and unafraid, we labor on – not toward a strategy of annihilation but toward a strategy of peace.

John F. Kennedy, excerpts from the American University speech, June 10, 1963

President John F. Kennedy's presidential portrait.

CHAPTER 10

The Secret Service: Abraham Bolden, True American Hero

"In order to sell that bill of goods to the American people, they came out with the cover-up. And they covered up everything that would probably point in another direction. They did that in hopes that the American people would buy that thing that they were selling called the truth, but it was absolutely falsehood."

"We can't just stand up when things affect us alone. We have to stand up wherever we find corruption in a democratic process. That's our obligation to the American people, our obligation to our children, and it's our obligation to God, to be the best people that we can be while we're on this planet Earth."

Abraham Bolden

PREFACE

Heroes come in many forms. Sports heroes are fine, in their own right, but Mr. Bolden is a true American hero. I have always been drawn toward men of fortitude, honor and integrity. Abraham Bolden is just such a man.

Abraham Bolden was the first African American Secret Service agent to be placed on White House detail. He was handpicked by President Kennedy himself to guard the president's own family.

Abraham was not on duty that fateful day in Dallas, and that haunts him to this day. He fully believes, as do I, that had he only been there, somehow, some way, he would have kept President Kennedy alive, even if that meant taking that fatal bullet himself. Mr. Bolden was subsequently set up by his fellow Secret Service agents to silence his whistle-blowing, damning accusations about drunk Secret Service agents that day in Dallas (accusations that were validated shortly thereafter).

Their blatant racism, drunkenness and womanizing, while on duty, left them unable to protect President Kennedy. In order to silence Abraham and protect their careers and reputations, the Secret Service agents had to deflect the accusations.

Mr. Bolden was subsequently set up and charged by the Secret Service with soliciting a $50,000 bribe to pass along a file containing incriminating evidence in a counterfeit scheme. The charges were false and were levied in an obvious attempt to silence Mr. Bolden.

> **He went through an American justice system that can only be described as a "third world kangaroo court." That is: guilty as charged, regardless of the absence of evidence or witnesses to substantiate the charge.**

The prosecution's main witness, Joseph Sapgnoli, whom Mr. Bolden had previously arrested, was a career criminal. He later admitted, under oath, that his testimony, incriminating Mr. Bolden, was 100% fabricated. Alarmingly, Spagnoli testified that he was forced to say these statements against Mr. Bolden under duress and threats from the Secret Service.

Yet, Mr. Bolden was still incarcerated, and no investigation into Spagnolli's perjured statements, or into the Secret Service, were ever made. Such was the blatant and desperate attempt to keep Abraham silent.

This was, after all, 1960s America, where African Americans were no strangers to a biased justice system. This was the time in history that you read about, when Whites, who had murdered Blacks, were found not guilty and released on an almost weekly basis. Blacks had no chance in such a justice system. They presumed that Abraham, a "Negro," once locked away behind bars, would simply slip into the night. They had no idea who they were dealing with.

"At the conference table and in the minds of men, the Free World's cause is strengthened because it is just. But it is strengthened even more by the dedicated efforts of free men and free nations. As the great parliamentarian Edmund Burke said, 'The only thing necessary for the triumph of evil is for good men to do nothing.'

And that in essence is why I am here today. This trip is more than a consultation--more than a good-will visit. It is an act of faith--faith in your country, in your leaders--faith in the capacity of two great neighbors to meet their common problems--and faith in the cause of freedom, in which we are so intimately associated."

President John F. Kennedy, May 17, 1961, Address Before the Canadian Parliament in Ottawa

Abraham Bolden A True American Hero

Fate and destiny took their turn throughout this story, including when Abraham first met JFK. Bolden, a "Negro" agent, living in Chicago in 1962, was assigned the derogatory task of guarding the toilet. Out of sight, out of mind. JFK arrived at McCormick Place, April 28, 1961, for a speech to thank the mayor of Chicago, Daley, for his recent support of JFK's successful campaign run for the presidency. At that time, the thought of an "African American" in the White House was a utopian dream; "Negros" were just trying to have the right to attend the same schools and colleges as whites.

Too much coffee brought JFK bounding down the stairs, entourage in tow, until he saw Bolden. He stopped mid-stride, spoke with Abraham for several minutes, then asked him if he would serve on his White House Protective Detail. Of course he would. "See you next week in Washington," was the response by the young president.

There are heart-wrenching and riveting personal stories about Mr. Bolden's willingness to lay his life down, not only for the president, but for the first lady and Caroline. Abraham was highly liked by Kennedy, who took a shining to him and introduced him to a "who's who" of White House movers and shakers, including his brother, Bobby, who offered him a job as an ambassador.

Appallingly, Mr. Bolden also witnessed on-duty Secret Service agents pick up women to have sex with, all the while supposedly protecting the president. On many occasions, there were also agents on duty too drunk to walk, let alone be called upon in an emergency. Indeed Abraham's fears were realized when it was discovered Secret Service agents on Kennedy's Secret Service back-up car, in Dallas that fateful day, were found to have been boozing all night at a strip club until 7 am, some never having been to bed at all.

Mr. Bolden was also subjected to rampant racism from his fellow Secret Service agents who did not like the fact he was working alongside them. They put a noose above his desk, called him "Nigger" to his face. They set him up, in an effort to silence his whistle-blowing about the drunken agents and the president's lack of professional Secret Service protection.

Fate & Destiny: Becoming The First African American Secret Service Agent, Hand Picked By JFK Himself

Holland: Let's start off at the beginning Mr. Bolden. You're the first African-American Secret Service agent, how did that come about? How did you meet Mr. Kennedy?

Bolden: Well, I became a Secret Service agent October 30th, 1960. And of course the president, at that time, was a senator and was running for the presidency and was elected in November of 1960. Well, the president ran a close race here in Chicago and he only won Chicago by about 8,000 votes, he won Cook County by 8,000 votes. And President Kennedy knew what a chore that was from Mayor Daley and I think that on the light of hand he knew that probably 7,999 of those 8,000 votes were "dead people." [laughter] But anyway, the president won by that margin there in Chicago.

So, the president was coming here to thank Mayor Daley for the work that the "machine" had done in putting him over in front of Nixon by that margin. Being a new agent, they assigned me to an "innocuous" spot over at the McCormick Place where the president was going to be speaking that night of April 28th, when he was coming here for the big banquet. Well, they put me out in front of a large room on the lower level of the McCormick Place, a place where I figured that seeing the president was slim to none.

And so about 8:30 that night on April 28th, 1961 the president was running a little late and his motorcade arrived at 8:30pm. I saw these cameras flashing up on the floor just above me; there were steps that were leading down the steps into this washroom and I was saying to myself, I sure wish I could be up there to see President Kennedy.

And all of a sudden at the top of the steps and walking down those steps towards me was the president of the United States, John F. Kennedy. And the first thing he wanted to do when the motorcade arrived was use the washroom and there I stood, right in front of the washroom.

It was such an ironic thing, you know. They thought that they were hiding me on that lower level of McCormick Place and that's where I met the president. So he stopped in front of me, John Kennedy stopped in front of me and smiled. He asked me, "Are you a Secret Service agent or are you one of Mayor Daley's finest?" And I smiled back; I told him: "I'm a Secret Service agent, Mr. President."

During the conversation he asked me, point blank, with a smile on his face, but I could see he was serious about it, he asked me if there had ever been any Negroes on the Secret Service White House detail in Washington DC. And I answered, "Not to my knowledge, Mr. President."

He asked me: "Would you like to be the first?" - And his eyes glittered when he said that because he knew what was going to be my response. I said, "Yes sir, Mr. President!" - And he said: "I'll be looking forward to seeing you in Washington DC"!

Abraham Bolden

Bolden: And he went on to use the washroom; he came out and he waved at me and went back up the steps. Oh man, what a beautiful day, I'm glad you asked me about that.

Holland: What a wonderful, wonderful experience. Was there anything about Mr. Kennedy that surprised you? Was he taller than you thought? Was he thinner than you thought, heavier perhaps?

Bolden: He was a little taller than I'd thought that he would be, and also his hair, I don't know whether there was any dye in there or not, but it seems like in person his hair was a lot redder than it appeared on television. It seemed like a darker brown on television, but it was actually almost red. That's nice. Of course the lights may have had something to do with it, but I got that impression also when I was in Washington DC that it was a reddish glow to his hair. And he had one of the most beautiful smiles than anybody could ever have -

very serious person - and I really enjoyed being in his company and working for the president of the United States.

Holland: That night, did you wake your wife to tell her what was happening?

Bolden: Oh, I woke my wife up, I'm telling you. We... oh, did I ever! [laughter] She probably heard me when I was getting out of the car in the garage and I think the rest of the neighborhood probably heard me too. I could never have imagined - you know, I had watched this young impressive Senator in his battle against Richard Nixon and all of the untruths that had been heralded his way and the improbability of him becoming president.

And I had a sort of "Esprit de Corps" with the president. I felt empathy with him because I felt that this president - I'd say he has within his heart a willingness to bring about peace and equality and justice for all Americans, and that's what he was standing for. That's what he said in all of his speeches.

And I got the impression that, listening to him, and the feeling that I've felt within him, that he was very serious about this and very honest. And he proved that he was, and then in the steps that he'd take towards forming full civil rights. And he was hated for that by the South, but he was loved for the stance that he took by most of your Negroes in the North.

Civil Rights; Being a "Negro" in the 50s - 60s. JFK Pro Civil Rights and His Fight For Change

Holland: Let's stay on civil rights just for a second. Let's go back a few years to 1957. Do you remember the "Little Rock Nine?"

Bolden: Oh, sure I do, sure. Yes, well, you know, the "Little Rock Nine" was in 1957, and Eisenhower was president at that particular time, and Governor Faubus was the governor at that particular time. Now, we had these nine Negro children who made applications to go to school and they were supposed to go to I think it was Central High School, wasn't it?

Holland: Yes, sir.

Bolden: Right, in Little Rock, Arkansas. And of course the governor was dead set against it and did not want these Negro children admitted into the school with the white children and there came a time when

President Eisenhower actually had to nationalize the National Guard force down in Little Rock and have them escort these young children into the classroom. Well, we know that worked out very well because many of them became leaders there at Central High School and went on to do some great things in journalism and other types of occupation.

Holland: How did that affect your life in those days when you heard of this struggle going on, not only in the South but it must have affected you personally living even in the Chicago in the North?

Bolden: Yes, well, you know, just prior to that we had the terrible murder of Emmett Till down in Mississippi and that was on a lot of people's minds.

Emmett Till (July 25, 1941 – August 28, 1955) was a youngster of 14 on a visit from his home in Chicago to Mississippi. On a dare from fellow kids who edged him on, Emmett, from the North and unaccustomed to the subservient roles Blacks were forced to play in the South, had flirted with an "older woman" who was all of 21 herself, but, white. He was dragged, kidnapped and murdered by a barbaric mob. No one stepped forward to stop it. Two of the mob were arrested and tried and were acquitted. Just months later they would boast in a magazine interview how they murdered Emmett. Because of the United Sates' "Double Jeopardy" statute, a person cannot be tried for the same crime twice; thus they lived out their lives free.

Emmett Till's murder was not unique in the South. The Klu Klux Klan ran rampant in the South with many members holding high office and controlling the outcomes of the investigations into the crimes. Thus was the climate of hate in the Southern States. It is said the hate was just as dominate in the Northern States as well, with the difference being, the North was covert while the South was overt.

Thus was the storm raging across the country when JFK and Bobby fought to bring change to Civil Rights. Thus was the magnitude of President Kennedy and not Nixon in the White House. The Kennedy's opted to do what was right regardless of the political consequences. Even if the whole world is against you, but they are wrong, that doesn't make you any less right.

Even if the whole world is against you, it doesn't neccessarily mean you are wrong.

Bolden: All down to Little Rock crisis and the bus rides and things like that. But I tell you, President Kennedy brought with him a lot of hope. But during the late 50s and the early 60s was a very troublous time in America, and many of the people of my race began to lose faith in the constitution and what it stood for. So my people were concerned.

And we were like in the wilderness; I think that the whole country was in wilderness, so to speak, and trying to solve the situation before that could probably bring down this country if some remedy hadn't been found. We had a young man that came along, Dr. Martin Luther King, who seemed to galvanize the thoughts and opinion of the majority and the minority too in America. He became the center of attraction of a movement towards an integrated society in which we now live today.

Holland: On the White House Secret Service detail, did you ever have any discussions about civil rights or anything outside of the Secret Service with anybody there, perhaps the president or Bobby?

Bolden: No, I didn't. I didn't discuss it as an issue, not the racism as an issue, although I experienced quite a bit of it being an agent in the United States Secret Service.

Secret Service Agents Call JFK a "nigger lover" / Outright Refuse To Protect Him Because Of It

I saw a lot of racism within the Secret Service itself and there were comments that were made that I overheard; probably they weren't intended for me to hear.

But I heard the president referred to by some of his closest agents as "nigger lover." I heard two of them talking, and they were saying – and this was going on in the White House – that if anyone would take a shot at the president or try to assassinate him they wouldn't do their job.

Abraham Bolden

Bolden: And this was mortifying to me; I couldn't believe I was hearing my ears. And the reason for that is that some of these agents were from the South and they were dead set against the policies and principles that the president stood for. Although what they were doing wasn't raising the stakes because, see, the Secret Service is not really protecting the man. What we are protecting, and I should have been protecting, was the office - the official office - the constitutional office of the presidency of the United States - which is above anybody that could ever come into that office.

And in assassinating the president or talking against the president, once he was elected and calling him these different names, what they were actually doing was making it a personal thing, which your bodyguards and Secret Service can't afford to do that. We have to keep our eyes on the total prize - which was the Constitution of the United States of America. They were racists. As a matter of fact, one of my supervisors told me - when we were in Hainesport, Massachusetts...

Holland: Harvey Henderson?

Bolden: Right, yes, Harvey Henderson. He looked me right in the eye and - is it okay, if I tell you and all the audience what is exactly he said?

Mr. Bolden has earned the right to say whatever he wants, so I simply said "Yes, sir," knowing full well what "word" was coming, the world needs to know.

Bolden: He says, "Bolden," he says "I'm going to tell you something and don't you ever forget it." He told me, he says "you're a nigger, you were born a nigger, you're going to die a nigger, and you'll never be anything but a nigger so act like one."

Now here is a man who was shoulder to shoulder with the president - who was standing on the side of the president's automobile - with those type of sentiments within the group itself. And so I found this to be very, very duplicite, if nothing else.

Holland: It must have broken your heart, sir, to know that those responsible for the life of a man held in high esteem by yourself and the country, would have sentiments like that.

Bolden: Well, to me, it not only broke my heart, but I saw it as a serious security risk. I saw it as a risk so predominant that before I left the Secret Service detail and went back to Chicago, I went in to the chief's office, UE Baughman in Washington DC, and explained what I had seen and what I had heard.

Urbanus Edmund Baughman was the chief of the United States Secret Service from 1948 to 1961, under Presidents Truman, Eisenhower, and Kennedy; he retired in 1961, two years before the assassination.

He is also on record for bizarrely stating that there was no Mafia in the United States for the previous 40 years. Remember that when we start to discuss Mafia involvement with the Kennedy assassination in the (Please see "Chapter 9 The Mafias Role; Lamar Waldron" for more information).

SECRET SERVICE TOO DRUNK TO PROTECT JFK

Bolden: I warned the chief of the Secret Service (UE Baughman) that the agents were reporting for work, drinking, and not really in any condition to protect the president of the United States. Some of them would be inebriated, having been up all night, and they were doing this in a terrible mood and drinking on the job.

They had a little hut in there, at Hainesport, Massachusetts, where the agents were staying while they were eating lunch or whatever. There was alcohol in those watch houses. I thought that this was really a security breach that was endangering the president of the United States, and I made no bones about it.

Because you have to understand this: I was a Secret Service agent sworn to uphold the Constitution of the United States of America. I did not swear to uphold the Secret Service or to uphold anybody who was doing something that would jeopardize that Constitution. So I pitched my cards with the Constitution of the United States which I had sworn to uphold. And that's the reason I got in trouble and had served time in the penitentiary.

And when they came to Chicago here in March of 1963 - and agents went down on Rush Street and had a drinking session all night long until about six in the morning - when the president was due here that night. I castigated those agents while we were in a meeting, along with several of the Chicago policemen and told them point blank: "What's going to happen is that you're going to get the president killed!"

Abraham Bolden

Bolden: I was ostracized because of my attitude. If you talk to any of those agents - there are a couple of them who are still alive - they would tell you that Bolden spoke out - he didn't bite his tongue when it came to the protection of the president of the United States.

Holland: Sir, have you been in contact with these fellow agents that you just spoke about since then, and have you been able to come to any terms with them?

Bolden: I have talked with a couple of agents - some within the Secret Service now, and some who were in the Secret Service when I was there. And, to a man, they all understand what happened to me and why it had to happen. Because a couple of those agents are out of the Chicago office here, and they know exactly what I was saying, although they declined my invitation to come out front and verify these things that I'm saying.

Because prior to the release of many of the documents that were declared "top secret" by President Lynden Johnson, these people know that I'm telling the truth, and they could verify what I was saying.

Then the federal government of the Congress investigated, and then certain documents were released that verified everything that I said. And so I have to keep on keeping on, because there's a greater thing that's at stake than just the back of one man or the death of me or the death of President Kennedy or anybody in my family, and that is the larger picture of the protection of the freedom, justice and equality that we have under the Constitution of the United States.

Holland: Have any agents ever come to you and expressed any remorse for what happened?

Bolden: Yes, yes. I talked with one agent shortly after I was released from the penitentiary. He testified against me at the trial, and he just came to me and said point blank: "Well, I had to do what I did because they put so much pressure on me." And I told him: "I forgive you man."

I understand how those things go down, because when you saw what the Secret Service did to me and finally made a better man out of me - if you would only understand that - they made a better man out of me.

What I went through alerted me, and it brought me closer and closer to the reality of what would happen if we lose these freedoms that we have under the Constitution of the United States. It made me more willing to fight to preserve these freedoms from any and all enemies of America.

Holland: You see, sir, this is what makes you a great man, because you've taken the negative, horrible things that happened to you, and you've turned it into something positive. Instead of getting down on yourself and letting that fester away at you, you've risen up beyond that.

The Juice: The Secret Service Covers Up The JFK Assassination

Holland: What is so explosive that they're still trying to cover up? Is it their own ineptitude or is there something more festering there?

Bolden: Well, some of those agents - I know absolutely about two of them - there were administrative reports that they submitted to the supervisor and special agent in charge of the United States Secret Service - they stood by and let those reports be re-dictated by the supervisor of the Secret Service in the Chicago office, Maurice G Martineau.

Maurice Martineau was the assistant special agent in charge of the Chicago Field Office, 1963 to 1969.

Bolden: Those reports were re-dictated as to have happened after the president was assassinated. You see, that's a very serious thing because they not only stood by and watched a felony committed, which is submitting a false report to a government agency, but they became a part of it.

Now for them to come forward and to give that information - they have to also give information that incriminates them - because they became a part of a conspiracy to hoodwink the American people.

THE ASSASSINATION

Holland: Sir, where were you November 22nd 1963 when you heard the news about JFK?

Bolden: I was in a night club over here in Chicago at 37th and Indiana. He served liquor and I was inside taking some handwriting samples from him because somebody had passed a forged government document to him in the payment for drinks. Normally, we have to take a handwriting sample from whoever had handled that particular negotiable instrument - to exclude them as being the party that forged the name of the payee.

So, I was standing there - and it was about 11:45 AM - that we were taking the handwriting samples - and suddenly there was an announcement. I remember it was on Channel 2 - that we called CBS here in Chicago - that the president had just been shot. Now at that particular time no announcement was made that he was dead - but that he had been shot.

But I knew right away - that under those circumstances - the president probably would have been killed - because I thought that his protection would not react, and they didn't.

Holland: Indeed, it was proven that most of the agents had been up all night drinking, some of them had not even gone to bed.

Bolden: That's right, absolutely. Absolutely. And when I made that charge - shortly after President Kennedy was assassinated - and I made the charge that those agents were up that night - see I didn't know for a fact - but I knew that by habit that's what they did, you see. I knew them. And so, as it turned out, I told the chief of the Secret Service, UE Baughman, that they would not react.

And if you look at the picture when that bullet struck the president in the head, they're still standing on the running board. Not one of President Kennedy's guards went to protect him.

Now (Clint) Hill was assigned to the first lady, Jacqueline Kennedy, and he was very alert. Clinton Hill and I were good friends. I always did think that Clint Hill was a very efficient agent, but I knew that those agents standing on the running board would be in no condition to react and they were not.

Holland: I would imagine you have run those scenes over and over in your head, perhaps putting yourself on that car that day. I should tell folks, Mr. Bolden was not on protective duty, he was not there; he was in Chicago, as he just said. Sir, had you have been there, would you have taken that fatal shot for Mr. Kennedy?

Bolden: I surely would. Not only was that my duty, that was my duty to do that under the Constitution of the United States, and nobody forced me to go into the United States Secret Service. It's the same as a soldier in uniform. They take many, many bullets from people all around the world. We have young men, 17, 18, 19 years old being brought back in flag-covered coffins.

The American people, who are in this country, have to have that same idea of sacrifice for the country that those soldiers have. Even though we have on the "anonymous suits" and all the different type of hats and things, we still are in a fight, and that fight is to protect the Constitution of the United States of America with our lives, if need be. President Kennedy, having been the chief executive of that Constitution, deserved all the loyalty given as a soldier would give for his country.

"To stand in silence when they should be protesting makes cowards out of men."

Abraham Lincoln

DIABOLICAL PLOT TO SILENCE MR. BOLDEN WHEN HE FOUGHT TO TELL THE TRUTH ABOUT THE ASSASSINATION

Holland: Sir, let's talk about the Warren Commission now. Did they ever contact you at all?

The Warren Commission was set up in 1964 by the government to investigate the JFK assassination.

Bolden: The Warren Commission never contacted me. I was only contacted by an official of the United States government after I was released from prison. I believe it was in 1979 when the Congress took up their investigation of the assassination. (The House Select Committee Assassinations)

Holland: I know you made an effort to contact the Warren Commission yourself, sir. I was wondering if we could talk about that and what led to your arrest just after that?

Bolden: I had told a couple of agents that the first chance I could get to go to Washington DC, I wanted to testify. The Warren Commission was sitting at that particular time. They were handling all the testimony. But according to what I was reading in the newspaper, they weren't handling anything concerning the investigations that we had investigated of live and growing programs and conspiracy to assassinate the president. I didn't hear some of the names that I knew had been associated with such conspiracies.

So, I wanted to go and to watch it in DC and contact J Lee Rankin, who was the counsel on the Warren Commission. I had an opportunity when I went to Washington DC on May 17th, 1964 to a Secret Service school. I was there actually to go to school. But the night that I arrived there, I tried to contact J Lee Rankin through the White House switchboard.

Now there was an agent with me, an Agent Gary McCloud, and he walked into the telephone booth next to mine, and, since I never heard the money drop - it was the old type telephone, and you could hear the ding-a-ling. Since I didn't hear that, I knew that he was listening to what I was trying to do and, as a matter of fact, I had to abort that call and try to set up some other means to try and contact J Lee Rankin, who was the counsel.

Now, immediately the next day before noon, the Secret Service went to my hotel room in the Willett Hotel, they packed up all of my clothes. I didn't know anything about this. They were going through my room, they packed up everything, threw it in my suitcase and everything.

In the meantime, Mr. Howard Anderson, who was the Secret Service personnel director, came over to the Secret Service school that was being held in the Treasury Building, and said that I was "needed" back in Chicago because they had seized a counterfeiting ring in Villa Park in Illinois which is a little suburb of Chicago.

I flew back with an Inspector McCain and McCloud, who was an agent going to school with me. I was met by several agents at O'Hare Airport, and they drove me into Chicago to the Secret Service office - all the time saying that they had discovered this "big counterfeiting plant" that's in Villa Park, and they needed my expertise as an agent in order to bring it to a close.

So, I came here (Chicago) and they sent me to the United States attorney's Office, and, to be frank with you, they had me snookered. I mean, I thought this thing was really an investigation. I didn't know what they had in store for me. But I sat there for about six hours. They didn't let me eat anything, talk to anybody for fear that they were telling me that one of the suspects might be in the building and recognize me and blah, blah, blah. They had a big pretext going.

The Evil Men Do

Bolden: About six hours later, Mr. Martinau, who was the supervisor here in Chicago, walked into the room and said, "We're going to charge you with soliciting a bribe." I almost hit the floor. I said, "What!? You know that's ridiculous!" And he looks me right in the eye with a little smile on his face. He says, "You prove it." Now, it's very difficult to prove a negative, especially when all of the records and things are in the hands of the person who is trying to send you away; you just can't do it.

And he was behind it. Mr. Martinau was behind the frame-up. Now whether or not he had the orders to do it from James Rowley, who was then the chief of the United States Secret Service– I believe that he was acting on the chief's orders, that was to silence me, to quiet me any way possible. I finally realized that they arrested me that night, on the 18th, locked me up on the "word" of two counterfeiters. These were men who had made a career out of criminal activity.

One of them, Joseph Spagnoli, had been arrested some 50 times! And Frank Jones had been arrested by me, as a matter of fact. He was awaiting trial for various convictions of which he would have gone to the penitentiary for the rest of his life. And these are the men that they put on me; I was supposed to have given one some "document" to give to the other one for $50,000 and it was ridiculous.

Kangaroo Trial In The United States Of America: Judge Tells Jurors Bolden Is Guilty And Expects Them To Return with A "Guilty Verdict"

Bolden: I would do two trials, and a strange thing happened in the first trial. The Federal District Judge, the Honorable Joseph Samuel Perry (1896 – 1984), called the jury out while they were deliberating as to what the verdict should be, after the evidence had been presented.

The judge called the jury out and said: "In my opinion the defendant is guilty of counts one, two and three of the indictment." And he tells the jurors, "Now go ahead and deliberate on the instructions that I just gave you."

In other words, he wanted them to deliberate on me being guilty above any other claim. Now, our Constitution is against that; the jury's supposed to make the decision. And when the judge did that, he in fact became a juror because he had voted and asked them to vote with him. Well, they didn't. It ended up in a hung jury.

I went to trial for a second time about a week and a half later. The judge scheduled a second trial. Now, during this trial the judge, knowing what happened during the first trial (a hung jury), about 5:30 that evening on August 12th, 1964, is when I went on trial on 64CR324.

Holland: Yes, sir.

Bolden: When the jury was deliberating, what he did was put me, my attorney and all spectators out of the building, He locked us out of the building - asked the guard to put the chains on the doors and the whole building was emptied.

And all the people who were in there were: the jury, the Secret Service agents, FBI agents, CIA representative, the jury and the judge.

The judge had said he was going home for the day and he was going to shut down the court. But, on the way home, I heard that the jury had just reached a verdict and I knew that it had to be guilty under the circumstances. They summoned me on September 4th, 1964 to a term of six years in the custody of a federal prison.

WITNESS ADMITS HE WAS FORCED TO LIE AGAINST BOLDEN BY UNITED STATES ATTORNEY, RICHARD SYKES

Holland: When did Spagnoli come forward and tell everybody that he was indeed perjuring himself and was lying?

Bolden: He did, yes, on January 20th, 1965. I turned 30 on January 19th and I really needed a miracle. My wife and I had done a little birthday party that we had here. We were just talking about the case. I really needed something to happen, because I knew that they were really out to send me away to the penitentiary and do some other things.

And, lo and behold, my attorney called me on the 20th, January 1965 and said that Spagnoli had just admitted perjury in your trial. I couldn't believe it. What possessed this man to come out like this?

Of course that helped me quite a bit and we got a court directive of Spagnoli's admission that he had committed perjury, and he further said that he had committed this perjury at the instigation of the United States attorney. He named the United States attorney, Richard Sykes and not only did he name him, he had a piece of paper that this attorney had given him to remember his testimony, what he was to testify to."

Holland: Sir, was there any criminal action taken against those gentlemen?

Bolden: Not any whatsoever! Not any! Not even an admonishment - not even an indictment; nothing happened. And when my attorney appealed the case before the Seventh Circuit Court of Appeals in Chicago, the chief judge of the Circuit Court of Appeals called this attorney, Richard Sykes, before them and questioned him.

He wanted to know if he solicited perjured testimony in my trial. The United States attorney took the fifth amendment and he said: "If I answer that question, I cannot answer it because of the chance it'll incriminate me." And do you know, they still affirmed the conviction and sent me away to prison for six years!?

Holland: And there was no recourse at all? Did the attorney general's office of the United States– I know Bobby was an attorney general at that point, did they try–?

Bolden: No, nothing.

Holland: Did he try to intervene on your behalf at all?

Bolden: No, he didn't - he didn't. Nobody tried to intervene on my behalf. And when I had written letters to about everybody that I knew who should– I wrote to many of the Senate, Senator Long from Missouri, who was in the Judiciary Committee at that particular time– I wrote to those people trying to get "someone" interested to stop this disregard of the court proceedings that I had just went through. (the obvious illegally solicited testimony of Spagnoli by a US attorney to falsely incriminate Mr. Bolden)

Because I knew that once the government got me in custody, they were not only going to imprison me, but they were going to take some very dreadful acts against me in order to assure that I'll not be available to say anything.

Holland: Let's talk about some of those dreadful acts.

HELL

"What the government does is, they try to put you in a position where the American people won't believe anything that you say. That affects your credibility in a negative way.

They could not kill me outright because there was just too much information, too much pressure on the case. It was widely publicized. So the second best thing that the government does, the second avenue that they take, is to declare a person insane."

Abraham Bolden

Bolden: And so, that was what I knew that I had to guard against. Once they hang that tag on you, then you're not believable. Like, if I were talking to you right now and had once been declared insane, nobody would believe anything that I said. So, this is where they wanted me. And they proceeded to try to do just that when I went to Springfield, Missouri. They put me in a psychiatric ward and forced me to take psychotropic drugs.

Holland: How did you manage to keep your spirits up, sir, and your sanity?

Bolden: The first thing that I had to do was keep those psychotropic drugs out of my system. So, I had to devise a way that I could take those drugs and remove them from my system. And I did that. I explained it, properly elaborated, in the book ("The Echo From Dealey Plaza" by Abraham Bolden).

There were certain procedures that I did in order to make sure that these drugs did not take a hold on me. Because I knew that the government– if they want to destroy your mind, they start out with the mild sedatives. Then they get stronger and stronger, the longer that you're there, until they put you in the condition that you don't know where you are, and what it's all about. Then you're in their custody for the rest of your life.

So, what happened is that after I had devised this plan - I had done my time, about 50%. Now they still wanted to continue on and try to declare me insane. And I think that they were somewhat puzzled why those drugs were not taking an effect on me.

So while I was in that psychiatric ward, which they threw me in– see they can throw you in now for 30 days in order to evaluate, and that's the way they take credibility. But, they're not supposed to give you any medication except ordered by the court. They violated that rule when it came to me.

So, they scheduled me for an insanity hearing. That is, the Chief of Classification & Parole put me on the list for insanity hearing which was to take place on or about August 7th 1967. The Chief of Classification & Parole, he was going to be the one who was going to sign the paper declaring that I was insane.

Now, it just so happens that a certain thing happened to him where he could not be there when I appeared before the board and they sent me right back to the ward, because he himself committed suicide! That's the person who was saying that he was going to declare me insane, he himself committed suicide the day before that I was supposed to appear before the committee.

It was impossible for them to go on with any procedure without the Chief of Classification & Parole there. He was the one who had to sign the document verifying that I had indeed been found insane. They were going to change my number to a psychiatric number and hold me for the rest of my life.

Holland: Do you feel that may have anything to do with your case, sir?

Bolden: His suicide?

Holland: Yes, sir.

Bolden: I think that what happened is– see there's a higher law than the law of man. There is also a "law of God," and I'm a firm believer in that.

"Look at how a single candle can both defy and define the darkness."

Anne Frank

Bolden: I had a lot of faith. As a young man, I was very religious, and I'm very religious now. I think that it was a retributive "act of grace" from God, and that's what saved me.

Holland: It's very emotional when I interview Mr. Bolden because he is very authentic. When you were down in the pits, sir, I know there were several things that took place, an "active" intervention, a fire specifically.

Bolden: Well, I was at 21 East. All of the inmates at Springfield, Missouri– that's a Medical Center in Springfield, Missouri– they have a "name" for this place, and they called it a tomb. That's where I was in that 21 East site– their "active division," there for the worst of criminals, people who have murdered and have done all sorts of treacherous things. Most of them are incurably insane or have been made so by the government as being incurably insane. There was a lot of screaming at night, a lot of hollering and cursing that was going on back there. It's just a madhouse, so they called it a "tomb."

And when they put me there, on my tenth day there, I remember this just as clearly as I can, it was about the 16th of July, and I had this "vision." That was a vision where I believe it was a holy angel from

God. It couldn't have been anybody but a holy angel from God, and I do believe in angels of God.

But "he" or "she" came to me in my room in a vision, a light, and told me not to worry, that I would be free from that steel door that they had me in and had me locked up. Ten days they had me in there without any clothes. I didn't have any clothes or shoes or shoelaces or anything like that. They hadn't let me bathe or come out of that room for 10 whole days. I couldn't turn the light on or off. They'd be set from the outside They flushed the toilet from the outside.

And so there I was. When I saw this vision, it told me not to fear, and that God had heard me, that God was with me.

The very next morning, there wasn't even eight hours between the vision and daylight, I heard the fire bells ringing in the ward. They were ringing loud, and the guards were running back and forth past my room.

I knew that something was going on because I could smell the smoke and I heard one guard holler to another one that there was a fire in one of the cells down near the end of the hall.

This guard who was still on his way there said it can't be. He said we don't have anybody in there. It's been vacant. And he says, "well, the room is burning." Everything in there was burning, the mattress and everything was on fire, and they couldn't figure out how that could be with nobody in there.

It made it necessary for them to come to my cell, and for the first time in those 10 days, the guard turned that key, and I walked out from behind that three-inch thick steel door, and to like it was almost like making parole.

Even though I was just walking into another lobby area of that ward, it was being outside was just like freedom.

And I tell you, nobody can tell you, can really explain to you how it feels to be alone with nothing but your thoughts and the lights being turned out at seven o'clock. Nobody talks to you except those who want to give you some medication or the psychiatrist come by and talk to you through the door– and the guards push you blankets and things in through a little slot in the door. It just was horrible, it was horrible, Brother Holland– and I wonder sometimes how I endured it.

After I came out of that situation, I sat across from one inmate that I had witnessed myself. He stabbed another inmate on the elevator that I was on, stabbed him to death, cut his guts out. I witnessed this and here I am, they put this inmate– his first name was James– I won't say his last name– but here this guy came over and sat down, and we had a conversation about that day that he killed another inmate. You can imagine how I felt at first when I recognized this guy, and I was in there with him.

Of course, I was on my guard, and the silverware that we were eating with, I wasn't afraid that he could do anything with that, because most of it was plastic or cardboard. But, we had a conversation and I tell you, I wouldn't take anything for that experience. It was a great experience for me. It was a learning experience too. And I came out of it, and for the rest of mankind, I believe I have something to contribute to mankind.

The First African American Pinkerton Detective

Bolden: But, I always loved law enforcement. I was enthused with it because we had a couple of men in the Navy; one was a guy they called Leo "Fats" Goodman and he was a deputy sherriff and a real nice guy. He weighed about 450lbs. But everybody loved Leo.

And there we had Lucius Hogan. Now, these people stayed about a block away from me and they were like part of the neighborhood mentors. You know, when the children would get in trouble sometimes, the parents would go and get one of them and say, you talk to this boy, you know. They were like policemen - very well respected and I admired them so much and they impressed me. I really wanted to be in law enforcement and that's the choice I made. Now I could have stayed in music.

After I graduated (BA in Music Composition) they offered me a job in Southeast Missouri where I had met my "Waterloo," so to speak, and I was supposed to report down there for choir director. (Mr. Bolden suffered a debilitating injury to his lip from an unexpected fall and was unable to continue to play trumpet at the level he was accustomed to afterwards). A job came through at Pinkerton National Detective Agency; I accepted that rather than go and accept the music job.

Holland: And you were the first African-American at the Pinkertons also, weren't you?

Bolden: Yes, isn't that something? You know I didn't know that. I had no idea and my wife happened to see this Pinkerton job in the St Louis Post Dispatch newspaper one Sunday. She was reading it, and at that time I was considering going down to Southeast Missouri. She says: "Well here's a policeman's job. You were talking about you might apply for a police job." She said, "Pinkerton is looking for agents for their detective agency."

I told her, "You know, Pinkerton's got a 'reputation', they don't hire no Negro agents, you know." She says, "Well you never know." She says, "Take this clipping out of there," and she cut the clipping out. She said, "You want to go over there in the morning and apply for the job?" I said, "Oh, okay…But I tell you now, they're not going to hire me, you know." So I put this clipping up in the lapel pocket of my Sears & Roebuck suit. I had a nice Sears & Roebuck suit that cost me $39.95 with two pairs of pants. Man, and I was sharp too. [both laugh]

I went up to Pinkerton National Detective Agency on the 12th floor at 705 Olive Street in St Louis, Missouri, and I walked in the office and I saw a young lady who was sitting there typing. I said: "I came to see about the Pinkerton Investigator job that you have open." And she looked at me and she says: "We don't have anything "open." And I said: "Yes you do." And I gave her this clipping that my wife had cut out of the paper and it said clearly that they were looking for an investigator.

Abraham Bolden: "And she looked at me and said, "We're not hiring people like you" - Well, back then, in those days, I knew exactly what she meant; she didn't have to elaborate and I wasn't going to give her any trouble, you know, and this was in 1956. I wasn't going to give her any trouble."

And, as I turned around getting ready to walk out of the office, this tall, sandy-haired European walked out and he asked the secretary, "So what's the problem"? And she said, "He came looking for a job and I told him we don't have "anything" open." And he looked at her and says, "Yes we do." And he told her, "So give him an application and have him fill it out and then come and talk to me."

So I filled out the application and I found out that this was the business director of Pinkerton. And I filled out the application. He looked it over and he asked me about my music career and everything and I told him what had happened, and he says, "Well, we'll give you a background check that'll take about two weeks."

And they called me up and told me to report to Pinkerton and I went over there and he says, "Well, Mr. Bolden, I'm going to give you a chance." He says, "Do the best you can because we don't have any Negro Investigators in Pinkerton, but you being the first one, I'll be expecting a lot from you now." I thought I won't let you down, Mr. Mertz, that's right.

And he gave me the job, gave me my badge and my star and everything and I became a Pinkerton detective. Man, was I happy [laughs]. I couldn't wait to go tell Leo Goodman and Lucius about it. I showed them my little silver badge and everything that they gave me. I felt real good about that.

Abraham Bolden: "At that particular time, being the first African-American wasn't very significant to me, you know. I didn't go over there and say I'm the first Black man and all this kind of stuff. I mean I realized that it was a milestone but I'm more proud of it now than I was then."

"Meet the "Jackie Robinson" Of The Secret Service" JFK introducing Abraham Bolden

> Holland: Let's talk about what President Kennedy said to Pierre Salinger sir.
>
> Bolden: Oh, isn't that something, yes. I was standing in front of the president's office on detail, on post in Washington DC, and the Cabinet was coming out of a meeting that they just held. And I happened to be standing right outside the president's door and when Senator Barry Goldwater came out through the president's office door, and they left it open. I reached in to close the door. President Kennedy was standing in the office and he was talking to his brother, Robert Kennedy.
>
> He looked up and saw me, and he came rushing over with his hands extending and he said, "Mr. Bolden, I see you made it here!" I was startled. You know, he remembered my name. He came, and he smiled from ear to ear and everything. He called his brother over and told him "I want you to meet Mr. Bolden, he's with the Secret Service, the first Negro."
>
> He said the same thing to Senator Barry Goldwater and here come Pierre Salinger (press secretary to President Kennedy). And he says, Pierre, come over here, I want to introduce you to somebody. Pierre came over, and President John Kennedy says, "I want you to meet Abraham Bolden, he's the Jackie Robinson of the Secret Service."

And I tell you, I almost burst into tears, to be equated with the icon like Jackie Robinson. I mean, I felt so good. I felt like the president was really telegraphing to me the fact that I would have to do like Jackie Robinson did, that he realized that what I was coming into, in being a pioneer, that everything was not going to be, you know, pie and sweetness. He realized that.

And so I think by equating me with Jackie Robinson, that was the message that he was really relaying to me, rather than Pierre Salinger so much.

Holland: Sir, you have achieved that and so much more. Let's stay on some happy times. Your first time on Air Force One?

Bolden: Oh, wonderful! And I'm sure that President Kennedy was the person that put me there, because we were leaving Hyannis Port on July 5th after celebrating the 4th of July down there, and this same supervisor who had told me that I was nothing but a "nigger," he told me that I was assigned to the president's Air Force One. Now, I knew that he would never put– not Harvey, he would never put me on Air Force One unless it was all inside of one of the jets, you know. [both laugh heartily]

Really, he would put me under one of the wheels maybe, but not inside. Anyway, I'm sitting on Air Force One, and I'm really looking at how it's laid out, all the equipment it has on it, and the president came out of his cabin as I sat there near the front of the plane, and he nodded to me, you know, and I nodded back at him.

I said, man, this is really something, being historical like this. Plus, I rode on the helicopter to get on Air Force One. I was about, I would say, let's see, oh, maybe six inches from the president. He was sitting and our knees were almost touching, and I was sitting right across from him, and I was looking right in his eyes, and he was looking, you know–

At one time I started to mention to him some of the problems that I had had, but I decided that would really be out of the way, because here is a man who's got Vietnam on his mind. He's got all of these problems of Russia and Khrushchev at him. Now I come up and say "somebody called me a..." I regard as highly insignificant. I felt that it best to handle that through the Secret Service normal chain of command, hoping that they would take some type of action, but they didn't.

PROTECTING JACQUELINE & CAROLINE KENNEDY

Bolden: Jacqueline Kennedy came out, and she had on a bathing suit, and she had a towel draped around her shoulder, and little Caroline was with her. She had Caroline by the hand, and I was sitting at a table, and it had an umbrella over it and two chairs, which were one of the Secret Service posts near the beach.

She walked up to me and says, "Mr. Bolden, would you watch Caroline while I take a swim?" I says, "Sure, Mrs. Kennedy." And she went off, down by the water. Caroline kept looking at me, and she kept looking at me, and finally she says, "What's your name?" [Laughs] I told her "Abraham." And she says, "Abraham?" And I said, "Yeah, like Abraham Lincoln." And she said, "Oh."

And then, with a little sand cup she had, she was putting sand in it with a little spoon, and she stopped and sat at the table across from me, looking inquisitive, and she says, "Do you have a daughter?" I said, "Yes, I do, and her name's Ahiva." She says, "Can I play with her?" I said, "Sure you can." I said, "But she's in Chicago and you're here." And she says, "I can go to Chicago."

She was so sweet. She was such a sweet little girl. And then Jacqueline came back and I heard her say to Jacqueline, as we were walking back up towards the main house, "Mummy, can we go to Chicago?" I thought that was so cute, that was so cute. She had on a little pink sand suit on.

Holland: That's beautiful.

Bolden: I don't know if she remembers that, yeah. Oh, I was very happy about that, and I wrote a letter to my wife and told her that Caroline Kennedy wanted to play with Ahvia. They're about the same age, you know. And, you know, it was just wonderful.

JFK AND BOBBY MAKE PROMISE TO BOLDEN; IT IS UN-KEPT;

Bolden: The Kennedys treated me so "royally." I talked to Bobby Kennedy while I was there in Hainesport, and he wanted to know why I didn't make an application for the FBI. I told him that I didn't think I was qualified because I was not even a lawyer nor an accountant. And he says, "Oh, those types of things could be waived, you know."

Yeah, he told me to look into it when I got back to Chicago. But, in the meantime, the president joined the conversation and asked me if I intended to make a career out of the Secret Service. And I told him that not really; I really wanted to be a Diplomat or something like that to one of the African nations. And he asked me if I spoke any of the African dialects. I told him no.

"Well, I tell you what, Mr. Bolden," he says, "you go to Berlitz Language School there in Chicago, I think they've got one in Chicago, or just outside of Chicago, and learn to speak one of those languages, and who knows. Before I leave office I might help you fulfill that dream." And I told him, "Thank you, Mr. President." And I'm telling you, I mean he was serious about this and so was I. So was I.

Holland: Do you still have that aspiration, sir, to become, indeed, a Diplomat?

Bolden: Well, I can't now because of the felony conviction. What I would like to see happen is that the current president, Barack Obama, if somehow or another they totally investigate this case, because there's much evidence of my innocence in the Secret Service files.

I know there would have to be, because I never committed any of the crimes. Now, I would hope that they would declare that my conviction was unlawful, reinstate me to the Secret Service and then let me resign.

See now, that's the way I would like to see it go, but the chances of that happening I think are slim to none, by as much as me meeting the president at McCormick Place [laughs]. So there is a slight possibility, see, because a pardon is one thing, but they want you to say that you committed a crime, and that you're asking a president to pardon you. Something like that. No, well, I might accept it but I would never say that I did something that I didn't do.

Holland: Is there anybody folks can write to?

Bolden: Yes, they can write to me at www.echofromdealeyplaza.net.

TRIUMPH AGAINST THE STORM

In a very real sense Mr. Bolden gave his life for President Kennedy and is haunted to this day by the assassination. He upheld the Constitution of the

United States with dignity and honor. He was railroaded by a corrupt justice system and triumphed. He is a role model for the ages.

> Holland: Is there anything, sir, that you would like to leave the people with?
>
> Bolden: Well, what I would like to leave the people with is this: when trouble occurs, when such things happen like this, assassination of presidents or leaders, heads of state, Dr. Martin Luther King, Malcolm X, whoever it is, we have to stand up and be alert, we who want to stand for democracy, we that want to stand for equality and justice.
>
> We can't just stand up when things just affect us alone. We have to stand up wherever we find corruption in a democratic process. And that's our obligation to American people, it's our obligation to our children, and it's our obligation to God, to be the best people that we can be while we're on this planet Earth.

Abraham Bolden is a Great Man and a True American Hero. A petition has been started to bring justice for Mr. Bolden at the web address below. Or simply Google: Abraham Bolden Petition.

---

www.petitionspot.com/petitions/abrahamwbolden/

CHAPTER 11

JFK: Oliver Stone's Hollywood Feature Film

In 1991, a Hollywood feature film was released that was so controversial it caused the United States Government to alter its policy on national security and release never-before-seen files, whose contents were so explosive that they were supposed to be kept under lock and key until 2033.

The Academy Award winning film "JFK" is quite simply Hollywood director Oliver Stone's cinematic masterpiece. Stone was driven to make this film, not only to satisfy his artistic prowess but also his passion for truth. "JFK" brought to light all the lore, all the myths, all the rumors surrounding the JFK assassination, and placed them in plain sight for the world.

There was such an outcry by the public after viewing "JFK" that the Clinton administration created the Assassination Records Review Board (ARRB). It was set up as an independent agency to re-examine for release the assassination-related records that federal agencies still regarded as too sensitive to open to the public. The Board finished its work on September 30, 1998, issued a report and transferred all of its records to the National Archives and Records Administration.

In this chapter I am going to introduce you to three of the best researchers connected with the JFK assassination; all were primary consultants to Oliver Stone's film "JFK."

- Jim Marrs
- Robert Groden
- Jim DiEugenio

We are going to go step by step through the scenes in JFK, all the tidbits that you may not be aware of.

Jim Marrs Author of "Crossfire," The Book Oliver Stone Turned Into "JFK"

Jim Marrs is simply the "Chairman of the Board" when it comes to assassination researchers. With his signature white beard, dark glasses and hat, he resembles an archeologist who just came in from the Sahara. And in true Jim Marrs fashion, he would be immaculate, not a speck of dirt. Perhaps the archeologist analogy is fitting. Jim has certainly been digging up information about the assassination in some of the most unexpected places. He has brought history to the public.

> Marrs: The thing started for me that very afternoon because – this is going to be amazing to young people today – but at the time of the Kennedy assassination every radio station, every TV station was broadcasting it – that's all they talked about.
>
> On 9/11, I remember you could kick over to the Cartoon Channel and you could watch cartoons – you didn't have to watch was happening on 9/11. But on that weekend if you turned on any media, newspapers, radio, TV, it was nothing but filled with the assassination information.
>
> They had people on there who had been witnesses in Dealey Plaza – and since then I've talked to maybe a hundred people or more who were there at the time, including former House Speaker Jim Wright who was a friend of mine, and they all said the same thing: They said there was a shot – a pause – two shots right on top of each other – a bang, bang-bang.
>
> Well even at that time I'm a Texas boy, I've been deer hunting, I even had some bolt-action rifles and I knew you don't get a bang-bang with a bolt-action rifle. You have to cock the bolt – you have to regain your

sight picture – you've got to pull the trigger – cock the bolt again, it goes bang: schick-schick-schick-schick-schick, bang. That's the best you can get. And so, at that time I thought, well, that's odd, how do you get a bang-bang if there's only one guy shooting a bolt-action rifle?

But then Sunday came and I'm sitting there watching television – and while they're going to transfer Oswald – and Jack Ruby steps out in the basement of the Police Station – with all these cops standing around – and Oswald handcuffed, spread-eagle with his hands out on both sides to these cops – and shoots him in the gut. You know and I'm going wait a minute. And then they tried to say that Jack Ruby didn't have any connection to anybody – that was at the time – but I knew better then, because I was in a fraternity in the university and I had been told by my older fraternity brothers – I'm not a big gambler I didn't really pay much attention but I'm listening and they said to me and others ,"If you want to get in a high stakes poker game go to Dallas and look up Jack Ruby," he said, "but be careful he's connected to the Underworld." (In those days "Underworld" was also used for criminal activity, Mafia, black market types of things.)

Now, I was a journalism student and I was a little bit more up on things. So right off the bat I knew something was wrong – fishy about this shooting – because you can't get a bang-bang from a bolt-action rifle. How does one lone nut get in the basement of the police station and shoot another lone nut? Why are they telling us that Jack Ruby is not connected to anybody when everybody I know, even my fraternity brothers, said he's connected to Organized Crime or the Underworld. I began to accumulate newspapers including the Campus paper, the Dallas papers, Forth Worth papers – I've still got all those original papers.

When the Warren Commission report came out – like an idiot – I was one of the few people that actually read it. [There were 26 thick books, each one being a volume of the report.] I started going through them and what I found out real fast was that the report would say one thing but when I'd go back in the volumes and check the testimony and check the documents, sometimes it was the exact opposite of what they said in the report. So I was real fishy about the report too.

How Oliver Stone Got Hold Of "Crossfire"

Holland: The book of course was "Crossfire." This was the book that was handed it to Oliver Stone in an elevator.

Marrs: That fellow had been a CIA Station Chief. It was John Stockwell. He had already been hired by Oliver Stone to help him research all of the information about the assassination, and when John Stockwell read my book "Crossfire," he took it to Oliver Stone, saying "Hey, everything you need is right in here."

JIM MARRS' "JFK" BEHIND THE SCENES STORIES

Holland: Jim actually worked as a consultant for Oliver Stone on the movie "JFK." Do you have any stories to tell us about meeting Oliver?

Marrs: Oh, we could spend the whole time talking about some of the stories – but, I will tell you a little "vignette" that I personally witnessed that blew me away and I don't think anybody has ever talked about it – in fact I don't think Oliver Stone really talked about this – although I remember reading one interview where he made some kind of oblique mention.

They were filming in Dealey Plaza – there in Dallas – and they were shooting some scenes inside the old School Book Depository. But now the School Book Depository, which is now on the sixth floor of the Sixth Floor Museum, which says that they're not taking any particular position on what really happened to Kennedy, but they've got that corner Plexiglased off so you can't get to that window and look out and see for yourself that there's no line of sight into the street and they've got the boxes all piled up – and you know about the only thing they don't have is a big neon sign saying "here's the sniper's nest" [laughter]

They [Sixth Floor Museum] would not allow Oliver Stone to shoot from that window – which I found kind of interesting because all he wanted was just a couple of minutes to shoot [a camera] through that window that everybody to this day "officially" says that was the window that Oswald was shooting from. And I'm thinking – well, you know, what's the deal!? Why won't they let him shoot through that window?

And of course, the problem was, that if you actually see the fact that the window is only less than a foot off the floor and that the window was only partially open – about a quarter of a way – and there's two two-inch pipes to the left of the window – it makes it a very awkward shooting position. And then there's a tree right in the line of sight – to the middle of the street – and maybe somebody just didn't want the public to see that. So, they made Oliver Stone go to the seventh floor and shoot out of the eastern most seventh floor window.

So, they had been shooting that morning, running the motorcade, and there was just hundreds of extras, all these people as the crowd, and they had been lining the street just like the crowd did on November the 22nd, and curving all around the intersection there at Houston and Elm Street.

They called a break and it was, as I recall, it was pretty warm that day and a lot of people didn't want to be standing there on the hot asphalt in the middle of the street. So they had all moved over and it was a huge knot of people, these extras, standing there right on the corner of Elm Street, right directly beneath the sixth floor and the seventh floor window.

And I was across the street kind of watching all this happening and I looked up – because I saw a movement in the window and they were up there trying, I guess to get their camera in position or whatever – and there's a huge plate glass window with no barriers – just one big plate glass window – and I'm not sure what happened – but apparently somebody leaned against the window or a ladder or a boom moved against the window and the entire big piece of plate glass popped out of that window!

And all of this is racing through my mind as it happened! It only took a few split seconds – but I'm going "Oh my god! That's going to fall down right in the middle of that knot of people and you know the casualties could be extreme." And this window is sailing down and then it caught a gust of wind and being a flat plane, it just kind of swayed over to the side and crashed into the empty middle of the street and shattered into a gazillion pieces.

Everybody, of course, just was shocked and they stood there and they looked – but nobody had been standing there – and it was just a bunch of glass lying in the street. Quickly some people came out and they were sweeping up all the glass and everything just kind of went on. But I'm sitting there thinking that's almost a sign that somebody bigger than us is watching over this production.

Holland: Divine intervention I was just thinking actually.

ROBERT GRODEN PRINCIPAL CONSULTANT TO OLIVER STONE FOR JFK

Robert Groden has dedicated his life to researching the JFK assassination in order to bring justice to those who really murdered President Kennedy on November 22, 1963. He made a solemn oath at President Kennedy's graveside in Arlington Cemetery and he has never faltered from it. Robert Groden is a noble, honorable man and was most gracious to come on Night Fright and speak with us.

The Zapruder film is the most famous 8mm home movie of all time; it was filmed by a fellow by the name of Abraham Zapruder. Robert was the first person to bring the Zapruder film to national TV in 1975, on "Good Night America with Geraldo Rivera." Robert helped bring about the "House Select Committee on Assassinations." Robert was appointed as Staff Photographic Consultant and is considered the primary expert for all photos and films pertaining to the JFK assassination. Robert was also senior advisor for the documentary series "The Men Who Killed Kennedy."

Holland: Let's dive in right away: Can you tell us how you got involved with Oliver Stone and "JFK"?

Groden: Well, Oliver was planning on doing the movie, "JFK" about a year before we actually started shooting, and he had called a lot of people for advice on the film and setting of the production, and every time he would call somebody, they would say, "Have you spoken to Robert Groden yet"? So he finally did; he called me up about a year before the assassination scenes were to be shot in Dealey Plaza.

So Ollie invited me down to Dallas and we spent a lot of time – went around to all the buildings, all the scenes relating to the case – and then he asked me if I would be involved in the making of the movie and I agreed. And he flew me down a few months before we actually started shooting and the rest is history.

We actually set up all the scenes – the art directors put the actual places back into the same condition they were at the time of the assassination and the accuracy was uncanny… just unbelievable.

DEALEY PLAZA EXPLAINED

Holland: Robert, can you take us into Dealey Plaza? Can you tell us the official Warren Report scenario; where the shots came from, where they originated from?

Groden: Dealey Plaza is a park-like area in downtown Dallas. It's been called the "Gateway to the West." It's one block by two blocks; on the eastern end is Houston Street, on the western end is the triple road underpass. On the southern end is Commerce Street, and on the north is Elm Street. Elm Street is where the assassination took place. I refer to that as the original "nightmare" on Elm Street.

The corner of Elm and Houston is where a building is located called the "Texas School Book Depository" – that building has been there for quite some time. There was a fire there – I think around 1917 and they rebuilt the building. It was originally six storeys, now it's seven.

Dealey Plaza – that's D E A L E Y – was named after George Bannerman Dealey; he was the first editor of "The Dallas Morning News," the newspaper. And he owned all the property that Dealey Plaza is now. He gave it to the city as a gift and when they built the Plaza, the park-like area there, they named it after him.

Assassination Shots

Groden: At the time of the assassination – during the entire event – the president's car was on Elm Street and it was heading from east to west and a series of shots rang out. Nobody knows how many, to this very day.

The actual audio recording of the shot that was made by the Dallas Police Department (please see "Chapter 7 Frontal Shot 21st Century CSI & JFK For Real / Dictabelt sound recording evidence") – quite by accident – shows a potential of fifteen shots being fired: the four shots that hit the president, the three that hit Governor Connally and all the others that missed.

Holland: Can we talk about those shots right now and how many you feel hit the car, and caused wounds, etc, etc. Because we know the official report from the Warren Commission says only three shots, and we all know that that's a load of bunk by this time.

Groden: Well, you're being kind... I refer to it as BS, but in fact nobody really knows how many shots were fired. The president was hit four times:

1. He was hit in the right, in the throat;

2. He was hit in the back, six inches below the shoulder line;

3. JFK was hit in the right temporal area – that's the shot that killed him –

4. Then he was hit a second time in the head, just above the hairline. During the middle of all these shots, Governor Connally was hit three times:

5. He was hit in the right shoulder by the armpit;

6. He was hit in the right wrist and

7. He was hit in the left thigh.

That's a total of seven shots between the two men, and that doesn't count all the shots that missed.

8. One of the shots that missed hit a curb and bystander named James Tague on his cheek.

9. A bullet struck the chrome over the windshield in the president's car.

10. Another one hit the windshield itself.

11. One hit the sidewalk on the north side of Elm Street.

12. Another one hit a small section of cement around a storm drain on the south side of Elm Street.

13. Another one hit the street much farther up to the east, and so on, and so on.

If you count them all together, there is certainly between 12 and 15 shots fired.

Now, because of the timeframe of the shooting – thanks to the Zapruder film – the maximum that could be fired by that weapon (The bolt action Mannlicher Carcano rifle said to be the sniper rifle) – given its restrictions for firing times – the maximum is three.

But we have so many more, that – and even the Government now has – for instance – 1978, has admitted at least a fourth shot. (Bob is referring to the House Select Committee on Assassinations which he was Staff Photographic Expert, their conclusion was 4 shots *not* 3 in Dealey Plaza and that JFK was probably assassinated by a conspiracy.)

So given that it's impossible for the weapon that was allegedly "found" on the sixth floor of the Depository, to be the sole weapon used in this crime.

Holland: Robert, do you feel like Governor Connally was a legitimate target in that car as well, or do you think he was just collateral damage, for lack of a better term?

Groden: You know, you ask a question that not enough people have actually asked; it's always been assumed that Governor Connally was hit by accident. I don't believe so. It is possible, but the reason for Governor Connally being hit might be to link Oswald to the crime.

Lee Oswald had nothing against President Kennedy – nothing; he admired him. But when Oswald was in the Soviet Union – he was on a mission – we had sent him there – he had worked for the Central Intelligence Agency (CIA) and he was sent to the Soviet Union on a mission. And while he was there, he wrote to the Secretary of the Navy and asked him to upgrade his "Dishonorable Discharge" (from the Marines) to an "Honorable Discharge."

The Secretary of the Navy wrote back and said well, "I am no longer the Secretary of the Navy and I can't help you." Well, the Secretary of the Navy had *been* John Connally.

So, if Governor Connally was hit on purpose, it would have been to link Oswald to this crime, because with President Kennedy there is no link.

How The Zapruder Film Was Broadcast on "Good Night America with Geraldo Rivera"

Groden: I started collecting everything written on it (the JFK assassination) and within a couple of years, I had amassed a massive collection of photographic evidence relating to the Kennedy case. And this was at a time when nobody really cared too much about the photographic evidence, so I had the field pretty much open to myself.

At the time there were only two other people that I'm aware of, that were involved in the photographic evidence: one was a man from Hartsdale, New York, named Richard Sprague (JFK researcher), and the other was Harold Weisberg (legendary JFK researcher and pioneer). So I started to correspond with some of the other people that were interested in this and within a short period of time, we had developed a lot of evidence.

In the mid-1960s… the late 1960s – I had started working for a company in New York and we were given the original Zapruder film by "Life" magazine to see if we could blow it up from 8mm up to 35. The idea was that they would use it within a professional documentary, which they never did, by the way.

Unbeknown to them at the time, an "extra" copy was made and that's what I released on national television. (Robert smiled and winked here indicating he just may have been the one who made the bootleg copy.)

Holland: Were you threatened at all once you released it?

Groden: Before I showed it on Goodnight America, Geraldo Rivera was given an ultimatum from "Life" that he better not show the film.

And he said, "Though the heavens fall, let the truth be known," and in fact, he told them, ABC, if they tried to prevent him from showing it, they could get themselves a new boy, he was going to resign – he would quit. But that's back in the days when he had some credibility.

So they ran it. And the next morning "Life," who had paid a quarter of a million dollars for the film, sent a one-time "permission" to show the film to Geraldo, after it had happened; they did that to protect the copyright. Essentially it made it look as if they had licensed it, but they hadn't really.

Holland: Why do you think they were trying to prevent the film from being shown? What was so explosive in the film?

Groden: The Zapruder film is a clock for the assassination; it shows us when the shots were fired, it's the visual photographic record of what happened. When the president was struck in the head in the head from the right front, he was thrown violently to the left and to the rear.

Now, there's one point which I must bring out… I must say it and I cannot say it enough. Every single doctor who saw the president at Parkland Hospital – every doctor, every nurse, every other eyewitness – said that the shot came from the right front, that the exit wound was in the rear of the president's head."

WHY WAS JFK ASSASSINATED; WHAT WAS HE THREATENING

Holland: Why was JFK murdered on November 22nd 1963? What was he threatening?

Groden: President Kennedy was threatening a lot. If you throw it all together into a big basket, it becomes the "status quo." In fact, the president was a threat to:

- the CIA
- organized crime
- the military
- big business
- the ultra-right wing politically
- the Federal Reserve System
- so many people

Our problem has never been to find out who wanted the president dead; the problem we've had is trying to figure out which one of them succeeded.

Holland: What is your scenario? What is your opinion on who had him killed?

Groden: It's like a menu in a Chinese restaurant, two from column A and one from column B. What it comes down to is that the House Assassinations Committee said it was organized crime, and they were right. The Senate Intelligence Committee vied that in fact it was the Covert Actions branch of the CIA – they were right. Many of the research community, myself included, feel that Lyndon Johnson was up to his big floppy ears in this, and I think we're right. In fact, it was all three. There may have been more, we don't know all the answers. We do know that the most likely answers are the three elements that I just said.

Organized crime wanted the president and his brother Bobby out of the picture completely. They knew that Lyndon Johnson wouldn't support Bobby; they hated each other.

Santos Trafficante, the mobster (boss of Tampa), said "You cut off the head and the tail dies." Bobby, being the tail, and the president being the head. It was a matter of survival for the Mob. It's considered an extremely risky thing for them to have tried, but then again, they wouldn't have existed if the president and the attorney general had continued their war. For them it was a calculated risk.

As far as the CIA goes, the CIA was going to be disbanded by President Kennedy. He felt that they were insubordinate, they weren't listening to him. He'd already had to fire the three people at the top: Allen Dulles, the Director and his two main assistants, Major-General Charles Cabell and Richard Bissell.

And you know – for those of you who may not be aware – I'm sure most of you by now are – that Allen Dulles' assistant, Major-General Charles Cabell, his brother was Earl Cabell, the Mayor of Dallas – the man who changed the motorcade route and got it to go in front of the Book Depository.

ROBERT GRODEN "JFK" BEHIND THE SCENES STORIES

Holland: Now that dynamic between you and Oliver, did you ever come to loggerheads?

Groden: Once… just once.

Holland: Can you tell us that story?

Groden: Yes, there was a scene shot on the sixth floor of the depository – where the character of Oswald (played by Gary Oldman in an outstanding performance.) was supposed to be potentially shooting and then taking off immediately after. That's not exactly the way it would have happened. The Government witnesses that were called said the man who fired from the sixth floor didn't run away right away; he stood there as if to admire his work before he left.

Oliver was really involved in shooting this critical scene and I kept trying to get his attention – I never could – and he shot it four times before I actually could get his attention.

So, I finally did and I explained that to him and he looked and he said: "Why didn't you tell me before?" He said, "You weenie?" I said, "I tried!" But that was the only time. We got along very, very well and I wish Ollie would do "JFK II" and tell the rest of it."

> Holland: Doctor Robert McClelland was on the show; he was one of the surgeons who worked on JFK. He also says, for sure, the shot came from the front, hit him in the forehead, took out the back of his head. None of this "magic bullet" stuff where a bullet comes in from the back of the head, does a u-turn and then goes right back out. It doesn't happen.

(See "Chapter 4, Dr Robert McClelland living history the surgeon who worked on JFK & Lee Harvey Oswald" for more information.)

> Groden: I had the honor of playing Dr. McClelland in the movie, "JFK." There were actually two of us; I'm the one who's actually in the "lifesaving scene" at Parkland when they're trying to save the president's life. There was a later scene where Dr. McClelland as a character appears at the Shaw trial in New Orleans – that's the real doctor; that wasn't me – it should have been, but it wasn't.

Jim DiEugenio Primary Researcher For Oliver Stone's "JFK" DVD

Jim DiEugenio just maybe the most knowledgeable person on the planet when it comes to the JFK assassination. Jim has the extraordinary ability to name names and dates at the drop of a hat. He knows his stuff. It is uncanny.

Jim, and fellow researcher Lisa Pease, published "Probe" Magazine. It was a series of articles dedicated to all of the assassinations in the sixties: JFK, Malcolm X, Dr. King and Bobby. Along with Lisa (who I have had the distinct honor of interviewing as well on "Night Fright,") Jim published a book hailed by Oliver Stone called "The Assassinations."

Never debate Jim on this subject matter with any expectations of winning; you won't. He is that good. He is driven, as all researchers are, by passion and the desire for truth, two of the greatest American qualities.

Jim's introduction to the JFK assassination came from an interview that New Orleans' DA Jim Garrison had done for "Playboy Magazine" in October 1967, that Jim read a decade latter in 1977.

> **Jim swears to me that his motivation for the purchase of the magazine was strictly for the article. Who am I to doubt him?**

If you listen to or read anything by Jim, you will learn details. He has never failed to reveal aspects of the assassination that had never been associated with one another. He takes an aspect, and not only has the ability to turn it upside down, but he turns it inside out as well. It is no wonder Oliver Stone sought him out for his research expertise and to add his proficiency to the "JFK" DVD.

NEW ORLEANS DISTRICT ATTORNEY JIM GARRISON

Earling Carothers "Jim" Garrison (November 20, 1921 – October 21, 1992) was the district attorney of Orleans Parish, Louisiana from 1962 to 1973. Oliver Stone's film "JFK" is based on the true story of Jim Garrison's investigation into the assassination of President Kennedy in the 1960s.

Right after the assassination, on November 22, 1963, Garrison received a tip from a Jack Martin, that a fellow called David Ferrie may have been the pilot to fly the JFK's assassins out of Dallas on the afternoon after the assassination, using a small private Cessna type plane. It is important to note that, at the time, Jack Martin was working for Guy Bannister, an ex-FBI agent and right-wing zealot, at Banister's office at 544 Camp Street.

Oswald had an office at 544 Camp Street, New Orleans in 1963. The Cuban exiles had an office there. And a fellow by the name of Guy Banister had an office there. Guy Banister was an ex-FBI agent who was organizing the anti-Castro Cuban exiles for the intelligence services. Banister was also responsible for overseeing shipments of weapons into Cuba in order to arm the covert anti-Castro revolutionaries who were committing acts of sabotage against the Castro regime.

Oswald having an office there is significant because both the anti-Castro Cuban exiles and Guy Banister were anti-Castro and anti-Communist zealots. However, we are told by the Warren Commission that Oswald was pro-Castro and pro-Communist.

It simply doesn't make sense that either Bansiter or the anti-Castro Cuban exiles would have put up with a pro-Castro and pro-Communist in an office across the hall from them. A more likely scenario is that Oswald was not really pro-Communist or pro-Castro, but was actually working for the US intelligence community and Banister. More than likely he was creating a cover for himself so he would be accepted into Cuba at a future date without any problems.

> **BTW there is a wonderful scene in the movie "JFK" that dramatizes this whole scenario about 544 Camp Street.**

Two days after the assassination, David Ferrie was questioned by Garrison about his whereabouts the day of the assassination. His answers were so bizarre and conflicting that Garrison decided to hold Ferrie for further questioning for the FBI's own investigation into the Kennedy assassination. Appallingly, the FBI released Ferrie without explanation.

Garrison waited three years until he once again returned to the Kennedy case. He was flying from New Orleans to Washington and happened to sit beside Louisiana Senator Russell Long. They started to chat, and the Kennedy assassination came up. Long said he never believed the Warren Commission report. That was the spark that lit a fire in Garrison to return to the JFK case.

This time Garrison had success. The connections between people started to solidify and led to the arrest and 1969 trial of Clay Shaw (played by Tommy Lee Jones in "JFK"). Shaw was found innocent of the charges but it is certainly worth noting that both the jury and judge believed that Garrison had proved that there was indeed a conspiracy in the assassination of President Kennedy, but fell short in proving the guilt of Clay Shaw.

DiEugenio: I guess the best way to talk about the Garrison investigation is I think – the first thing you probably want to talk about is a guy named David Ferrie. David Ferrie had known Oswald since the mid-'50s because Oswald, at this time, had been in New Orleans and he had joined something called the "Civil Air Patrol" which is kind of like "ROTC" for high school kids.

Holland: In Canada we don't have that. "ROTC" is kind of the "Air Cadets" folks, here in Canada, and it's kind of like that where 15, 16-year-olds would join.

DiEugenio: At this time, 1955, 1956, Oswald (an exceptional performance by Gary Oldman in "JFK") first meets David Ferrie. Now this is an absolute certainty and people who always really disliked the whole thing about Garrison always try and deny this. But there's no questioning it today. There's even a picture, I think more than one of this.

Because then, of course, the question becomes why would a Right-Winger like Ferrie be associating with Oswald? Why would a Communist want to join the Civil Air Patrol because what Ferrie was doing in the Civil Air Patrol was "interesting" these young men into going into the military, which is of course what Oswald did.

So, Oswald knows Ferrie from his Civil Air Patrol days. And then when he goes back to New Orleans in April of 1963, he meets up with him again. And so it's this association that Jim Garrison gets tipped off on, on the weekend of the assassination. An assistant DA named Herman Coleman talks to a guy named Jack Martin and Jack Martin tells him this association between David Ferrie and Lee Harvey Oswald. And he tells Garrison about it. Garrison calls in David Ferrie to question him, and Ferrie, as you saw in the film, gives him this incredible cock-and-bull story about why he drove to Texas.

Ferrie says he went to "go ice-skating," okay. And then he said "Well, we went to go goose hunting." And so Garrison says …

Holland: Did you bag any geese?

DiEugenio: How could you shoot at geese? You didn't bring any shotguns.

Holland: Ferrie says to Garrison, "We forgot them."

[both laugh heartily]

DiEugenio: And so Ferrie then gets turned over to the FBI – because in those days, Garrison actually believed that the FBI was actually investigating this case. Which of course was absolute complete hogwash. Hoover never did any investigation of the JFK case and he goes ahead and turns him over to the FBI. The FBI then goes ahead and lets Ferrie go.

And so Garrison goes okay, I guess I was wrong. But he never loses his interest in the JFK case. So he then starts reading a lot of the books – reads all the Warren Commission volumes, and then has that famous meeting with Sen. Russell Long, which is depicted in the film.

So now he really goes back into the case. And this is in October and November of 1967. And this is when he makes an incredible discovery about 544 Camp Street – finding that [building] on one of Oswald's flyers – more than one I think, actually.

And then Garrison walks down to 544 Camp Street and he puts it all together. Oswald wasn't a Communist. If he was a Communist, why would he be working out of Guy Banister's office in New Orleans. And by the way, there's that other thing that I discovered in my book that is this – that that particular flyer, the Corliss Lamont flyer.

Corliss Lamont was a wealthy progressive who lived in New York and wrote a series of pamphlets on leftist and liberal causes. I think there were about 16 of them. And this one was called the "Crime Against Cuba" and it was basically about the "Bay of Pigs." Here's another problem with this, the "Crime Against Cuba" pamphlet. "The Crime

Against Cuba" pamphlet was originally published in the summer of 1961, and it went through four editions in just 1961 – all right. And here's the capper. If you look in the Warren Commission volumes, Oswald had the first edition.

So here comes the question: How could Oswald get the first edition of this pamphlet in the summer of 1963 if it was sold out by the summer of 1961!?

And I provided what I think is the answer: Because Corliss Lamont had an order from the CIA for that pamphlet in 1961. They ordered 15 copies of it. So, one solution to the paradox is that the CIA had it – gave it to Bannister – and Bannister gave it to Oswald – not knowing that Oswald was going to stamp the 544 Camp Street on it.

When Garrison discovers this, this whole 544 Camp Street thing, he then begins to track down all the people that were seen at 544 Camp Street. And that's people like – in addition to David Ferrie – there's also people like Kerry Thornley. (Author who penned a book based on his friendship with Lee Harvey Oswald, BEFORE the assassination of President Kennedy.) There's also people like Sergio Acarcha Smith. (An anti-Castro Cuban Exile associated with violent exile groups who plays a prominent role in the assassination.)

This leads them into this whole nexus of the CIA and these anti-Castro Cubans who are working together in this. First of all, it was the "Bay of Pigs" then it became "Operation Mongoose."

Operation Mongoose

After Fidel Castro took over Cuba in 1959, many Cubans fled to the US. These folks are called "anti-Castro Cuban exiles." They wanted to go back to Cuba to overthrow Castro and reclaim Cuba. The CIA agreed and, ominously, so did the Mafia.

The Mafia had been operating all the night clubs and casinos in Cuba and making a fortune before Castro took over. Now suddenly that source of revenue was cut off. They wanted it back and were willing to do anything to achieve that goal including working alongside their nemesis, the CIA.

So, the Cuban exiles, the CIA and the Mafia all ended up working together on one common goal: to topple the Castro regime and take back power and control. The operation was headed by military intelligence leader Col. Ed

Landsdale, who had been also in charge of covert ops into North Vietnam. This was called "Operation Mongoose."

> Holland: Can you just give a brief synopsis of Mongoose?
>
> DiEugenio: Mongoose was after the Bay of Pigs and after the investigation of the Bay of Pigs. Kennedy "okayed" this secret war against Cuba – headed by Air Force Colonel Edwin Lansdale, who is really CIA – although he was ostensibly working in the Air Force – he was really a CIA operative. Operation Mongoose was meant to put pressure on the Cuban regime, Castro's regime, so as not to export revolution and Communism into South America.
>
> And its peak was for about eight or nine months and then it was shut down after the Cuban Missile Crisis in October of 1962. Kennedy tried to move a lot of those operations offshore. He didn't want them operating off of American shores ... because of the deal he had made with Khrushchev.

JFK promised Soviet Premier Nikita Khrushchev that he would NOT invade Cuba in exchange for the removal of the Soviet's nuclear missiles. Please see Chapter 3 "Ted Sorensen The Man Who Saved The World Really" for more information.

> DiEugenio: So Garrison discovered all this stuff and of course this is another "thing." What the heck was this Communist doing mixed up with all these CIA guys and these anti-Castro Cuban exiles? So this is another thing of course that chipped away at Oswald's image of supposedly being a communist, when in actuality he was really working as a CIA agent provocateur and also an informant for the FBI. So these are the discoveries that Garrison makes. And all of this takes place in late 1966, early 1967.
>
> And then, of course, New Orleans' reporter Rosemary James and the "New Orleans States-Item" newspaper, basically blow the cover off of Garrison's investigation. And that was probably the beginning of the end, although you could argue that the CIA and the FBI were already on to what Garrison was doing. Because they were already sending undercover operatives into his camp to spy on him, to plant microphones in his offices, to go ahead and do everything they possibly could to make sure that whatever progress he was making would be at first surveilled and then subterfuged.
>
> So, Garrison was being stymied. His office was infiltrated. His office was secretly miced. There were tapes. The FBI was taping him and

setting up transcripts, sending them to Hoover. We have this because we know the secretary was actually typing up the transcripts of the recordings. This was an article I did for "Probe Magazine." This went, of course, all the way up to the trial. Hugh Aynesworth, Houston, Texas investigative reporter actually tried to bribe some of the Clinton witnesses. I should explain who that is. The Clinton –

Holland: Yeah, it's not Bill Clinton.

DiEugenio: No, it's not Bill Clinton. [both laugh]. The Clinton witnesses were people who lived in this small town about 125 miles north of Louisiana, New Orleans, Louisiana where they sighted Clay Shaw, David Ferrie, and Lee Harvey Oswald. First, in a little town called Jackson, then, in a little town about 15 miles away called Clinton. And then Oswald went back to Jackson again.

And so there were literally dozens of witnesses who saw all three of them. And these witnesses were very compelling – I mean, *very* compelling. And there were actually some of these witnesses that testified against Clay Shaw at his trial.

Well, Hugh Aynesworth actually went up there and tried to bribe Sheriff Manchester, a witness who had verified that he saw Shaw, Ferrie and Oswald together), the town's Sherriff, into turning on Garrison.

These are the kind of things that the other side went to, to make sure that Garrison was not going to succeed. And this went on all the way to trial when the CIA Station in New Orleans actually went ahead and then they moved a Teletype Machine into the office. And they actually started monitoring the trial for the CIA. And James Angleton, the counterintelligence chief of the CIA, actually did "name traces" on the Jurors who were being interviewed to serve on the trial.

And the CIA came to the conclusion that unless Garrison was subverted, that Shaw was going to be convicted. We actually have this in their own words now. And so they went ahead and started sanctioning what they called "task forces" in which they were going to go ahead and make sure that this did not happen.

And one of the things they did was, they sent in "propaganda" experts into New Orleans. Because at the beginning, Garrison was actually getting some good press in New Orleans, especially by the New Orleans States-Item newspaper. They had a couple of reporters who are actually sympathetic to Garrison.

What happened of course is that once the CIA decided to go into heavy subversion, those two guys got transferred off the Garrison beat. I know this for a fact because I interviewed one of them. Yeah, they got transferred off the Garrison beat. And if you can believe it, they started covering high school football games.

So now the CIA began to control the media. And by the way, this was no mean feat because until Garrison took on the Kennedy assassination, he was one of the most popular politicians in Louisiana. In fact, he very easily could have become the Governor of the State or the Senator for Louisiana. In fact, the Governor at the time actually wanted Garrison to run with him as the Lieutenant Governor candidate. So it really took a lot to really go ahead and smear the guy because he had such a great history up until the time. But this is what they did:

They basically went *all out* to go ahead and muddy up his name – accuse him of all these ridiculous Mafia charges – that he was hiding Carlos Marcello (New Orleans's Don) and all this other stuff – this bunch of junk. And this is what managed to actually begin to turn the tide. The tide begins to turn in about April of 1968 with the local press in New Orleans, led by people like Rosemary James and others and WDSU, which was owned by the Stern family which was heir to the Sears fortune.

I had mentioned, glowingly above, about Jim's exceptional skill in bringing aspects of the assassination never thought as associated together and then seamlessly connect the dots between them all. The paragraph above is a perfect example.

DiEugenio: Let's call it the covert things that were happening to Garrison's investigation, his office, etc. that was meant to go ahead and make sure that Shaw would not be convicted. And they succeeded, and I could go in even further with what they did to some of Garrison's witnesses.

Garrison suspected that a man named in the Warren Commission as "Clay Bertrand" was really New Orleans business man "Clay Shaw." This was crucial to Garrison's trial against Shaw, because it was that man named in the Warren Commission, Clay "Bertrand," who tried to get legal help for Lee Harvey Oswald right after the assassination of JFK. It would prove a connection between Shaw and Oswald.

When Shaw was arrested and booked by New Orleans Police Officer Aloysius Habighorst (actor played by Odin K. Langford in "JFK"), Shaw was specifically asked if he ever used any "aliases." Shaw responded, yes, "Clay Bertrand."

During the trial, when Officer Habighorst was called as a witness to verify Shaws' alias as "Bertrand," his testimony was disallowed by the court as Shaw's lawyer was not present when Officer Habighorst asked Clay Shaw if he had any aliases. That was 1969. Today it is commonly held by those on both sides of the debate that "Clay Bertrand" was indeed "Clay Shaw."

> Holland: Go ahead if you want, and give a couple of examples.
>
> DiEugenio: Aloysius Habighorst – a guy who actually testified that Shaw admitted that his nickname was Bertrand. His alias was Bertrand, the booking agent.
>
> Habighorst almost got run over by a truck as he was going into the courtroom. And there's a famous picture of him in my book where he has the sunglasses on. I asked his wife why he had sunglasses on. She said because it was covering a black eye because he almost ran over by a truck the day before. See these as a kind of things that were being done to Garrison's witnesses. He couldn't protect them because of these forces that were at work.
>
> In other words, they never really stopped going after Garrison. So I would say that we have today – I'd say 40 to 45% of what Garrison really had. And the stuff that we have today is pretty darn good. I mean, we've been able to put together some really interesting stuff.
>
> For example, about Rose Cheramie that could have never been written unless the ARRB declassified all these things. We've gone even further than what the House Select Committee did in just that part of the story.

Please see Chapter 2 "Seven Smoking Guns – Rose Cheramie – forewarned that assassins were on their way to Dallas to kill Kennedy one day before JFK was assassinated" for more information.

Jim is bang on when he states that they never really stopped going after Garrison in a continuing campaign to smear his reputation. As late as 1973, a former Garrison investigator, Pershing Gervais, said that Garrison had accepted monthly bribes to keep quiet about illegal pin ball operations in New Orleans. The case went to trial and Garrison was found not guilty.

Gervais had been living with his wife and two children in Vancouver B.C. under the name Paul Mason. According to Gervais, he had been given a fake job at General Motors of Canada for $18,000 annually which in today's dollars would be around 200K.

He declared that the US Justice Department had asked him to report and spy on Garrison. Gervais ended up asking New Orleans reporter Rosemary James, mentioned in the interview above, to interview him so he could "come clean." James arrived in Vancouver for the interview where Gervais stated he had been paid $22,000 ($250K today) annually to undercut Garrison's case. He had been specifically chosen by the Justice Department for the task as he was "the one who could get him."

RUTH AND MICHAEL PAINE & GEORGE DEMOHRENSCHILDT

The best way to quickly describe George DeMohrenschildt's role (played by Willem Oltmans in "JFK") in this story is to say that he was Lee Harvey Oswald's CIA "handler" during Oswald's stay in Dallas up to the assassination of President Kennedy.

> **Why is this important? Because The Warren Commission said Oswald acted on impulse and had no connections to a conspiracy in the assassination of JFK. So, what then, was a CIA operative doing taking care of Oswald?**

George DeMohrenschildt (April 17, 1911 – March 29, 1977), was born in the Soviet Union. His father was persecuted by Stalin, and the family fled to America. During World War II, it was rumored that DeMohrenschildt was a Nazi spy living in America. It is important to note that many pro-Nazi sympathizers hated Communism far more than Nazi Fascism and opted to side with Hitler in order to rid the world of the "dreaded Communist plague."

A perfect example of this is when the Vatican "got in bed with the devil" and signed an agreement called The Reichskonkordat in 1933. This agreement had the result of giving Hitler the prestige he desired on the global stage to be heralded as a credible world statesman. The Vatican saw the threat of Communism as far greater than that of Hitler and were fooled into signing their "deal with the devil."

You will be surprised to learn that DeMohrenschildt was closely connected to Jackie Kennedy. When Jackie Bouvier was a little girl she was often seen sitting on DeMohrenschildt's knee calling him "Uncle George." I mention this only to show how George had friends in high places in the power elite of America.

DeMohrenschildt had no knowledge of the assassination and was in no way involved. His sole role in all of this was strictly to watch over Oswald. He was as shocked as everyone when Oswald was arrested and charged with the assassination of JFK. He believed to his dying day that Oswald was a "patsy."

Edward Jay Epstein interviewed DeMohrenschildt, On March 29, 1977. In the interview DeMohrenschildt admitted that, in 1962, he was requested by Dallas CIA agent J. Walton Moore to look out for Oswald, "I would never have contacted Oswald in a million years if Moore had not sanctioned it."

Shortly after the interview ended, on the same day, DeMohrenschildt received a request for an interview with Gaeton Fonzi, then an investigator for the House Select Committee on Assassinations.

Late that afternoon, DeMohrenschildt was found with his head blasted open from a shotgun. The coroner's verdict was suicide.

In our interview together, Jim talks extensively about how DeMohrenschildt connects with an often overlooked couple in the JFK assassination, Ruth and Michael Paine. It was Ruth Paine who got Oswald the job at the Texas School Book Depository in Dallas, and it was from Ruth Paine's garage that the alleged assassination rifle, Mannlicher Carcano, was taken.

> DiEugenio: Ruth and Michael Paine were ostensibly friends of a guy named George DeMohrenschildt. George DeMohrenschildt was basically Oswald's best friend in the Dallas area when Oswald comes back from the Soviet Union. He introduces Oswald to Ruth and Michael Paine, who are his friends and Oswald becomes a kind of "cohort" of this White Russian community (this means anti-Communist Russia, like the anti-Castro Cuban exiles). Oswald's supposed to be a Communist sympathizer, right!?
>
> And he's hanging out with these people who want to overthrow the Communist revolution in Russia and bring back the Royal Family. You know, everywhere you look in this case, you've got to smile. Did they really expect you to believe this stuff? So, anyway, that's who Oswald is supposed to be hanging out with in this Dallas / Fort Worth community. And the Paines are a part of it.
>
> Now, Ruth Paine's objective from the very beginning seems to have been to separate Oswald from his wife. Because she immediately befriends Marina Oswald and her excuse was that she wanted to take Russian lessons from Marina. After the Oswald's go to New Orleans in April 1963, Ruth Paine then picks up Marina – and I think this was September the 23rd of 1963 – brings her back to Irving Texas where Ruth Paine lives and that is the instance where Oswald gets separated from his wife.
>
> So, approximately two months before the assassination – Oswald, this whole image of him as a loner is now cinched because he literally is

alone now – he only visits his wife on weekends while he's living in this apartment in Dallas during the week. And its Ruth Paine also gets him his job at the Texas School Book Depository.

Because Oswald has put his name in a Texas Employment Agency and the call came in for a different job that paid him a higher rate of pay – but Ruth did not give him that message! And instead she got him this job at the Texas School Book Depository, which of course just by this "amazing cosmic stroke of coincidence" happened to be right on the motorcade route when JFK comes into town.

And then "of course" it's Ruth Paine's garage that becomes the home of all this Oswald evidence that implicates him. So this is what I mean. The Dallas plot was not going to fail. They basically pulled out all the stops for Dallas.

Holland: And Ruth Paine's sister had CIA connections.

DiEugenio: Ruth Paine's sister was actually working for the CIA. "Somehow," Ruth didn't know that – because when Garrison asked her that before his Grand Jury, "Why is your sister's file Top Secret at the National Archives?" Ruth says: "Oh, is it?" Garrison goes yes, and he says: "Do you have any idea of why they would want to keep it Top Secret?" She answers, "Oh no, no… I don't have any idea." "Do you know where she works?" And she says: "No."

Now, what's so hard to believe about that, of course, is right before Ruth went to New Orleans she was staying with her sister for about nine days. And this was in Maryland, a little town right outside of Langley, Falls Church, which is … it's a "bedroom community" for the CIA. They all lived in Falls Church, and drove into Langley.

So, "she didn't know" where her sister worked – right before she picked up Marina – never asked her sister. Okay, and then, of course, like I said, it's [Ruth's] place that becomes a home for all of Oswald's evidence. And then she's told the police when they got there: "We've been expecting you." And then her and Marina left and let the police go ahead and rummage through her house, not just one day, but two days – Friday and Saturday. So this is what I mean. It's very hard to look at what happened in Dallas and not say, "Boy, they really pulled out all the stops on this one."

Then there's also Mary Bancroft. Mary Bancroft was Allen Dulles' girlfriend, who was the best of friends with Michael Paine's mom. (Allen Dulles was the Director of the CIA, Kennedy fired him because of the Bay of Pigs fiasco.) So I think that is really, really, interesting that Allen Dulles was in Dallas right around the time of the assassination and his girlfriend Mary Bancroft – not just his girlfriend, but she actually worked for him as a spy in the OSS and the CIA. Ruth Forbes Paine I think was her name. (the OSS was set up during World war II and was the predecessor to the CIA)

Jim DiEugenio "JFK" Behind The Scenes Stories

DiEugenio: Because Oliver took such a pasting on the movie, he wanted me to do an essay on the new documents that were released by the Assassinations Record Review Board. That was the Agency of the Government that was created out of the controversy surrounding "JFK" because at the end of the movie he put that famous title up that, the files of the House Select Committee on Assassinations are sealed until the year 2029. So because of that, Congress passed a law saying that the Federal Government had the go-ahead to unleash all the documents that they had been holding, all these years.

So, Oliver wanted me to do an essay on the release of the DVD informing the audience of some of the developments that tended to back up some of the ideas that went into his film. Oliver really liked it a lot. Now "JFK," as films go, I think it's a pretty good movie.

By the way, since we're talking a little bit about the movie, I should say one of the immortal highlights of the film is during the trial scene when Jim Garrison talks about the Single Bullet Theory (the "magic bullet"), and he says: "devised by an ambitious Philadelphia lawyer named Arlen Specter." Here's a little bit of insider information:

That actually wasn't in the script. But when they went down to film that scene, Kevin Costner was reading it and rehearsing it. And he said "Oliver, come on, I can't say this." He goes, "What do you mean? Come on, they didn't really say this – that the bullet came in down here – that it went up here." He didn't believe it. He didn't want to make a fool out of himself, right.

Holland: He's referring the "magic bullet," folks.

DiEugenio: So Oliver had to get his research assistant, and she, Jane Risconi, had to show him: "No really, they do say this" And she's showing him in the Warren Commission volume: "See, it's here, it's here … see, it comes in here. It goes out here"

So, Kevin Costner goes, "Who thought up this idea?" And she goes, "Well, Arlen Specter." And he goes: "Well, let's put his name in the script." So they rewrote the script right there and then put his name in the screenplay. And that's how he got in the movie.

Holland: There was a controversy over that too. I heard he was thinking about suing Costner.

DiEugenio: You know, you can't libel somebody, if you tell the truth.

Clay Shaw Jim Garrison

Jim DiEugenio

Lee Oswald in New Orleans

Lee Harvey Oswald

Pamphlet Case Sentence Given

Lee Oswald, 23, 4907 Magazine, Monday was sentenced to pay a fine of $10 or serve 10 days in jail on a charge of disturbing the peace by creating a scene.

Oswald was arrested by First District police at 4:15 p. m. Friday in the 700 block of Canal while he was reportedly distributing pamphlets asking for a "Fair Play for Cuba."

Police were called to the scene when three Cubans reportedly sought to stop Oswald. Municipal charges against the Cubans for disturbing the peace were dropped by the court.

CHAPTER 12

Assassination Noise: Breaking Down The Myths

I'm not a conspiracy theorist. I'm a conspiracy empiricist because that's what the data forces you to conclude. There's no other possibilities consistent with the laws of physics.

NASA Physicist Paul Chambers

I wasn't going to do this chapter for fear of angering those in the JFK research arena who have laid ground work all of their lives at a time before data mining on the net was even a dream. In those days when one did research, there were no key words to type in and quickly ascertain only the info you needed. In those days documents were snail mailed, read, assessed, and then commented upon and re-snail mailed back. This was the challenge of communication and the exchange of ideas between researchers in those days.

Today, in mere seconds you can sift through relevant documentation and cipher out what is factual and what is a stretch. But let me say this. The researchers, to each one's credit, questioned everything, turning it upside down and all around and then handing it off for someone else to do the same.

It was the time of Vietnam, lies hidden from our youth. It was the "golden age" of the CIA where agents operated freely on their own accord, committing murder and overthrowing of governments, often without elected officials' knowledge or permission. It was the time of Nixon and Watergate, when even the president couldn't be trusted. It was the time of the Iran – Contra scandal, where operations were carried out covertly by subordinates, leaving the government "plausible deniability." It was then and still remains a time of challenge to reach the truth.

> **I'm going to take on some of the loftier claims that have come to my attention over the years. These assessments are based on my interviews with those "in the know," behind the scenes, and from what I have read over the years, and good ol' common sense.**

MILITARY COUP D'ÉTAT

For a long period of time it was suspected that JFK's assassination was a coup d'état orchestrated by disenfranchised members of the Joint Chiefs of Staff, and with good reason.

As mentioned in Chapter 3 "Ted Sorensen, The Man Who Saved The World, Really," Sorensen stated that during the October 1962 Cuban Missile Crisis, a few of the "Hawkish" Joint Chiefs, mainly those aligned with General Curtis LeMay, were heatedly insisting on military invasion of Cuba, damn the consequences, even if it escalated to nuclear war.

When Kennedy opted for the peaceful blockade as a step to deter the Soviets and Cuba, in the hopes of averting the end of the world, they became furious with what they perceived as a weak response. Ted went on to state that there was a concern that these "military hawks" were getting out of control, and JFK wanted to rein them in. Certainly, coups in other countries have happened for less. Without question, there was motive, thus why it has been entertained as a viable "conspiracy theory" for the assassination.

However, Ted stated empathically that the elected representatives of the people, the government, were always in firm control. It is my belief as well, that quite simply, the people surrounding Kennedy, his handpicked "New Frontier" team, would not have stood for a coup. Kennedy was their personal friend.

There is no way Ted Sorensen, Robert McNamara Secretary of Defense, in charge of the military, Dean Rusk, Secretary of State, Kenny O'Donnell, Dave Powers, his own brothers Bobby and Ted Kennedy, et al, would have stood by while the military murdered their own commander in chief and took power.

President Kennedy watches B-52 bombers in Florida. General Curtis LeMay, the Air Force Chief of Staff and JFK's frequent antagonist, 1962 (Associated Press)

The most important person that would have never stood by while a coup took place was the actual Chairman of the Joint Chiefs of Staff himself, General Maxwell Taylor. General Taylor was handpicked for that role by JFK, precisely to keep the other Chiefs in line and to maintain a clear line of truthful communication between the military and the Kennedy administration.

> **Taylor was so close to the Kennedy family that Bobby named a child after him. There is no way a coup of this magnitude could remain covert and take place without coming to the surface and exposed for all to see.**

It is the premise of Oliver Stone's film "JFK" that a military coup took place with the assassination of President Kennedy and with Vice President Lyndon Johnson waiting in the wings to assume power.

PRESIDENT LYNDON JOHNSON

It is no secret that V.P. Johnson wasn't well liked by Kennedy's handpicked New Frontier team. His skirmishes with Bobby Kennedy are legendary, second only to Bobby's confrontations with Jimmy Hoffa.

If Johnson was involved, at any level, of a coup, why then did he go out of his way and insist that all of Kennedy's New Frontier team remain at his side after the assassination, especially Sorensen and McNamara? If indeed Johnson was waiting in the wings to assume the presidency after master minding a plot to kill the president, wouldn't he have brought in his own people and gotten rid of Kennedy's people, people he knew disliked him, for fear that they might investigate the assassination themselves and find out he was behind it?

> **Bobby and others did launch their own investigations privately and Bobby in specific was told it was a Mafia hit.**

Georgia Senator Richard Russell was a member of the Warren Commission. When the Commission was about to release its conclusion, Senator Russell refused to sign the document stating he simply did not believe in the Commission's so-called "single bullet theory," what we now call the Magic Bullet Theory.

President Johnson, somewhat dismayed that a member of his handpicked blue ribbon Warren Commission would dissent from the Commission, and in an attempt to clarify Senator Russell's position, decided to give him a phone call on September 18, 1964. Senator Russell was adamant about not believing the Magic Bullet Theory and stated to Johnson: "I don't believe it!"

President Kennedy and Vice President Johnson. (Associated Press)

What is explosive is what came next: Johnson's own admission about what he personally thought about the Magic Bullet Theory. Johnson's response to Senator Russell was astounding. "Neither do I!" he thundered.

White House aide Marvin Watson is on record as saying that President Johnson personally disclosed to him that he was "convinced that there was a plot in connection with the assassination." Watson continued the revelation stating, "President Johnson felt that the CIA had something to do with this plot." ("Breach Of Trust" page 449)

> **Why would Johnson even remotely continue to indicate that there was a conspiracy? Would he not fear that the Justice Department might open up the case based on his allegations and thus create an unwanted investigation that could lead right back to him?**

If Johnson was indeed the first president to be a mere puppet of the military-industrial complex, does it not follow then that all subsequent presidents have been as well? Carter, Clinton, Obama? Did "we the people" lose control of the country and never get it back? Those very military people, that were around in 1963, are all gone now and a completely new generation of people, many having been born decades after the Kennedy assassination, are in place. To draw a line of generational continuity from one generation of military to the next, to the next, to the next, to infinity, is unfounded.

Secret Service Agent Driver Bill Greer

Let me clear up a misconception that has been making the rounds on the internet. There are those who claim that the Zapruder film (the film of the Kennedy assassination that was used in the movie JFK) shows the driver, Secret Service Agent Will Greer, turning around and shooting the president with a gun in his hand. In fact it does not. The illusion is due to the low-quality reproduction of the film, the sun that day, and shadows.

Greer did turn towards the president, apparently surprised and somewhat mystified when he heard the shots ring out. Greer did the exact opposite of his limited Secret Service training by bringing the president's limo almost to a stop, providing snipers an almost stationary target. Greer was trained to gun the car out of harm's way. He didn't. Were he or other Secret Service agents part of a conspiracy to assassinate the president? No. Absolutely not. Others claim he was slowing the limo to let the Secret Service agents, who were standing on the dash boards of the Secret Service protective follow up car directly behind the president's limo, to get onto his car to surround the president and protect him.

ZAPRUDER FILM ALTERED

There is another theory circulating that speculates that the individual frames of the Zapruder film were meticulously painted over in order to mask the kill shot coming from the front of President Kennedy. Supposedly the conspirators painted in a blood splatter pattern that they presumed would show the kill shot coming from *behind* President Kennedy. In so doing, they would have successfully thrown off researchers looking for a frontal shot.

The only problem is that the Zapruder film does show a frontal shot, and the blood patterns are consistent with that of a frontal shot as well. The Zapruder film was and is the best evidence to show, conclusively, multiple shooters and thus a conspiracy in the Kennedy assassination. Check out Chapter 7 "Frontal Shot 21st Century CSI & JFK For Real" where we discuss this very subject.

> **If one had access to such a film, instead of altering it, wouldn't it be more prudent to destroy it completely? What's more, there are other films taken by bystanders that day of the assassination. When those films and the Zapruder film are played back simultaneously, they all line up in sync.**

If we are to accept the above theory that the Zapruder film was altered, that would mean that someone would have to have known in advance who was going to film the assassination that day, then gotten all the cameras from those people, collected all the film, and then altered them all.

Sorry, folks, but this theory falls into the same category as the theory that "ice bullets" were used to kill Kennedy so they would melt away and leave no traces, or the theory that the guy with the umbrella in the Zapruder film had a poisoned dart that killed the president, or that other classic "documentary"

Zapruder film frame 298 showing the driver looking back at the wounded in the limousine. (Zapruder Film © 1967 (renewed 1995) The Sixth Floor Museum at Dealey Plaza

online that declares with absolute certainty that the Bush family was behind both President Kennedy's and John Jr's deaths, murders they were forced to commit to gain membership in some elite covert society.

Theories like these just cause the mainstream to question the credibility and, rightly so, the sanity of legitimate JFK researchers. It does a disservice to the whole community.

> **Look, bottom line, I like James Bond as much as the next person - but I know when the movie ends and the lights come on and am ushered back into reality.**

"JFK: Beyond The Magic Bullet"

This was a documentary produced and directed by Robert Erickson. It was meant to prove that the "magic bullet" could have actually happened. It is best to let an expert explain why the conclusion from Erickson's documentary was false. None better than NASA physicist Paul Chambers. For more on his findings and his proving a frontal shot, please see Chapter 7 "Frontal Shot 21st Century CSI & JFK For Real."

> Chambers: There was a very good test done by a group in Aniline, Australia a few years ago, sponsored by the Discovery Channel. They lined up two dummies. One was a gel man, which is a ballistics gel put over a skeleton. They had two of them lined up, you know, horizontally.
>
> Everyone says, "Well, my God, Kennedy and Connally were lined up perfectly for the shot." Okay fine, but the problem is the vertical path that the bullet has to take.
>
> They hit the first dummy in the back. It comes out his chest. It doesn't come out his throat. You can see clearly in the video, the bullet coming out his chest. So, sorry, not consistent right there.
>
> It goes on to hit Connally, punches through his body, breaks his ribs. Everything's good, then the bullet hits his wrist. We have a gel, simulated wrist. It bounces off.
>
> But the real bullet that hit Connally, goes through him, shatters his wrist, leaves three grains of fragments inside which exceeds the amount the bullet could have lost, so two grains. You've already got three in his wrist, plus some fragments in Kennedy's neck, plus it lodged in his leg.

Paul is bang on here; I watched the show in amazement and was astounded that the documentary announcer had the audacity to say:

> Documentary Announcer: Amazingly, Alex (the TV show's expert sniper perched atop a hydraulic lift-bucket shooting below at a non-moving, stable target) has replicated the "magic bullet" shot.

It's simply not true. Alex, the sniper, did not. It's an outright lie. But why?

In the show, the video clearly shows that the shot enters Kennedy's back and exits his chest. Remember, the Warren Commission's claim is that the "magic bullet" entered Kennedy's back between the shoulder blades and exited through JFK's throat in the front, not his chest, because that's where the real wounds were on the president's body. What does the announcer say about the TV show's bullet?

> Documentary Announcer: It struck Kennedy in the neck–

No, it did not! Erickson clearly shows their bullet entering the dummy's back, in between the shoulder blades, approximately 6" below the back of the neck. At no time does the show's bullet even come near dummy's neck, back or front.

> **The word "neck" is used by the show to trigger, in your mind, confirmation of their testing to re-create the Magic Bullet Theory. If you are not that familiar with this**

Frame from 1:16:46 of "JFK: Beyond the "magic bullet" showing the track of the expert shot exited the "JFK" dummy at the chest level

theory, you might say to yourself, "that sounds correct, wasn't there a 'neck' wound or something associated with JFK and the 'magic bullet?'"

According to the Warren Commission's Magic Bullet Theory, the "neck" wound is an *exit* wound not an *entrance* wound, and it is found on the *front* of JFK not on his *back*.

Documentary Announcer: –streaking through to Connally.

So what's wrong with this? Erickson clearly shows their bullet as it "streaks through" the JFK dummy's chest, approximately at the sternum, not a foot above where the real wound was in JFK's neck.

Notice once again their use of language. They don't mention "exit wound." Instead they use "streaking through."

The show can now avoid using the word "chest" to describe where their bullet exited the JFK dummy replica from. This lets Erickson off the hook in facing the truth: their multi-million dollar attempt at proving the Magic Bullet Theory has failed, and failed miserably.

So, quite simply, they chose to lie and misinform. How the mainstream media can continue to get away with this over and over again is mind boggling.

What this does prove beyond doubt, is that the angles that supposedly prove the Magic Bullet Theory are indeed wrong. It is what we have known all along; a shot that enters at the angle where it did on JFK's back cannot exit JFK's throat without traveling upward once inside his body.

In order for the bullet to change course and deflect upward, it would have to have hit something hard. The only thing hard enough for that is bone. If it hit bone, the bullet would have to deform. Yet this "magic bullet," Warren Commission CE399, the bullet they claim did all the damage, has no such deformity, and on top of that, (are you ready for this one?) nor did it have any blood or tissue on it!

Furthermore, if that bullet did travel upwards to the president's neck, it would have exited JFK's throat, then traveled up into the sky, missing Connally completely. It would not have been found conveniently lying on a Parkland Hospital gurney in pristine condition with no blood or tissue on it, as though it had been fired into cotton or water to be planted later.

There is other crucial information left out of Erickson's documentary as well.

- In the show, the test shot is fired from a Mannlicher-Carcano rifle, as was the original alleged "magic bullet" shot. There are, however, many discrepancies. The scope is newer and hi-tech, rather than misaligned and basic, as it was on the original.

- The show's rifle had its barrel end gaffer taped firmly to a railing and held solid on a tripod, instead of handheld as it was originally.

- President Kennedy was a moving target and not stationary, as was in the show. That's a huge difference and advantage, just ask any hunter.

- Erickson's sniper, Alex, had ample room and was not cramped, pushed up against a wall, bending over at a bad angle, as was the case in the original sniper's nest on the sixth floor of the Texas School Book Depository.

- There were no time constraints, giving the test sniper all the time in the world to aim and target.

- Alex also fired practice shots in advance of the final shot.

Try as they will, they could not duplicate the "magic bullet." Bottom line, the show's bullet entered almost where the original "magic bullet" did, in the upper back shoulder just to the right of JFK's vertebra, but it did not exit the throat. It exited the chest. Erickson glossed over that completely. Why? Simply because the angle from the sixth floor sniper's nest is too steep to enter Kennedy's back and exit his throat. To achieve this scenario, the sniper would have to be standing at street level, almost level with the car. We know that is one scenario that never happened.

> Chambers: So the whole thing collapses like a house of cards. And as you discussed, there was only three casings found at the School Book Depository. Four shots means another shooter, and that means, as you said, a conspiracy. And just that information alone forces you to that conclusion.
>
> I'm not a conspiracy theorist. I'm a conspiracy empiricist because that's what the data forces you to conclude. There's no other possibilities consistent with the laws of physics.

OPEN WINDOWS IN DEALEY PLAZA

There is a theory that all the open windows in Dealey Plaza were a clear indication that something was amiss in the president's protection November 22, 1963. Unfortunately this theory falls flat as well, if you look at any photos of JFK's motorcades throughout his presidency. Hawaii and Ireland are great examples.

There were always windows open along the routes. Very often JFK rode in an open-roofed car, and often actually sat perched on the back trunk, his feet on the back seat. He was wide open for any sniper attack. The Secret Service did their best to keep up, running alongside the car, but often not in sight or anywhere close enough to assist the president should an emergency arise. It was just the way they protected the president in those days. Today the president travels in an armored car that some say could withstand a small nuke. Different era, different methods.

THE THREE TRAMPS

Minutes after the shots rang out in Dealey Plaza and the motorcade was speeding President Kennedy to Parkland Hospital, the Dallas Police cordoned off many areas of the plaza, and started to round up suspicious-looking people. Just behind the picket fence, on the grassy knoll, is a parking lot with several train tracks running through it. There were several train box cars parked on a track siding that happened to contain "hobos."

Hobos, are homeless folks, who, in those days, when long-distance car travel was still in its infancy, used empty train box cars to travel from one place to another instead of hitchhiking like most do today. The Dallas Police took three men off of a box car, and walked them through Dealey Plaza to the Police Station at the corner of Main and Houston Streets for questioning.

It was a good call by the DPD, as the vast majority of witnesses heard the shots coming from the grassy knoll, and had raced up there seconds after the assassination in order to get the shooter. It would make perfect sense, therefore, that an exit strategy for the assassins may include a quick, convenient train ride out of Dallas. While trudging across the plaza, these three men and their police escort were photographed many times.

Here is where the problem started to arise. The three men were questioned and then released. When early researchers tried to find out who they were, no evidence of their police files or questioning was found. When these same early researchers came upon the photographs, they noticed that, for "hobos and tramps," their clothes looked brand new and not dirty and worn. Next,

Walking the three tramps through Dealey Plaza. (Photo by Murray Large)

the researchers started to examine the faces of the three tramps. Many became convinced that they were looking at CIA operatives E. Howard Hunt and Frank Sturgis, later to gain fame as the Watergate burglars working for President Richard Nixon. Another tramp was thought to be Johnny Mafiso Rosselli. Another was believed to be Charles Harrelson, a known Mafia hit man.

He was also actor Woody Harrelson's father; it must be stated clearly that Woody Harrelson had very little to do with his father while growing up and absolutely had nothing to do with JFK assassination.

Oliver Stone's film, "JFK," covers the possibilities of the three tramps somehow being involved in the assassination as late as when the movie came out in 1991. As it turns out, all of the above was unwarranted speculation and completely inaccurate.

In 1992, author and researcher Mary La Fontaine exposed that the three tramps were in fact really...well...just that, three tramps. It seems that the Dallas Police had misfiled the reports and questioning of the three and had rediscovered the files in 1989, consequently releasing them to the public.

Let's not forget that up until around 1998, files were always hard copies, kept in a filing cabinet or storage box, and were always notoriously misfiled. This has since changed with digital online filing and search engines.

The president and first lady in the limousine with the plexiglas bubbletop on

During research, Mary had come across the files and the names of the three tramps: Gus W. Abrams, Harold Doyle, and John F. Gedney. Even Stone now admits that, with this new revelation, he got that one wrong.

Limousine Bubble Top Roof

Older theories about the assassination believed that the Secret Service was somehow complicit in the assassination of JFK. One of the theories for evidence was the removal of the plexiglas bubble roof top that sat atop JFK's presidential limo, allowing any snipers an unobstructed, pristine target in the open car.

The bubble top roof was used on occasions when there was adverse weather conditions. In truth it was rarely used. Under the sun it would act like an incubator holding the sun heated air in the car. Maybe a dozen cars had air conditioning in those days. The president's was one of those, but it was woefully inadequate. So, it was used solely to keep the president dry in the rain.

Indeed it had been a torrential down pour that morning in Dallas before the president arrived. So how and why was the bubble top removed? Here is the true story.

A young news reporter by the name of Jim Lehrer, (the same Jim Lehrer that now has the profoundly respected PBS news show), was present that day at Dallas Love Field airport, assigned to cover the arrival of Air Force One and the president's entourage. Jim is quoted as saying that he clearly saw that the bubble top was originally on the president's limo before the plane landed. Lehrer approached a Secret Service agent and casually asked if the bubble top roof on the president's limo was going to be on or off during the upcoming motorcade through downtown Dallas. This was strictly for photographs and television cameras covering the motorcade so they could adjust their camera's aperture accordingly; absolutely nothing sinister was intended.

A Secret Service agent who knew Jim, cordially greeted him and quizzically said he simply wasn't sure. The agent radioed the downtown area where the motorcade would pass, to see if there was rain. The response came back that, no, indeed, everything was clear; the sun was out. The agent turned and ordered other Secret Service agents to remove the bubble top roof. It was as simple as that. No conspiracy. If it was still raining, the roof would have remained on. Now that the sun was out and the temperature rising, it was off.

As noted that the bubble top roof was not bullet proof and made only of plexiglas. However, should it have remained on the car, it would have caused grief to the snipers targeting Kennedy. Regardless, the assassins were primed to kill the president. Had the bubble top been in place they would have shot at the car anyway, but with less accuracy. Consequently, the bullets piercing the Plexiglas would be misdirected, ricocheting everywhere. It would have been an absolute blood bath inside the car that probably would have seen Jackie Kennedy and Nellie Connally shot to pieces, along with countless bystanders.

Jim Lehrer goes on to say that around midnight at the Dallas Police station, after the assassination, that same Secret Service agent came to him in tears and said "Oh Jim, if only I hadn't removed the bubble top."

CHAPTER 13

Montréal & the Assassinations of JFK, MLK, RFK

CIA MKULTRA Mind Control In Montréal

McGill University, in my home city of Montréal, is a legendary bastion of celebrated scholars such as Canadian Prime Ministers, Nobel Laureates, and US national security advisors.

McGill also has a dark past, perhaps one that the administration would like to keep in the shadows, erased from the glorious halls of higher learning at McGill. It is a past that will shock you and horrify you. Worst of all, it's true.

I am talking about the CIA mind control project of the 1950s and 1960s infamously known as MKULTRA. These covert, barbaric experiments took place in the heart of Montréal, behind locked doors, at Montréal's prestigious McGill's Allen Memorial Psychiatric Hospital, right here on Canadian soil.

Psychiatric patients were used as experimental animals and were induced with the psychotic, mind-altering, and often lethal drug LSD. They also used hypnotic suggestion combined with the LSD on their human lab rats in an attempt to alter their reality, to what end, one can only postulate. The experiments of

McGill psychiatrist Dr. Ewen Cameron are well-known and horrifying. But, there was another one before him, someone who had met Cameron. He too was a McGill graduate in psychiatry. His name is Dr. Renatus Hartogs.

We know today that Dr. Hartogs worked with the CIA in both Montréal and New York on what we would call today "mind control." In those days however, it was advertised as "behavior modification," under the guise of the possibility that "troubled youth" could be veered off their path of delinquency. Desperate for test cases, he solicited New York's Catholic orphanages, offering money to the administrators in order to secure "test patients."

> **These administrators, who were charged with protecting these children, and were governed by the highest of moral standards, readily agreed and turned over their kids in droves.**

Lee Harvey Oswald In Montréal

Let's go back to Montréal, and the summer of 1963. Prior to the November 22, 1963 assassination of JFK, Lee Harvey Oswald was documented as handing out pro-Castro leaflets, not only in New Orleans, but right here in Montréal, Canada at the corner of St. James and McGill. He is witnessed by a Canadian Customs official, a professional who was trained to remember and recognize faces. Coincidence you say? Maybe. But just for the sake of exploring further, let's continue. (See Chapter 8 "CIA Guilty As Charged" for more information.)

James Earl Ray In Montréal

Let's fast forward four years from 1963 to 1967 (Expo '67 for all of you Montréalers) to a place still in Montréal and directly around the corner from that place where Oswald had been spotted in 1963. James Earl Ray, the purported assassin of none other than Dr. Martin Luther King Jr., is also documented as frequenting a bar at 121 rue de la Commune West. It is claimed he met several times with a shadowy figure by the name of "Raul." Ray always deflected guilt for Dr. King's assassination away from himself and onto to this shady figure, Raul.

On April 4, 1968 Dr. King fell to a single assassin's bullet at the Lorraine Motel in Memphis. James Earl Ray was sought for the murder and was finally arrested and convicted. He would die in prison in 1998.

Another "coincidence", interestingly enough, Raul was alleged to be seen in Dallas in 1963 only a few days prior to JFK's assassination. Raul had been seen giving Dallas night club owner and Mafia bag man, Jack Ruby $20,000 in Ruby's very own Dallas Carousel Club. Jack Ruby would gain infamy when 3 days after JFK's assassination, he would shoot dead Lee Harvey Oswald in a Dallas Police station. Was the $20,000 payment for a hit on Oswald? Or just another coincidence? Let's keep going and see what else transpired.

RFK & Sirhan Sirhan

Only two months after the assassination of Dr. King, June 1968, Bobby Kennedy was gunned down in a hotel kitchen in Los Angeles by what the authorities called just another lone-nut gunman, Sirhan Sirhan. Allegedly, Sirhan, a Christian Palestinian, was enraged at Bobby's support for Israel.

The fatal bullet that entered Bobby's head was shot from behind him, from no further than two inches away and entered his head from behind his right ear. Sirhan was *never* closer than three feet from Bobby and never..., *never behind* Bobby, *always* in front. There were also 14 bullet holes from a gun that carried only nine bullets.

> **There is so much more to this story and is the source for another book. What is important is that it has long been speculated that Sirhan Sirhan was under "hypnotic suggestion" or specifically, "MKULTRA mind control," when he allegedly assassinated Bobby Kennedy. A programmed assassin trained to carry out a task when given certain keywords as "triggers." The movie "Manchurian Candidate" covers this type of scenario.**

Back To Montréal

Now, let's bring it all back full circle. The Warren Commission was set up to investigate the assassination of President John F. Kennedy. The Commission's thesis was that Lee Harvey Oswald was nothing more than a disenfranchised youth and malcontent who had acted alone.

Therefore, it was *imperative* that The Warren Commission get expert testimony to attest to Oswald's "unstable behavior." None better than a psychiatrist that had treated Oswald when Oswald was a "delinquent" teenager. In Oswald's early teenage years, because he had skipped school so much and repeatedly got caught, it was decided he would have to see a psychiatrist.

Now, guess who his psychiatrist was? Our previously mentioned McGill alumni: one *Dr. Renatus Hartogs*! It was Hartogs' testimony, solicited by the Warren Commission, that nailed Oswald as what has become known as "the lone-nut assassin."

FROM THE WARREN COMMISSION REPORT

Justice Delany declared him a truant, and remanded him to Youth House until May 7 for psychiatric study.

In accordance with the regular procedures at Youth House, Lee took a series of tests and was interviewed by a staff social worker and a probation officer, both of whom interviewed Mrs. Oswald as well. 218 Their findings, discussed more fully in Chapter VII of the Commission's report, indicated that Lee was a withdrawn, socially maladjusted boy, whose mother did not interest herself sufficiently in his welfare and had failed to establish a close relationship with him. Mrs. Oswald visited Lee at Youth House and came away with a highly unfavorable impression; she regarded it as unfit for her son. On the basis of all the test results and reports and his own interview with Lee, Dr. Renatus Hartogs, the chief staff psychiatrist, recommended that Lee be placed on probation with a requirement that he seek help from a child guidance clinic, and that his mother be urged to contact a family agency for help; he recommended that Lee not be placed in an institution unless treatment during probation was unsuccessful.

(http://www.archives.gov/research/jfk/warren-commission-report/appendix-13.html)

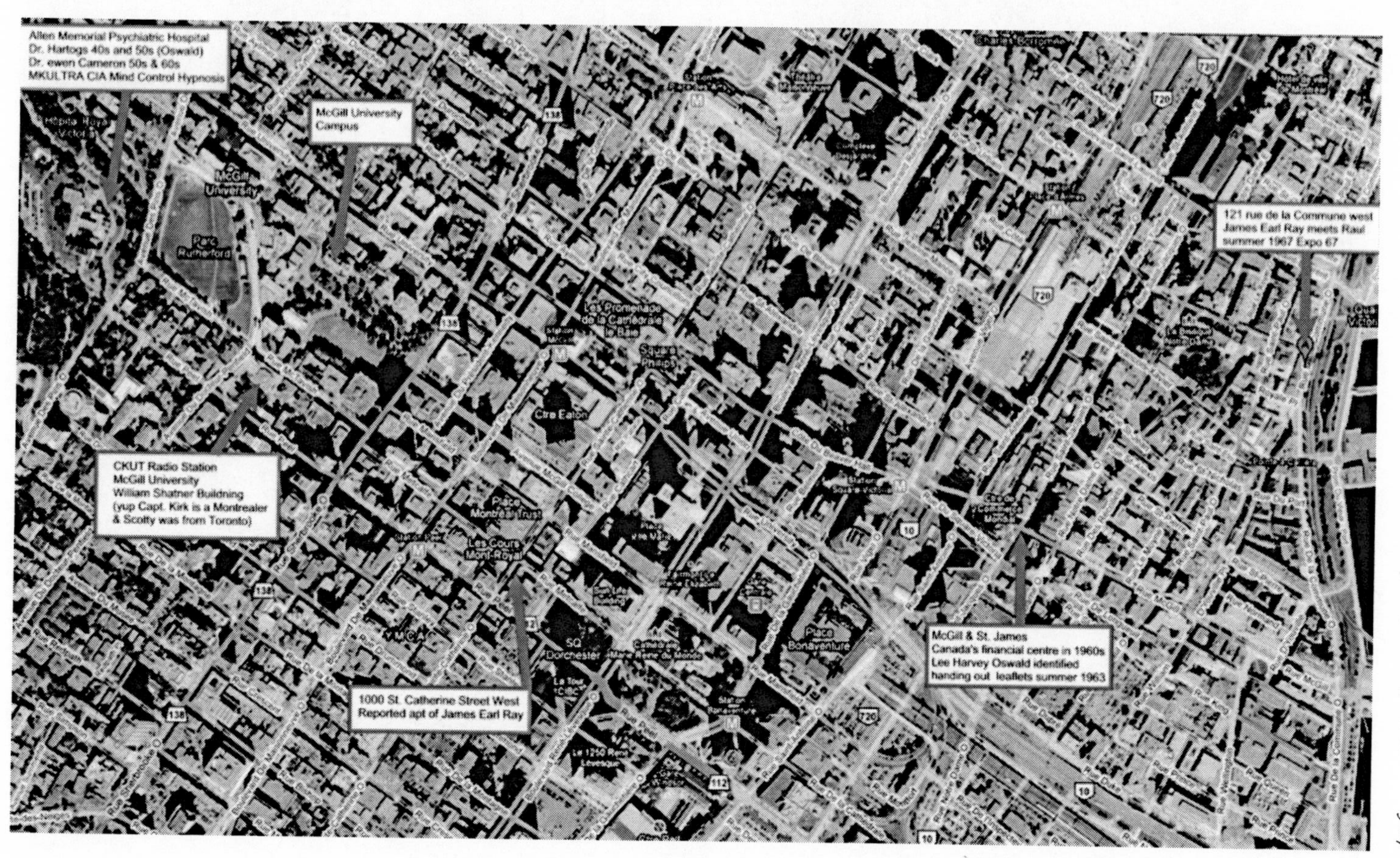
Allen Memorial Psychiatric Hospital
Dr. Hartogs 40s and 50s (Oswald)
Dr. ewen Cameron 50s & 60s
MKULTRA CIA Mind Control Hypnosis
McGill University
Campus
McGill University
Park Rutherford
CKUT Radio Station
McGill University
William Shatner Buildning
(yup Capt. Kirk is a Montrealer
& Scotty was from Toronto)
Ctre Eaton
Place Montréal Trust
Les Cours Mont-Royal
SQ Dorchester
Place Bonaventure
1000 St. Catherine Street West
Reported apt of James Earl Ray
McGill & St. James
Canada's financial centre in 1960s
Lee Harvey Oswald identified
handing out leaflets summer 1963
121 rue de la Commune west
James Earl Ray meets Raul
summer 1967 Expo 67

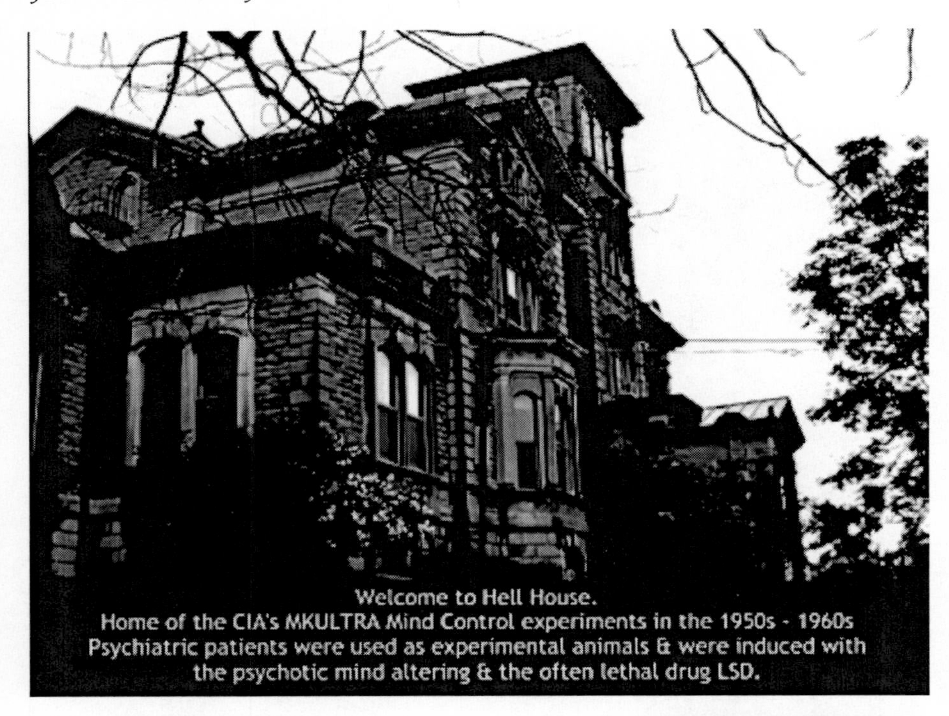

Welcome to Hell House.
Home of the CIA's MKULTRA Mind Control experiments in the 1950s - 1960s
Psychiatric patients were used as experimental animals & were induced with the psychotic mind altering & the often lethal drug LSD.

1967 (Expo 67) James Earl Ray, purported assassin of Dr. Martin Luther King Jr, meets several times with a shadowy figure "Raul"at bar at 121 rue de la Commune west. Ray always deflected guilt for Dr. King's assassination away from himself & onto "Raul".

Montreal - summer 1963 - the finacial capital of Canada. St James is to Canada what Wall Street is to the US. Montreal was & is the centre of orgainized crime in Canada. Prior to the coming November 22, 1963 assassination of JFK, Lee Harvey Oswald,the purported assassin of JFK, is documented handing out pro Castro leaflets not only in New Orleans but...right here in Montreal, Canada at the corner of St. James & McGill. He is witnessed by a Canadian Customs official, a profesional trained to remember & recognize faces.

CHAPTER 14

MY OWN PERSPECTIVE

I was dead set against writing this chapter. I am not a "researcher," and this is not a book of my original research. This book is intended solely to inspire a new generation to "question everything" and, as a consequence, achieve more than they ever thought possible of themselves. It is written as an historical document on Ted Sorensen, Abraham Bolden, Dr. McClelland, James Tague, Bev Oliver, and others who shared their real stories, in their own words, and not from third or fourth-person interpretations. This book is not about me, but about my desire to let "those who were there" speak. Above all, it was intended for the reader to be exposed to the information and decide for themselves.

However, inevitably one of the first questions from folks about this book is, "Who killed JFK?" So, for all those who have asked me that question, I will jump head first into the fray. As I take a deep breath into my lungs and hold it, and as I say on Night Fright, "strap in, and hang on; here we go."

There Is Never Just One Reason In Politics

In politics, every step and movement is assessed, calculated, spun around and reassessed again. When the US went into Iraq, it wasn't just for weapons of mass destruction (WMD) or oil; that would be too simple. Honestly, it was to shake things up from the status quo in the Middle-East. Someone once said that the best defense is a good offence. On September 11, 2001 we were on the defensive. So, we took the fight off our soil instead of sitting back and waiting for the next attack. Act; not re-act.

There were a variety of reasons to go into Iraq and Afghanistan. We wanted to get rid of a dictator, Saddam Hussein, who had openly gassed hundreds of his own people in the Iran–Iraq war in the 80s. He caused the first Gulf War by invading Kuwait. He "disappeared" hundreds of prisoners in his prisons and was actively seeking a nuclear bomb to shore up his prestige in the region and around the world. And make no mistake, once he achieved his goal, given his reckless track record and temper, it wouldn't have been long before he would use that weapon. What would the consequences of that action be? Do we sit around and wait for that to happen and *re-act*? Better to act and take out the risk completely, like the Israelis did with "Operation Babylon" when they bombed Iraqi Osriak nuclear reactor just outside Baghdad on September 30, 1980. Take out the risk, and you sleep easier at night.

Saddam was also actively seeking some kind of partnership with Al Qaeda. Even though the two were ideologically at odds with each other, eventually some sort of mutually beneficial partnership would have risen, especially when Saddam had WMDs. Al Qaeda would have "looked the other way" for a liaison with someone with a weapon that could murder "the Infidel" en-mass. In return, Al Qaeda would have supplied Saddam with the perfect, successfully tested, tactically accurate, delivery system: suicide bombers.

A good analogy for terrorist groups is organized crime. It's like the Montréal chapter of the Hells Angels, Montréal Mafia and Irish West End Gang coming together for common causes (drugs) to form the "Consortium." Think of it similarly, in make up, to New York organized crime's "Commission." Eventually bad guys will stop warring with each other and come together if they find it mutually beneficial.

Q: Who Killed JFK?

A: The Mafia, CIA, anti-Cuban exiles, military intelligence. End of chapter. thanks for reading. lol.

Sounds absurd doesn't it? All these groups working together? But remember "Operation Mongoose." Remember what I stated about adversaries working together "against Communism." Operation Mongoose is where we find exactly that, all of these groups actively working together for a common, single goal: to assassinate Castro and return to Cuba for power and money. (See Chapter 11: "JFK, the Movie, Robert Groden, Jim DiEugenio, Jim Marrs / Operation Mongoose")

THE REAL QUESTION THAT NEEDS TO BE ANSWERED IS *WHY*

So why was Kennedy killed? Again, it wasn't for just one reason. More than one person wanted him dead. A good indication of that comes from Ted Sorensen's comments on who pulled the trigger.

> Sorensen: I don't know, nobody really knows and I try to avoid reading most of these so called "conspiracy books." The fact is that Kennedy had enemies in the Right Wing, particularly because of civil rights, and because his American University speech indicated that he was taking a more accommodating position toward the Soviet Union. He also had enemies among organized crime, as did his brother Bobby. He also supposedly had enemies among Communists in both the Soviet Union and Cuba, although I don't think either one of them would have thought that they would gain by Kennedy's removal. All I meant to say in the book ("Counselor") was, "Considering the number of enemies that he had, in the military and intelligence circles in the United States, Lord knows they had reasons to get rid of him. They had opportunities to have access to arms, to reach out to the kind of weird and confused individuals who can be recruited for that kind of work. I don't make any accusations, because I don't believe in making any accusations without proof."

Let's go over that list Ted just mentioned and see if there are any commonalities between them and see if we can find a place to begin.

1. ORGANIZED CRIME

By far, this group probably had the biggest motive. There was a war raging against them and they were losing, big time.

> Waldron: The mafia tried to kill JFK first in Chicago, motorcade cancelled, Tampa, motorcade went ahead but the godfather there found out that authorities knew, so the hit was cancelled. Succeeded in Dallas, the phony evidence pointing to Fidel's, believed by many.

> Mafia got away with murder, but now, as people can read, I mean, Marcello eventually, once he was finally in prison, he just admitted, "I had the SOB killed and I would do it again. He was a thorn in my side. I wish I could have done it myself. (Chapter 9 "Mafia, Lamar Waldron")

2. The Right Wing

They were enemies of civil rights and fearful that JFK was relinquishing the country over to Communist sympathizers. Right away we know of Joseph Milteer, a white supremacist and member of the radical extremists "The White Citizen's Council Of Atlanta." He boasted to an undercover police informant, William Somerset, that Kennedy was going to be killed from an office building with a high-powered rifle, which is precisely the way JFK was assassinated. (Chapter 3 "Ted Sorensen the Man Who Saved the World Really") The following took place in Miami, November 9, 1963, a mere 13 days before Kennedy would be assassinated in Dallas.

> Somersett: (undercover): How do you figure the best way would be to get [JFK]?
>
> Milteer: (supremacist): From an office building with a high-powered rifle

Lee Harvey Oswald would be charged with the assassination of President Kennedy only 13 days later on November 22, 1963, allegedly having committed the assassination with a high-powered rifle from an office building.

3. US Intelligence Circles

E. Howard Hunt, Gerry Hemming and Frank Sturgis were all CIA agents or operatives. Even though Hunt denied being involved with the assassination, his son, St. John Hunt tells a different story based on a confession told to him by his dying father. Here is the story from Mark Lane.

> Lane: St. John Hunt's mother said to him that his father had been in Dallas (November 22, 1963). St. John Hunt said, "When my father was dying he said to me, 'Mark Lane was right. I and the CIA were involved in the assassination. I have to tell you that now.'" It wasn't exactly that many words; [he] just said that I was correct and he had played a part. And St. John Hunt said that to me in writing actually.

The following is what was confessed to Mark Lane from CIA hit man Gerry Patrick Hemming:

Lane: I told him exactly what Marita Lorenz had said; it was a two-car caravan, Sturgis was there, he was there, the Novo brothers were there, other Cubans were there, went to Dallas and in Dallas, Eduardo, who is E. Howard Hunt, paid Sturgis off for the operation.

He said "All right, so what's the question?" I said "Is that true?" He said "No." He said "It was a three-car caravan. Everything else is true." So that was Hemming's statement to me.

Holland: And Mark, you mentioned that E. Howard Hunt paid everybody. Where did the money come from? Where was it financed out of?

Lane: Well they assumed since Hunt was CIA and they were all working for CIA, they just presumed it was made available by the Central Intelligence Agency.

Holland: Any speculation Mafia dollars may have been involved?

Lane: Well, I don't see any indication to that at all. You know at that time, you've got to remember, at that time the Mafia and the CIA were working together in planning the assassination of Fidel Castro and various things.

4. CUBA & THE SOVIET UNION

Ted Sorensen didn't really believe that either Cuba or the Soviets were involved with the assassination of JFK and neither do I. I do believe, however, that early on there was information flooding in that represented that viewpoint, reports that Oswald was pro-Castro and trying to gain access to Cuba. Oswald had also gone to visit the Soviet consulate in Mexico and had met with the head of Soviet Black Op assassinations Kostikov. (Chapter 8 "CIA Guilty As Charged - Mark Lane")

Lane: The CIA met with Earl Warren and gave him a briefing. And this is what the CIA said, this is the legend they gave him: "In September of 1963 Lee Harvey Oswald went to Mexico City. He went to the Cuban Embassy and we have absolute proof of that. Then he went to the Soviet Embassy and we have proof of that. We have photographs of him and we have a tape recording of him when he called the Soviet Embassy from Mexico City." It was right there.

He called them and he said he wanted to see Kostikov "Is he in? This is Lee Harvey Oswald calling." In other words, the tape recording showed that Oswald had a relationship with Kostikov.

> Valeriy Vladimirovich Kostikov. The following quote is from the CIA directly to the Warren Commission: "Kostikov is believed to work for Department Thirteen of the First Chief Directorate of the KGB. It is the Department responsible for executive action, including sabotage and assassination." (Documents from the Mary Ferrell Foundation)

Avoiding World War III – Why The Cover-up?

The above was also the scenario VP Johnson feared when he became president only moments after JFK was assassinated. Was it a communist plot? Was the United States also about to be hit by a nuclear attack? Was Cuba involved at some level, threatening to rekindle fears of the previous year's missile crisis? The initial intelligence flooding in after the assassination was both chaotic and dangerously unsubstantiated, more impulse and reaction than level-headed analysis.

Let me go back to 9/11 for a moment. Remember all the misleading info on 9/11. Let's look at the White House underground bunker. I did an interview with Lt. Col. Robert Darling, who was deep below the White House in the bunker, manning the phones and communications that day. He had Vice President Dick Cheney perched directly behind him and Secretary of Defense Condoleezza Rice sitting beside him.

A report came in that a civilian passenger jet was on a course that would take it directly into the White House. Cheney had ordered two F-18s to track and down the aircraft. Moments later another report came in that the plane was down somewhere over Pennsylvania. Now remember, this was 2001, with all the best communications in the world in place in the White House bunker. When word reached VP Cheney that the plane was down, he asked all present to state their full name and rank for what he believed would be a "Congressional Investigation." Cheney believed, as did everyone in the bunker, that the American F-18s had shot down the plane.

It was only after the fact that they all learned that the plane was downed by the efforts and bravery of its passengers, and that the Air Force jets had not even been close enough to down it. And that was 2001, not 1963.

> Lane: And Warren went out, and we have the minutes of the first meeting of January '64 where he talks to the staff, the lawyers, where he says basically "Truth is no longer our objective. We cannot have 40 million Americans die because of our investigations." And there's a record of this. I have those minutes. It was top secret at the time, I have them now. And he's talking about 40 million Americans. He didn't say why, but how were 40 million Americans going to die?

Ominously, on November 22, 1963, moments after President Kennedy was assassinated, the intel rushing in also had both Soviet and Cuban covert prints all over it. This is the reason why it was essential for the US to have a lone shooter at this time, in order to down play any chance of a conspiracy until all of the facts had been gathered and a complete investigation taken place. But that could take years. So, it really came down to a choice between a cover-up or the possibilities of World War III.

National security won out and the cover-up began. That was the reason for the cover-up back then, but what about now? Why continue the cover-up when we know more of who Oswald was, and that it was not the Soviets or Cuba behind the assassination?

MISSILES STILL IN CUBA – WHY THE COVER-UP CONTINUES TODAY

Part of the deal to end the Cuban Missile Crisis was to have the Soviets dismantle all missiles in Cuba and return them to the Soviet Union. This would be officially monitored by United Nations Weapons Inspectors. One problem: Castro refused to allow any UN officials on the island.

JFK was being hounded by the United States military that the missiles were still in Cuba long after they were supposed to be taken out. It is my perspective that they were never completely taken off the island and are in fact still there. There may not be the same numbers perhaps, and the ones that remain may not even be fully operational. But, why, in the name of G-d, would we open up that "can of worms" again and risk nuclear holocaust?

After all, we have lived with Castro's Cuba for decades now; the Soviet bloc has collapsed; there is far less tension between the opposing super powers than in the past 60 years; so let sleeping dogs lie. Why poke the dog? To what end and advantage? There is none.

This is why I believe that the true reason behind keeping many of the JFK files closed for so long, 75 years so far, is to allow Castro time to die. As blunt as this may sound to you, Castro is an unpredictable loose cannon. During the Cuban Missile Crisis, he actually told Khrushchev to release the missiles and let them fly at America. He boasted to Ted Sorensen that he wanted them sent in a surprise attack during the crisis! With a guy like this at the helm, why chance it? Wait until he is dead and gone. Chances are, once that happens, and it has been established that we are dealing with a sane and rational post-Castro Cuba, within a short period of time, full disclosure will be forthright.

It has long been my thesis that the cover-up of the Kennedy assassination continues based on the presumption that the nuclear missiles, some of them at least, were never removed from Cuba and remain there to this day. It seems that my thesis is corroborated below by investigative reporter Chuck Goudie of ABC. The following headline is from his report filed April 5, 2012:

> *"It was widely thought that all the missiles were removed and taken back to the Soviet Union and the silos all dismantled. That does not appear to have been the case."*

(http://abclocal.go.com/wls/story?section=news/iteam&id=8610254)

Robert Groden, principal consultant to Oliver Stone for "JFK," stated the following on the nuclear missiles still in Cuba:

> Holland: Robert, I'm going to ask you a question I've never asked any other guest before on the JFK assassination. Do you think that there's still missiles in Cuba that were never removed, and perhaps – just perhaps – that's why the cover-up remains, because people figure, well, you know, we've lived with Cuba for so long, why open up a Pandora's box once more?
>
> Groden: Wow... not only is that a question you've never asked anybody; nobody's ever asked me that either. I think it is a very, very strong likelihood that they were not completely removed. I have thought that before and I think it now. We have no proof that they were actually removed. The fact that the whole issue is, Castro never used [them], proves nothing.
>
> At this stage of the game, we'd still be under the same threat we were then. The IRBMs, the ICBMs, whatever, were... Any major city on the East coast of the United States — or from the center of the United States — would have been a target, easily reachable by any of these missiles. President Kennedy knew it. I'd like to believe that they were all taken out, but we have absolutely no reason to believe that they were.

Lamar Waldron's book, "Legacy Of Secrecy," is being made into a Hollywood film starring Leonardo DiCaprio and Robert De Niro, and what this research shows on the missiles in Cuba.

> Waldron: They were beating up on JFK in the press claiming missiles were still in Cuba. JFK had tried to get those UN weapons inspections. Fidel would not allow them. JFK was going through the UN. What was he going to do? You know, I mean there was no way to prove a negative, that there weren't those missiles without those inspections.

AND IN THE END...

Why should we give a damn? There are those that say Jack Kennedy was nothing more than a playboy, never worked a day at an honest job in his life, a womanizer who cheated on his family. There are also those that decry that Dr. King was nothing more than a subhuman who was undeserving of a Nobel Peace Prize, and, like Kennedy, had many extramarital affairs. There are those who say Bobby Kennedy was a snobby little puke, born with a silver spoon in his mouth, arrogant and disrespectful to his office.

All I know is this: Is evil real? Unquestionably. All one has to do is look at the Holocaust to see how evil raged across the world under the guise of National Socialism: The Nazis. No country was unscathed. Even my own country, Canada, turned away boat loads of Jews fleeing the Nazi juggernaut. Canada had a policy for the Jews wishing to flee certain death and immigrate to Canada. When asked how many Jews, women and children, they would be willing to accept between our borders, the Canadians' curt response was "NONE is too many." Yeah, polite, liberal Canada, second largest land mass of a country in the world, couldn't find room for a few women and children, and turned them around and sent them back to certain death. So don't try to tell me evil doesn't exist. It does, and is running rampant once again, with the world being more anti-Semitic than anytime in history.

It is said you can't see the light without the dark. Goodness without evil. There is some merit to this. If we we were on a fully lighted stage, and someone entered with a lit candle, it is doubtful we would even notice. However, if you put us all onto a stage, immersed in suffocating blackness, unable to see our way, then someone entered with that same candle, that candle will shine the brightest it has ever shone. The 60s were like that. For John, Martin, Bobby, and *especially* for Ted Sorensen, for one brief shining moment we were all inspired by the light

REFERENCES

Kennedy: The Classic Biography (Harper Perennial Political Classics) by Sorensen, Ted (1999) William S Konecky Assoc.

Counselor: A Life at the Edge of History by Sorensen, Ted (2008) Harper Collins

Plausible Denial by Lane, Mark(2011) Skyhorse Publishing

Nightmare In Dallas by Beverly Oliver and Coke Buchanan (1994) Starburst Pub; First Edition

LBJ and the Kennedy Killing by Tague, James T. (2013)TrineDay

The Echo from Dealey Plaza: The true story of the first African American on the White House Secret Service detail... by Bolden, Abraham (2008) Crown

The Killing of a President: The Complete Photographic Record of the JFK Assassination... by Robert J. Groden (Nov 1, 1993) Studio; First Edition edition

Crossfire: The Plot That Killed Kennedy by Jim Marrs (2013) Basic Books; Revised Edition edition

Destiny Betrayed: JFK, Cuba, and the Garrison Case (Second Edition) by DiEugenio, James (2012) Skyhorse Publishing; Second Edition edition

Legacy of Secrecy: The Long Shadow of the JFK Assassination by Waldron, Lamar and Thom Hartmann (2009) Counterpoint

JFK and the Unspeakable: Why He Died and Why It Matters by Douglass, James W. (2011) Orbis; First Edition

The Man Who Knew Too Much: Hired to Kill Oswald and Prevent the Assassination of JFK Richard Case Nagell by Russell, Dick (1992) Carroll & Graf Pub; First Edition edition

Head Shot by Chambers, G. Paul (2012) Prometheus Books; Reprint edition

Enemy of the Truth, Myths, Forensics, and the Kennedy Assassination, Fiester, Sherry (2012) JFK Lancer

Mark Sobel, Director of "The Commission" film starring Martin Sheen, Sam Waterston, Ed Asner, Martin Landau, Joe Don Baker

Someone Would Have Talked by Hancock, Larry (2010) JFK Lancer

The Assassinations: Probe Magazine on JFK, MLK, RFK and Malcolm X [2012] James DiEugenio, Lisa Pease (2012) Feral House

Jacqueline Kennedy: Historic Conversations on Life With John F. Kennedy by Kennedy, Caroline and Beschloss, Michael (2011) Hyperion

Breach of Trust: How the Warren Commission Failed the Nation and Why by McKnight, Gerald D. (2005) University Press of Kansas; Reprint edition

Beyond the Fence Line: The Eyewitness Account of Ed Hoffman and the Murder of President Kennedy by Casey Quinlan and Brian Edwards (2008) JFK Lancer

House Select Committee on Assassinations Volumes

In the Eye of History, Medical Evidence in the Assassination of President Kennedy by Law, William (2005) JFK Lancer

The Day Kennedy Was Shot" by Bishop, Jim (1968)

From Love Field: Our Final Hours with President John F. Kennedy by Nellie Connally and Mickey Herskowitz (2003) Rugged Land

Documents from the Mary Ferrell Foundation

Lightning Source UK Ltd.
Milton Keynes UK
UKOW03f0246231014

240526UK00001B/135/P